Also by Thane Rosenbaum

Nonfiction

Saving Free Speech…from Itself
Payback: The Case for Revenge
The Myth of Moral Justice: Why Our Legal System Fails to Do What's Right

Novels

How Sweet It Is!
The Stranger Within Sarah Stein
The Golems of Gotham
Second Hand Smoke
Elijah Visible

Anthologies

Law Lit: From Atticus Finch to The Practice, A Collection of Great Writing about the Law

Advance Praise for *Beyond Proportionality*

"In *Beyond Proportionality*, Thane Rosenbaum presents a *cri de coeur* in defense of Israel's right to defend itself and against those who, out of ignorance and antisemitism, seek to deny Israel that right. Both enlightening and maddening, the book must be read by anyone willing to stand up for Israel as well as all those interested in knowing the truth about the Gaza war."

–Michael Oren, Former Israeli
Ambassador to the United States

"Thane Rosenbaum's defiantly heroic courage in the face of so much fecklessness, and the witty ironic drive of his quick-step insight into its origins, is both bracing consolation for the despairing and invigorating inspiration for the daring."

–Cynthia Ozick, Winner of the National Book
Critics Circle Award and PEN/Malamud Award

"Forcefully, and from the high ground, Thane Rosenbaum parses the laws of war that govern Israel's response to the savagery perpetrated against it on October 7, 2023, and pierces the cruel hypocrisy of those who claim that Israel committed genocide. Along the way, he provides a cornucopia of evidence supporting the conclusion that Israel took precautions to spare civilian life beyond what international law requires."

–Michael Mukasey, Former Attorney
General of the United States

"In this age of misinformation and disinformation, *Beyond Proportionality* is a brave and necessary contribution to the public's understanding of Israel's wars in Gaza, especially since it has been so grossly distorted in mainstream media and on university campuses. Thane Rosenbaum has given us much to think about Israel's moral dilemma, duty to its people, and Jewish survival."

–Abraham Foxman, Longtime National
Director of the Anti-Defamation League

"A necessary book that addresses a moral and military question: What can a nation do to defend itself against terrorists who pay no mind to the laws of war? Must it value the lives of its enemies more than its own citizens?"

–Jeb Bush, Two-term Governor of
Florida and Presidential candidate

"*Beyond Proportionality* is a searing defense of the laws of war against those who would twist them into weapons. Thane Rosenbaum exposes the moral hypocrisy Israel faces fighting terrorists who turn civilians into shields—and violate every law meant to protect those civilians. As a scholar of urban warfare, I can say plainly: this book gets it right—and it could not come at a more critical time."

–John Spencer, Chair of Urban Warfare Studies,
Modern War Institute at West Point

BEYOND PROPORTIONALITY

ISRAEL'S JUST WAR IN GAZA

THANE ROSENBAUM

A WICKED SON BOOK
An Imprint of Post Hill Press
ISBN: 979-8-88845-789-4
ISBN (eBook): 979-8-88845-790-0

Beyond Proportionality:
Israel's Just War in Gaza

Cover Design by Cody Corcoran

This book, as well as any other Wicked Son publications, may be purchased in bulk quantities at a special discounted rate. Contact orders@posthillpress.com for more information.

This is a work of nonfiction. All people, locations, events, and situations are portrayed to the best of the author's memory.

Post Hill Press
New York • Nashville
wickedsonbooks.com
posthillpress.com

Published in the United States of America
1 2 3 4 5 6 7 8 9 10

For Alan Kadish

CONTENTS

INTRODUCTION

"J'accuse!"—The Case Against Israel

At the turn of the nineteenth century, a political scandal in France galvanized public opinion all over the world. Known as the Dreyfus Affair, at its root was the inexorable display and mass hatred of Jews. This same antisemitic fervor, which a few decades later would materialize into the Holocaust, had been around for two millennia. Occasionally, it would manifest itself in pogroms and mass expulsions. Along the way, it went from latent to lethal, and emanated from a lie.

This time, however, the antisemitism was organized, sanctioned by the government, fueled by the press, and openly embraced by many people who regarded themselves as highly cultivated and civilized. Artists and intellectuals took a special interest in joining the mob. And it came pre-packaged with an easily disproved conspiracy theory involving a treasonous Jewish military officer.

Jews in France had long enjoyed the full panoply of civil rights. Indeed, during the French Revolution, France had become the first European nation to emancipate its Jewish population. For nearly a century, French Jews had participated in every facet of cosmopolitan life among the professional classes and cultural elite. But suddenly, they found themselves facing a backlash unlike anything they had experienced before.

The Dreyfus Affair made the unspoken hatred of Jews not just acceptable but fashionable. Seemingly overnight, Jews in France went from being socially accepted and having a sense of security to being on the receiving end of wild denunciations for their clannishness, duplicity, greed, and dual loyalty.

And much like Nazi Germany, the nerve center of these societal convulsions burned brightest on university campuses, in the pages of the mainstream press, and wherever artists and writers congregated. The fact that it all originated from an easily disprovable lie was of little concern. The case against Dreyfus was merely a pretext to something far worse.

Captain Alfred Dreyfus was an officer on the French military general staff accused of passing state secrets to Germany—the despised aggressor nation that during the Franco-Prussian War of 1870 had humiliated France and annexed Alsace and Moselle. Someone had to be blamed, and Dreyfus, a high-ranking Jewish officer, fully assimilated yet perceived as a foreigner, was an easy fall guy even though there was no actual evidence of his wrongdoing. The French legal system relied upon forged documents—manufactured by military counterintelligence—to falsify his guilt. The letters were not even in Dreyfus' handwriting.

That's not to say there was no spy within the ranks of senior military officers. But it wasn't Captain Dreyfus. Two years after he was court-martialed for treason and shipped off to Devil's Island, a notorious tropical hellhole where many prisoners died of disease and malnutrition, the French Army uncovered evidence implicating the true culprit—Major Walsin Esterhazy, who had sold secret documents to the German Embassy. But by then the nation was awash in anti-Jewish bigotry. Dreyfus should have been exonerated instantly. Instead, he was returned to France to face a new trial, where he was once again convicted and given an enhanced sentence.

Newspapers around the world covered the trial and its aftermath. A slogan representative of the times referred to Dreyfus as "the Jew who is everywhere but belongs nowhere." It should come as no surprise to learn that the Dreyfus Affair roughly coincided with the publication of *The Protocols of the Elders of Zion*, another forged document, this one alleging a Jewish conspiracy to conquer the world.

Events shifted dramatically when one of France's leading intellectuals, the novelist and playwright Émile Zola, wrote a lengthy front-page essay—famously titled "J'Accuse…!"—in which he charged the French government and legal system with a coverup. Zola wrote, "Here…are the facts which explain how a miscarriage of justice could be made; and the moral evidence, the financial circumstances of Dreyfus, the absence of reason, his continual cry of innocence…the hunting for the 'dirty Jews,' which dishonours our time." Given the public embarrassment to the nation's institutions, Zola himself was brought to trial and convicted of libel. He fled to London.

Eventually, the obsession with Dreyfus dissipated. The French government and its people finally came to recognize that they had been handed a convenient excuse to shift blame away from France's military and rest it instead with a familiar villain. National regret ensued, and by 1906, Dreyfus was exonerated, and his rank restored.

But anyone familiar with these events can't help but see the parallel with what is happening today. The global reaction to Israel's eighteen-month-long war in Gaza has had many of the same elements: heightened emotions, irrational arguments, distorted histories, the rejection of obvious truths, forged documents, falsified facts, misapplied laws, antisemitic stereotypes, and worldwide anti-Jewish rage. But instead of a single Jewish officer serving as the focal point, this time it was the Jewish state, and its professional military, who stand falsely accused—and with much the same imagery. Thus, Israeli Prime Minister Benjamin Netanyahu is often depicted as drinking the blood of Palestinian children.

Such fabrications are all the more paradoxical given the events that preceded and fully justified Israel's retaliatory war against Hamas. These sensationalized condemnations completely overlook and ignore what started the conflict in the first place. On the morning of October 7, 2023, southern Israel was invaded—by land, air, and sea—by six thousand Palestinians from Gaza. Most were terrorists with Hamas and Islamic Jihad, but many were ordinary civilians. It was a planned and coordinated attack that lasted several hours and targeted the concertgoers at the Nova Music Festival, most of whom were young peace-loving Israelis.

This breach of Israeli's sovereignty and the attack against its people also included families that lived in neighboring towns and *kibbutzim*. The carnage was otherworldly—1,200 murdered, many burned alive and gang raped, and 250 kidnapped, including the elderly and young children.

Almost instantly, the barbaric crimes committed against the Israeli people on that day were subordinated to the casualties of war in Gaza brought about by Israel's swift and overwhelmingly forceful retaliation.

Indeed, the charges against Israel surfaced not long after the massacre itself. On October 8, the day after, thirty-one student groups at Harvard blamed Israel for the attack, holding it "entirely responsible" for the mass slaughter. International tribunals, foreign ministries, human rights organizations, and the mainstream media quickly turned against Israel. Even its greatest ally—the United States—one-sidedly pressured Israel to end the fighting quickly in a seeming attempt to save Hamas from the consequences of its own actions.

These toxic antisemitic emotions never simmered down. To the contrary, the international Jew-hating campaign—clearly well-funded and organized—attracted enormous crowds. The world went on an anti-Jewish rampage with hundreds of thousands of mainly young people screaming for the end of Israel, impugning "war crimes," "genocide," "mass starvation," and "disproportionate force"—all the while remaining wholly ignorant of the protocols of international humanitarian law and not having much of a grip on the facts either. A wide assortment of people, many of whom claimed to be experts—and who therefore should have known better—instantly prejudged Israel as having created the conditions that justified the attack and, in its military response, violated international law.

The *Washington Post*, on October 8, went out of its way to justify what had taken place in Israel the day before: "The coordinated attack by Hamas…comes after months of worsening tensions over violence at Al-Aqsa Mosque…as well as continuing resentment of the punishing blockade and occupation of Palestinian lands."[1] That same day, *NBC News* reported, "Despite pleas from the United Nations and human rights groups, Israel has maintained a land, air and sea blockade on Gaza since 2007…. The International Committee of the Red Cross considers the blockade illegal and says it violates the Geneva Convention…. The U.N., various human rights groups and legal scholars, citing the blockade, consider Gaza to still be under military occupation by Israel."[2]

Also on October 8, National Public Radio quoted a pro-Palestinian activist with the following unchallenged statement: "The Palestinians who live in the Gaza Strip, the vast majority of them—they've been refugees living inside of Gaza for 75 years. And this is, of course, compounded by decades of military occupation and, in the last decade and a half, a brutal siege of the Gaza Strip, which has held 2 million Palestinians there hostage."[3] Raz Segal, who directs genocide studies at Stockton University, told *Time* Magazine that Israel's response was a "textbook case of genocide."[4]

All of these statements are either factually untrue or profoundly misstate the applicable laws. Most people shouted falsehoods and spoke irresponsibly without having any knowledge about the relevant legal doctrines. What the laws of war actually hold when it comes to the position Israel finds itself in was completely foreign to those screaming the loudest. Many of those calling to "free Palestine from the river to the sea" had no idea which river and sea they were talking about or where, for that matter, Palestine was located.

Actually, there is much to consider and digest when it comes to the war in Gaza. But few took an interest in understanding what the law requires. And those who were knowledgeable about it feigned ignorance or outright lied—with their lies amplified a hundredfold by a compliant global press. Meanwhile Israel's efforts to defend or explain its actions were dismissed as "Zionist disinformation."

This is the reason I have written this book—to disentangle lies from truth, myth from fact, and to bring some clarity to the legal norms of warfare that are constantly misapplied and invoked against Israel whenever it is forced to defend itself against terrorism.

Israel has now fought Hamas in three separate wars, and Hezbollah twice. After each conflict, the combined forces of the legacy media and alleged legal experts make inflammatory accusations against the Jewish state. They present a very different battlefield, an altered reality where Israel ultimately loses the war—measured in spilled ink, and not blood. It is a world war of defamatory words and political propaganda.

Each time, the fighting methods of the terrorists who are Israel's enemies are exempt from legal scrutiny. The targeting of Israeli civilians is perfectly acceptable. The same is not true when evaluating Israel's military response, however. Its adherence to the laws of war is discounted and discredited. In the wars that Israel gets dragged into, the killing of Palestinian civilians is elevated from collateral damage to crimes against humanity.

The double standards and distortions must, finally, come to an end—although that's unlikely. But at least there should be some serious discussion about how international humanitarian law and the laws of armed conflict apply in these situations. This book seeks to fill that gap.

As a threshold matter, it must be asked whether Israel was fighting a just war of self-defense in Gaza, and whether it was waged in a just manner. The doctrine of "Just War Theory"—essentially, the ethics surrounding the right to go to war, and to wage the conflict honorably—has a long history rooted in classical and Catholic tradition and is mainly derived in its modern form from the work of the seventeenth century Dutch legal philosopher Hugo Grotius. Today it is associated most closely with Princeton moral philosopher Michael Walzer and his landmark book, *Just and Unjust Wars: A Moral Argument with Historical Illustrations*. Walzer himself, who opined at various points during the conflict, has largely recognized the justness of Israel's war aims in Gaza, and the moral dilemma that Hamas' terrorist tactics present to the Jewish state.

Many other considerations then follow, which are covered throughout this book. The Geneva Conventions and their updated Protocols concern the protection of civilians and who qualifies as a civilian. The Convention on the Prevention and Punishment of the Crime of Genocide is the United Nations' adopted definition of genocide, and it outlines what is to be done when such crimes against humanity are discovered.

There are intersections among the laws of armed conflict, international humanitarian law, and human rights law—which are especially present in the wars fought between Israel and Hamas. Hamas and Islamic Jihad are nonstate terrorist groups who continually launch wars of aggression against the Jewish nation-state. Is Israel even required to comply with military doctrine given Hamas' nonstate status? How about the repeated rejection and open defiance of the rules Israel respects but Hamas flouts—most especially, in bypassing battlefields in favor of urban settings, and inflicting terror against ordinary civilians?

Article 51 of the United Nations Charter grants member states the right to self-defense. But are there restrictions placed on that right when a member state is at war with an enemy that threatens limitless aggression? Hamas has made good on those threats over the years. It is not mere conjecture or idle talk. Giddy Islamists never seem to tire of warfare. Perhaps Israel should be given a free hand to eliminate the threat—once and for all. The deadly consequences arising out of Israel's response should, perhaps, fall on the entity that started the fight and has no intention of ending it.

More questions require clarification. We hear a lot about the obligations of an occupying army to provide humanitarian aid, electricity, water, and medical supplies during wartime. But what does "occupy" mean, and how much aid, if any, and to whom, was it Israel's burden to supply? Nations under siege are not usually well fed. What happens when aid is hijacked by terrorists and never makes it to benefit the civilian population?

Does it make sense that Israel should be feeding and hydrating its enemy? No Jew lived in Gaza on October 6, and Israel is still at war with Hamas. Why then isn't Hamas legally and morally responsible for the care of its own people?

What about the use of civilians as human shields and the willingness of civilians to serve in that capacity? Who counts as a civilian, and when do civilians who voluntarily choose to provide material aid to an enemy lose their protected status? Gazan teenagers make up the fighting force of Hamas in large numbers. Are teenage terrorists to be regarded as children when Israeli soldiers can't demand to see the IDs of those returning fire?

Then there's the misuse of the word "proportionality." Must Israel and Gaza yield the same number of civilian casualties? Is that what it means to conduct a fair and proportionate war? What constitutes proportionality? Is it determined by disparate casualty counts—large and uneven numbers of civilian deaths is proof of disproportionality? Perhaps Israel should be allowed to go beyond proportionality—which is how most wars are actually won—given the asymmetric challenges of taking on terrorists.

There has been a quiet debate in Israel since the 2006 Lebanon War whether to formally implement what became known as the Dahiya Doctrine, named for a suburb of Beirut that even in this most recent war with Hezbollah has been a hotbed of terrorist activity. At the time, the Israel Defense Forces took a hard but critical look at the military and moral reality of the way in which terrorists fight wars—surrounded by human shields. Indefatigable enemies are always betting that Israel would not dare risk taking civilian lives. This is the cowardly new world of warfare that terrorism has perfected. In order to eliminate the threat to its own people, however, perhaps the IDF had the military and moral authority to, actually, take the dare.

The Dahiya Doctrine is a no-holds-barred green light to flatten wherever it is that terrorists are based and their weapons are stored. Civilians would be placed on notice that Dahiya, and other such urban compounds, should only be entered at one's own risk. Israel is not going to hesitate undertaking what is militarily necessary—even if civilians are proximately too close to the action.

For proportionality purposes, what matters most is the military value of the target. Once a target is identified as highly valuable and a military necessity, is there a formula that guides a nation in making its proportionality assessment? How many are allowed to be killed before an army is required to walk away? In Gaza, body counts are abysmally inaccurate, if not wholly fabricated. Is Israel bound by the math skills of its adversary?

Perhaps most importantly, when the focus is only on the number of dead Palestinians, the question must be asked: Do Gazans have any agency? Are dead Gazans the fault of Israel alone? Gaza is no ordinary battlefield, and Gazans are no ordinary civilians. Gaza is a densely populated urban minefield unlike no other. It is the very essence of asymmetric warfare: both sides are fighting under entirely different conditions, protocols, and valuations when it comes to human life. Fighting a war in Gaza presents singular strategic and tactical challenges. Should a state in Israel's position be held to impossible standards in preventing civilian death?

What would other countries do if faced with the same existential and moral dilemmas while at war with an unconventional, suicidal enemy? It's easy to demand strict compliance with international norms when it's not your soldiers being asked to undertake the risk of engaging in an abnormal war. Mitigating the risk to civilians stationed as pawns in cluttered warzones demands split-second decision making. It is a near impossible task.

This and more will be discussed throughout the book. Yet, I am under no illusion that the issues raised and answers offered within these pages will change many minds. You either believe that the Jewish people are entitled to self-determination in their ancestral homeland—with the right to defend its people from outside attack—or you are of the view that twenty-two illiberal Arab and Muslim states are not quite enough: Israel must forfeit its state to make room for another Islamist theocracy. If Israel has no right to exist, then applying international law to justify its war in Gaza, or condemning Hamas for violating those laws, will have few sympathizers.

Those who have twisted the facts and misstated the law are gambling that Israel's haters will never be dissuaded from the certainty that the Jewish state is guilty. Meanwhile, indoctrinated students, progressive activists, and social justice warriors are all too easily persuaded that Israel is nothing but an illegal settler colonial enterprise. Search engines are available to round out gaps in their knowledge. They simply have no interest in filling those gaps. They are not seeking a panoramic view of the Middle East. They will settle for a myopic one where Israel is forever slandered and demonized. The Jewish state should not receive a fair trial. A truthful recitation of historical facts is unnecessary. The laws of war are nothing but a nuisance if it absolves Israel of its alleged crimes.

What we have seen is the same toxic environment that existed during the turn of the twentieth century when the hatred of Jews was a globally shared obsession. Alfred Dreyfus paid a price for being a convenient object of scorn. More than a decade later, the antisemitic fever subsided, only to be revived several decades later during the Holocaust. Today it is being revived again.

Israel has already been judged guilty in the public sphere. There is still the possibility that international tribunals will apply the law and facts fairly. But that is unlikely, too. Given the past history of Israel's wars in Gaza and Lebanon, some degree of culpability will be found. Israel's many critics are never above manipulating the facts and misapplying the legal doctrine. As it so often happens at the United Nations, every opportunity to denounce Israel is never to be wasted.

Israel is not guilty of anything. It was attacked on October 7 by six thousand genocidal Palestinians that left behind 1,200 dead Israelis and took 250 hostages to Gaza, including a six-month-old baby. Among the dead were teenage girls who had been gang raped and infants that were beheaded and burned alive. Parents were murdered in front of their children; children were killed with their parents, excruciatingly, watching. Boyfriends saw their girlfriends raped. Soon, they would be murdered, too. The elderly, some Holocaust survivors, were kidnapped by today's Nazis who go by the name Hamas.

It's all too difficult to grasp.

What do the laws of international humanitarian law say when the carnage is Jewish? Do they not apply to protect Jews and punish their enemies? Equal protection under the law was not awarded to Jewish faculty and students on college campuses all throughout the 2023–2024 academic years. And international tribunals are unlikely to treat Israel in the same way it would treat a true genocidal nation—which is largely to ignore the crime altogether. Like so many double standards when it comes to Israel, the legal protections invoked on behalf of Gazans are not reciprocated for the Jews who perished on October 7.

What possible explanation can justify this disparate treatment? Well...Israelis, obviously, deserved it. Had it coming. How could Palestinian terrorists and civilians possibly restrain themselves? The world, apparently, reserves its harshest judgment for the rare occasions when Jews kill Muslims in self-defense.

Israel's critics paid scant attention to the events that provoked Israel into war. And they care little for the military imperative that requires Israel to deter its enemies from ever attempting such a brutal assault again. It is a duty owed to the Jewish people and citizens of Israel. October 7 was grotesque, and Gazans should have been prepared for Israel's reply. Deterrence is not established without suffering. After October 7, no one should have deluded themselves into believing that Gaza would ever look the same again. Israelis are forever changed, too.

David Suissa, the Editor-in-Chief of the *Jewish Journal* reminds Gazans, and Israel's critics, that they had to know that Israel's response to October 7 was not, and should not have been, measured. "The most important word in the Middle East is not power or honor or religion. Those are important, but the supreme word is 'deterrence.' Deterrence is how sophisticated people say 'scared sh-tless.'"[5]

Yet, global public opinion, and especially the arbiters of international law, seem to believe that Israel didn't have the right to send such a message. Its right to self-defense is ultimately an empty, qualified right. It exists, of course, but can't be exercised. The word "ceasefire" was shouted on college campuses before Israel even began its counteroffensive. World governments, including the United States, counseled Israel that it should exercise "restraint," "de-escalate" the conflict, and seek "diplomatic solutions."

No such similar cautionary words were uttered after 9/11.

The talking point that is taken as gospel is that Israel has no right to an existence in the Middle East at all. After its creation, nearly one million Jews were expelled from Arab nations where they had lived for millennia. Many migrated to Israel, their ancestral homeland. And, yet, despite the ironclad testimony of the Old Testament, and archeological evidence buried deep in the land itself, Islamists and progressives will tell you that Jews are not indigenous to the Middle East. They are trespassers, white oppressors, rapacious land-grabbers. Palestinians should be given free rein to attack and kill Israelis at will—precisely what happened on October 7—and "by any means necessary." Jews, especially if they are unrepentant Zionists, have no right to self-defense at all.

Taken to its logical conclusion, Israel is not permitted or even able to engage in a just war in the Middle East. The presence of a Jewish state, and its people, is prima facie unjust.

That's hard to reconcile with what was immediately said after October 7. Many foreign ministries and heads of state acknowledged Israel's right to defend itself. But it was a nebulous, non-specific right because it came with a catch: Israel was free to retaliate, but not if it meant killing Palestinians, including terrorists (a word that is itself considered evidence of a colonialist mindset; after all, one person's terrorist is another's freedom fighter).

No one said that outright, but no other inference makes sense. Collateral damage of any degree in Gaza causes instant fury. Military necessity doesn't seem to matter. No amount of proportionality will be accepted. The Jewish state finds itself in a Kafkaesque quandary: Israel has the right to enter into wars so long as there are no Palestinian casualties of those wars. Its wartime conduct is so circumscribed, any action taken it its own defense is summarily a war crime.

It is as if all that had happened on October 7 was forgotten. The nation acting in self-defense, and pursuant to international humanitarian law, is vilified as the aggressor. Dead Israelis didn't count; the killings of terrorists, however, were unjustified acts of aggression. The belligerency that gave rise to Israel's entry into a just war was downplayed, disbelieved, or appallingly excused.

A grotesque amount of savagery took place on October 7. It should have resulted in sustained universal outrage. Punishing Gaza and ordering the release of the hostages should have been a global priority. Instead, the ringmasters of organized antisemitism blamed Israel for what Hamas did ("rape is resistance") and preemptively condemned Israel for the retribution yet to come. Instead of sympathy, Israel received a litany of accusations: war crimes, genocide, mass starvation—none of which were justified, and each was unsupported by the laws of war and blind to logistical realities. Wars and genocides are two separate things. Israel was involved in the former, no matter how Israel's enemies persist in conflating the two.

Hamas made it very clear that what it achieved on October 7 would be repeated—"again and again." The Israeli hostages hidden in the underground labyrinths of Gaza were not returned. Rockets continued to be launched at Israeli population centers. At no point did Hamas or Islamic Jihad lay down their weapons.

Under those circumstances, Israel was under no legal obligation to bring the war to an expedited conclusion without first achieving its military objectives: to eliminate Hamas as a recidivist terrorist organization on its border, deter future Palestinian attacks, rescue the hostages, and reclaim the bodies of the Israelis that had been killed.

Given the brutality of October 7 with hostages in Gaza held captive by civilians, rockets launched daily at the Jewish state, and terrorists threatening a repeat performance, Israel was not obliged to follow any rules at all. To suggest otherwise is preposterous. No other nation would possibly think that the laws of war could strictly apply to such a surreal situation of national peril. Israel's wartime actions in Gaza have largely been in compliance with the relevant military doctrines. But that's a testament to its commitment to humane values and the rule of law. Israel should be commended for its restraint. Accusations against it are baseless and obscene.

Those charges stem largely from the death toll of Palestinians. More than half are terrorists, however, with an additional 30 percent comprised of friends and relatives of those terrorists. Clearly Israel is targeting Hamas and not the civilians of Gaza. The life expectancy of a Gazan depends largely on whether they have a relative who is a member of Hamas and is being targeted by Israel. Civilians are getting killed because terrorists like to keep their friends and family close by at all times.

That's Israel's fault?

The International Court of Justice (ICJ), which is under the auspices of the United Nations, prosecutes member states. The charges are generally filed by affiliated nations that often have no connection to the subject matter of the proceeding. South Africa, for instance, later joined by Ireland, has brought an action before the court accusing Israel of committing genocide.

The International Criminal Court (ICC), which also resides in the Hague, has a different purpose. It prosecutes heads of state or rogue generals, as individuals, held responsible for violating international law and committing crimes against humanity. Usually, a panel of experts are assigned the task of investigating wartime conduct or alleged human rights abuses. They draft detailed reports and make recommendations to prosecutors whether charges should be filed.

Warrants for the arrest of Israel's prime minister and defense minister have already been issued. This is the first time that leaders of a democratic nation have been charged under the ICC.

In both courts, genocide is the primary and most serious allegation. Israel is accused of both intentionally mass murdering and starving Gazans, along with failing to supply them with humanitarian aid. These cases represent rare instances in which genocide is being alleged in the context of an ongoing war. Even in prior cases involving the mass murder of ethnic Muslims in Bosnia and Herzegovina, courts concluded, with the exception of the killings in Srebrenica, that Muslim deaths were primarily casualties of war. There was no evidence of a specific intent to eradicate Muslims from the former Yugoslavia.

Unless there is some radical redefinition of genocide, it is difficult to see how these courts can rule differently in the genocide charge against Israel. Gazans are casualties of a war. The collateral damage from Israel's war in Gaza does not meet the legal standard for genocide.

Like the Dreyfus Affair, we have all witnessed in Israel's latest war the rush to judge the Jews. Facts and legal doctrine don't matter. The French military needed to refocus the public's attention away from its national security failures. Dreyfus was naturally chosen because he was a high-ranking officer, and a Jew, who could be readily demonized with little difficulty. It was not much of a stretch to agitate the public over a Jewish traitor. A scandal involving a cadre of incompetent generals could never compete with the time-tested antisemitic fervor of the Dreyfus Affair.

Like the corruption within the French military, the plight of the Palestinians is of little actual global importance. No one seemed to mind when Egypt illegally occupied Gaza from 1949 to 1967. And unlike Israel, Egypt had no legal claim on the land whatsoever. The self-determination of Arabs who had lived in once British-occupied Palestine was never uttered until *after* Israel reclaimed the Gaza Strip in 1967. The ancient prejudice against Jews is timeless, always predisposed to reactivation. Israel's wars in Gaza became the perfect rallying cry.

Old-school Christian antisemitism hasn't aged well. Christ-killers no longer cuts it. Islamists and progressives searched for their own crucifixion. And they found it in Israel's astounding first seventy-seven years of existence. The "Nakba"—the "catastrophe" brought about by Israel's creation—is less about Palestinian displacement than it is sheer embarrassment. Only the states that signed the Abraham Accords are Israel's admirers. Far too many nations in the Middle East, outside the orbit of the oil-producing states, have resigned themselves to being left behind. Israel serves as an odious reminder of their stalled progress.

Resentment weighs heavily on this newfound antisemitic revival. Interrupting Israel's march toward global greatness is most definitely a motivation. The anti-colonial impulse to promote the Palestinian cause is a cynical ruse. The hatred of Israel transformed Palestinians into a human rights priority. Wiping off that smirk on a Zionist's face. Finding ready excuses for third-world failures. Normalizing Islamist fantasies. Anything to remind the Jewish people not to get too cozy about their ancestral homeland.

CHAPTER 1

Judging a Nation, and a People, as Guilty—Regardless of the Facts and Law

Let me be clear at the outset and state, emphatically, what should be obvious to any rational thinking reader: I am not in favor of killing children, Palestinian or otherwise. And I don't know any Jew or any Zionist who is.

In another time, on a different subject, with less libelous implications and bad faith—and with Jews, preferably, not among the accused—such qualifying language would be unnecessary. Who wants to see children killed as casualties of war? Yes, civilian death is a tragic but unintended consequence of fighting a just war. But women and children are *never* the intended targets of an army with any honor. Murdering civilians, as a war aim, is an indisputable and indefensible war crime.

Israel derives no benefit from Palestinian casualties of war. If it could be avoided without surrendering the Jewish state to slaughter, if terrorists and their enablers could be excised from Gaza and killed in action without endangering the life of a single Palestinian child, Israelis would be overjoyed. They would benefit, both morally and politically, from precision killings of only those who deserve it.

Every single civilian death is a dagger used by the mainstream media to demonize the Jewish state. In no other conflict zone, in all of world history, has the death of civilians been as painstakingly scrutinized and fiendishly falsified as in Gaza. No other army has had the eyes of the world—in the form of United Nations investigations, international tribunals, and nongovernmental organizations, such as Human Rights Watch and Amnesty International—been as laser focused in condemning the manner by which an army defends itself against an implacable foe that also fights dirty.

Civil War General William Tecumseh Sherman—who notoriously marched through Georgia, burning farms throughout the state after setting fire to Atlanta, all for the ostensible purpose of starving the Confederate Army—infamously added to the vocabulary of armed conflict when he noted, "War is hell." He wasn't saying anything that everyone on this planet didn't already know. From biblical battles to the Trojan War to the Allied bombing of German cities during World War II, civilians die—and many of those civilians are women and children. They are called casualties of war or "collateral damage"—the term of art signifying civilian death at wartime. If civilians are killed, it is collateral to the war aim, incidental, and, in most cases, very much undesired. It is the unfortunate, hellish consequence of combat. Every war ever fought has produced collateral damage—even in wars where civilians were not sacrificed as human shields, as they are in Gaza.

All nations that have been dragged into a war by an aggressor and come out of the conflict victorious should be looking upon Israel's existential and military dilemma with more sympathy. It's a good thing that America, for instance, has been spared this kind of hypocritical wartime inspection. Had the United States been treated similarly, we would all have been speaking either German or Japanese since the middle of the last century.

Israel's past wars against multiple neighboring countries that fought with conventional militaries—1948 War of Independence, 1956 Suez Crisis, 1967 Six-Day War, 1973 Yom Kippur War—did not warrant the same attention because Israel was vastly outnumbered in each campaign, and many of the battles were fought in deserts or in the sky, quite a distance from urban areas. The word "Palestinian"—either the people or as a homeland—was scarcely mentioned back then because a country called Palestine never existed, and until the late 1960s, the people who lived there were referred to as Arabs from either Syria, Jordan, Egypt, or British-occupied Palestine. To say "Palestinian," for most of the twentieth century, referred to the Jews of the Middle East. The Palestinians of today, at the time, were neither a political cause nor a separate people. The world saw these conflicts as the continuation of ancient hostilities. Civilians invariably were killed during these campaigns—both Jews and Arabs. But it was a wholly expected outcome, treated no differently from casualties of other wars around the world.

That changed dramatically in the twenty-first century, when Israel found itself fighting unconventional, asymmetric battles against nonstate actors: terrorists—Hamas and Islamic Jihad in Gaza, and Hezbollah in Lebanon. These entities wholly ignored the laws of armed conflict—the agreed-upon principles for warring nations, and the Geneva Conventions and its updated Protocols, which dealt specifically with prisoners of war and civilians.

Israel, a tiny country surrounded by ruthless enemies, was presented with a new challenge. While its army respected international humanitarian law, its latest adversaries paid no attention to the rules regarding war. Terrorists don't bother with military doctrines or protocols on how one treats prisoners, hostages, and civilians. Instead, the laws of warfare that nation-states rigorously observe are seen as opportunities for them to exploit.

Rules can be leveraged against those who follow them. One side fights with voluntary restrictions; the other weaponizes those restrictions. Without ground rules, the advantage always goes to whomever is reading from a different playbook. It makes for a maddening and morally confusing battlefield. There are no terms of surrender when one side embraces martyrdom and when ceasefires are routinely broken. Warfare becomes a game without a time clock or fixed ending point.

The asymmetries also distort public perceptions. Yes, terrorists are lawless and barbaric. But they're also vastly outnumbered and overmatched. The Jewish state doesn't have that many global friends to begin with. Palestinian terror groups embrace their underdog status. It's more fashionable to cheer for terror and root against a nation-state fighting under a flag bearing a Star of David. Israel's enemies already had well over two thousand years of practice.

Each of these more recent wars were started by either Hamas or Hezbollah acting not on their own but as pawns of the fanatical Iranian regime. Israel was repeatedly placed in a defensive position on entirely new and largely untested legal and moral terrain.

In this new universe called Fourth-Generation Warfare, where a nation-state faces a rogue nonstate actor, one set of civilians are natural targets while the other, as noncombatants, are protected. Terrorists believe that civilians are fair game and act accordingly; military professionals know that such conduct receives a court martial. It is their job and duty to distinguish between combatants and noncombatants. Meanwhile, the terrorists Israel faces make no effort to protect their own civilians. They are cannon fodder, deployed and exploited as human shields. Human beings no better than sandbags, and a most potent tool of propaganda.

When Israel is the state actor, the judgment of blame is a foregone conclusion.

In the minds of terrorists, it is the asymmetry itself—the mismatch in arsenals, the considerable advantages one side possesses—that provides a license to kill or kidnap whomever they wish, in whatever manner they choose. Having disadvantages leads to leeway. As we learned on October 7, 2023, Hamas, and far too many Gazan civilians, believed that atrocities such as the torching of Israeli infants and gang raping teenagers were legitimate targets and acceptable war aims. They even filmed it all in real time—sometimes using the cell phone cameras of their victims, blanketing contact lists, torturing loved ones. These are not warriors with honor; they are sadistic savages.

The goal was not to win a war, but to send a message of terror: "Look what we can do to you; look what we are willing to do. We will target your women and children; we dare you to do the same."

Israeli military strategists have given civilian death a great deal of thought. They have had to. It presents a profound moral quandary of how to fight Hamas and remain a moral army. Israel has learned many lessons from years of fighting terrorists in urban settings. It is very difficult to imagine a rationality to these battles. A moral calculus. A strategic justification to do what a nation must to defend its own people, while, at the same time, blocking out the outside noise, the cascading crowds shouting "shame," which have their own motivations. Israel's critics aren't saying anything that is especially profound or that hasn't already been considered. Killing civilians in Gaza is not a regression to barbarism; it is a moral compromise Israel makes out of military, existential necessity.

And it is not the first nation to make these moral assessments. There is a wide body of legal and military doctrine, the aforementioned Just War Theory, which sets forth rules that guide nations in deciding whether entering the fight is justified—*jus ad bellum*, the justness of going to war in the first instance. Once engaged in conflict, there is another ethical consideration: whether an army is conducting itself justly—*jus in bello*, the justness in the manner an army chooses to fight.

How do you fight antagonists such as Hamas, Islamic Jihad, Hezbollah—especially when the unenviable task falls on Israel, a country not afforded the usual privileges of statehood, where the call for a "ceasefire!" arrives early to snatch victory away? Customary rules collide with double standards. What other nations can do with a sharp sword and a simple handshake, when it comes to Israel, there's a lot of red tape and fine print.

Neither Sun Tzu nor Carl von Clausewitz, the seminal military theorists of their respective eras, ever conceived of Palestinian terrorism and the way civilians may be integrated into a war plan. Ordinarily, armies are charged with protecting its nation's civilians. But no one is guarding the Gazans. And far too many Gazans don't seem to want protection. Most accept their role in the war effort, and they do so uncomplainingly. Israel faces a military landscape where the tactics of war and the logic of loss are completely inverted. War colleges and academies are feverishly taking notes, trying to make sense of it. The moral dilemma has little precedent and no good solutions.

Here's Israel's fate: Rockets and missiles can be fired at its cities indiscriminately. Citizens butchered in broad daylight. And when Israel retaliates, the first faces it sees are noncombatants. These all constitute war crimes, but when was the last time you heard an international tribunal in The Hague empaneled to prosecute Hamas for war crimes? Terrorism comes with its benefits. A blanket pardon. Accountability to no one. The lowest of expectations on how to fight fairly.

Yet, Israel's self-defense is held to the highest standards of wartime scrutiny. Nearly every move it makes raises all manner of global condemnation.

It runs along a predictable course. Not unlike what happened during the last war Israel fought with Hamas in 2014, after October 7, 2023, world leaders, initially and emphatically, stated that Israel had the right to defend itself. But even before Israel began its ground invasion into Gaza, sentiments had changed. Suddenly, Israel was being cautioned to "de-escalate" and exercise "restraint."

No such cautionary warning to exercise restraint was ever asked of the United States in its mission to annihilate the Nazis of Germany or the kamikazes of Japan. When United States Coalition forces eliminated ISIS from Mosul in 2017, resulting in the death of as many as eleven thousand Iraqi civilians, no global condemnation followed, and there was no second-guessing about an absence of restraint.

What began as short-lived empathy for the Israeli people quickly devolved into charges of war crimes and genocide—the very same crime that was given its own universal name, the Holocaust, when it came to the mass murdering of Jews. With a simple flip of the historical switch, now the Jewish state was being referred to as Nazis and charged with committing the same offense. South Africa's charges before the International Court of Justice was laced with symbolism and poetic injustice.

The International Criminal Court had its own plans. Warrants for the arrest of Prime Minister Benjamin Netanyahu and his Minister of Defense, Yoav Gallant, were issued, both accused of crimes against humanity—the very same charges brought against the topmost surviving Nazis at Nuremberg. It may have come as a shock that the court also sought to indict the mastermind behind the October 7 massacre, Hamas' military leader in Gaza, Yahya Sinwar, along with his deputy, Mohammed Diab Ibrahim Al-Masri (Deif), and the political head of Hamas, Ismail Haniyeh. (All three had already been assassinated, not that anyone expected their appearance before the court.) Despite decades of terrorism, involving the slaughter of civilians and the Israeli Olympic team and the hijacking of planes and cruise liners, world courts had never before shown any interest prosecuting Palestinians.

The impulse to punish terrorists is especially dampened given the anti-colonial crosscurrents of these times, where terror groups are often viewed as liberation movements and granted every courtesy as resistance fighters. A terrorist can be assassinated with impunity (i.e. Osama bin Laden); warriors dedicated to decolonializing also benefit from an entirely more favorable reading of international law.

A similar indifference is visible with the mainstream media's coverage of the wars between Israel and Hamas. Legacy outlets like CNN mentioned the Israeli prime minister's name thirty-one times more often than the names of Hamas' leadership in Gaza and Qatar, and nine times as often as the president of the Palestinian Authority in the West Bank.[6]

What is to be drawn from these disparate presentations? One side, Israel, was violating international norms; the other, terrorists from Gaza, were merely plying the tools of the terrorists' trade—tossing Jewish babies into ovens and gang raping Israeli teenagers.

The double standard is deafening.

Muslims kill Muslims all the time, whether in Syria, Yemen, Iran, Iraq, or Afghanistan. The media rarely finds such mass killings newsworthy. Half a million Arabs in Syria are dead (the recent ouster of Syrian president, Bashar al-Assad, uncovered a mass grave filled with over one hundred thousand dead bodies, some belonging to American and British citizens); there have been 377,000 deaths so far in Yemen.

Nothing but silence.

Israelis are defending themselves against terrorists. A disputed death toll of forty-eight thousand, the majority of whom comprised of militants and their families, generates worldwide headlines and leads to demands for the ending of the Jewish state.

Surely much of the disparity in global outrage may be attributed to latent antisemitism that since World War II has had no respectable outlet. But the way in which Hamas fights its wars plays a part, too. Hamas has turned theaters of war into stadium shows, lowering the bar on what victory looks like. Battlefields are where blood is spilled, but Hamas is interested in newsprint and digital film. Turning the world against Israel and instigating revulsion over dead Palestinians is how Hamas ultimately fights and wins wars. No other army has ever measured victory in such twisted, zero-sum terms.

In wars where insurgents are dressed like civilians out for a walk, indistinguishably out of uniform with faces cloaked in keffiyehs, body count is its own endgame. Dead civilians as a war strategy. Yes, revolting to Western eyes, but not incongruous to the Muslim Brotherhood of Gaza. Dead Palestinians hold the world's attention entirely because the killing is being committed by Jews. Israel's claim of self-defense will never erase the images of tiny coffins or grieving mothers cradling dead infants.

This is not an altogether original strategy. Islamists know that the West has no stomach for dead civilians—especially children. Muslims might have full faith in the *Akhirah* and the blessings that come with martyrdom, but Western thinkers will never believe the sacrifice of children to be acceptable wartime losses. Hamas knows this, exploits it, and has no compunction about placing its own people in harm's way if it leads to Israel's isolation.

When the smoke clears and the body count is revealed, squeamish Westerners will more readily blame Israel than Hamas—not entirely because the collateral damage was brought about by Israeli weapons, but because there is utter disbelief in Palestinians doing such an unspeakable thing to one another.

The events in the Middle East take place thousands of miles away. But distance does not suspend disbelief. The human mind limits what it will allow in. It is the reason so little was said and written about the Holocaust until the late 1960s. Despite firsthand accounts, the Nuremberg Trials, documentary footage, depositions from death camp guards, photographs of skeletal corpses piled high, blood-soaked ravines and mass graves, the cremated ashes of millions, and all those unaccounted-for shoes and gold teeth, it took nearly twenty-five years for the world to confront the enormity of what the Nazis had done.

The barbaric tactics of terrorists are similarly difficult for the mind to fully grasp, and so we compartmentalize at a remove. Children as human shields? Parents so demonstrably irresponsible and unfit? Young people brainwashed to welcome death so soon after their lives have begun? It forces questions that are too unseemly to ask. Is it possible that Muslims place so little value on their own lives? How deep is their primal lust for Jewish blood? Is there anything they would not do to claim an Israeli life?

The Gaza Health Ministry, an arm of Hamas, is the only entity permitted to chart the Palestinian death toll. There are no independent fact-finders—not the press, not the International Red Cross, not even the United Nations. In counting the dead, the Ministry makes no distinction between combatants and civilians. It treats every Palestinian death the same and, in doing so, conflates categories that are always separated in times of war. Terrorists are counted as civilians. Cold killers and sleeping kids measured the same, as if the IDF is targeting both. Fudge the numbers. Shamelessly lie. The sum is all that matters. No other ledgers of loss, by any other entity, is created.

To the West, grieving Palestinian mothers makes for excruciating film footage. I want to believe it is agonizing for Palestinians, too, but perhaps not in the same way. What I do know is that liberals in the West conclude that the moral costs are too high to allow Israel to finish the job—no matter who they are aiming at. And when these wartime stratagems are released to the public, Hamas moves its chess pieces along the board, and Israel is hamstrung in making its next move. Delay could cause another Israeli death. So, it stands before the world demonized, delegitimized, friendless—all according to Hamas' grand plan: to cast Israel as a pariah state.

The disparity in the death toll leads to the false charge that Israel is committing genocide. A redefinition of a crime applied to Israel alone. How trivializing it then becomes. Whenever people get killed—for whatever reason and regardless of circumstance—a genocide has been committed. Plane crash: genocide. COVID: genocide. Soldiers killed in action: genocide.

There is a danger in lowering the bar to the point where the original sin loses all meaning. The Biden administration capitulated to DEI and CRT initiatives, which diluted the meaning of racism. Suddenly, everything and everyone was "racist." Israel's self-defense against Hamas, misconstrued on college campuses and in street protests, has trivialized and normalized the word "genocide." Is collateral damage now a synonym for genocide? Because they are two very different things.

The conflation of the two is why Israel's critics, like Senator Bernie Sanders, focus exclusively on the disproportionate death of Gazans. The greater the disparity, the easier it is to justify halting the shipment of arms to Israel. "Disproportion" is constantly invoked in Israel's wars with Hamas, as if it positively constitutes war crimes, or worse, genocide—at least in the public square.

But the legal concept of proportionality does not depend on a balancing of ledgers. The final death tally at the end of a war does not have to add up to the same number. The asymmetrical nature of a war in which one side has air-defense systems, like Iron Dome, and the other conducts its operations within densely populated urban areas, will undoubtedly result in unequal casualty counts.

But death tolls in themselves are not dispositive of war crimes. A victorious army can miraculously avoid having any casualties at all—soldiers or civilians—and it would not prove that the war was fought unjustly. Death tolls can be lopsided without violating the rules governing proportionality. That's because proportionality assessments are focused more on what an army was aiming at and less on the results. Everyone already knows that wars leave dead bodies behind.

Disarming the Israeli Defense Forces (IDF)—depriving them of offensive weapons such as artillery shells, bunker busters, and precision-guided bombs—is one objective of Israel's critics: neutralizing its capacity to kill Palestinians. But for many, Israel's deployment of defensive weapons is just as objectionable—because it protects Jewish lives, and thus magnifies the disproportion in the body count between Arabs and Jews. Israel's air-defense missile systems—the Iron Dome, David's

Sling, and Arrow—ensures that Hamas rockets and Hezbollah missiles rarely reach ground. Detonations in the sky will not result in dead Israelis. And, frankly, that upsets a lot of people, especially the members of the Squad—and six other congressional House members—who, in 2021, voted against funding the Iron Dome for Israel. Obviously, if you are counting bodies, having an Iron Dome makes it an unfair fight.

A specific category of disproportion is the linchpin of what drives Israel's detractors: the plight of "innocent civilians" in Gaza. As a longtime law professor and legal analyst, I have had some interest in this area of international humanitarian law—probably because it is so widely misunderstood. In fact, during Israel's last major war with Hamas, back in the summer of 2014, I played a role in widening the conversation—and turning it into a controversy.

If the ledgers of loss consisted of Hamas terrorists on one side and IDF soldiers on the other, the inequality in death tolls would seem less objectionable—even if there were fewer dead Israeli soldiers than terrorists. What invariably catches the world's attention is not the killing of combatants, but that innocent civilians are among the dead. It is the civilian status of dead Gazans—especially women and children—that is the primary indictable offense leading to charges of Israeli genocide and war crimes.

It's also the preoccupation of mainstream media and human rights groups. Killing terrorists is one thing; civilians are not supposed to be on stage in theaters of war. Great care must be undertaken to protect them. After all, civilians are presumed to be innocent—hence, "innocent civilians." If one is not dressed in a uniform and carrying a weapon, then he, or she, can't lawfully be killed in battle.

But the presumptive innocence of *all* civilians isn't entirely true. Not all are alike. The post-World War II Geneva Conventions—especially the Fourth Geneva Convention, Article 4, which defined "protected persons"— addressed the matter of the treatment of civilians during wartime. An invading army may not mistreat or use the local population as hostages. The premise is that civilians must be removed from the fields of battle because they have no business being there. And they cannot be used as pawns. Wars are fought among combatants, only.

The problem is that the drafters of the Geneva Conventions—four separate treaties that protect victims of war and soldiers who are taken hostage—back in 1947, never anticipated the special situation presented in Gaza. They understood civilians in the ordinary sense. Most Gazans, however, are decidedly not ordinary civilians. There are, of course, Gazans who would qualify as innocent civilians, having no formal role with Hamas. But wartime conditions do not stand on formalities. There are Gazan civilians who provide material aid, support and comfort to Hamas. When civilians join the fight, even in capacities that do not require them to fire weapons, they may have intentionally surrendered their civilian status.

What the Geneva Conventions had in mind are "innocent" civilians, which has little to do with the wearing of uniforms. No members of Hamas or Islamic Jihad are wearing uniforms. Civilian can serve a deadly purpose without weapons or portfolio.

There is another feature of Gaza that was not considered by the original drafters of the Geneva Conventions. In the ordinary course, civilians have no interest placing their lives at risk. If they find themselves in harm's way, someone must have put them there.

Not in Gaza, however. Gazans have agency, and they exercise it. Hamas hasn't hijacked the population. Most are not under duress or house arrest. When civilians are presented with humanitarian corridors in which to shelter with their families, far too many refuse to leave their homes. The IDF provides evacuation warnings of impending airstrikes or ground operations—essentially, informing the enemy, "Here's our playbook. This is what we are planning to do next." Hamas appreciates the heads-up. But most Gazans ignore the warnings. They choose to stay put, holed up with terrorists. Unfathomably, many are prepared to become martyrs for the Palestinian cause.

Should Israel be legally and morally responsible for the deaths of those who reject a safe passageway and instead choose to die?

Hamas boasts that Palestinians rejoice in sacrificing themselves and their children. Impressed into national service as an auxiliary citizens' army. Brainwashed battalions reporting for duty. Their one assignment: get killed.

This has been the source of profound moral confusion. Those who live in Western nations cannot accept that Palestinians, especially parents, would make that choice for themselves and, most especially, their children. It defies the survival instincts of our species. It's one thing for Hamas wanting to turn ordinary citizens into weapons for PR purposes. But civilians volunteering to participate in madness? Enlisting children to commit suicide? Convincing Muslims that in death they are being delivered to a better place? Simply unfathomable if one is ensconced in a cozy apartment on Park Avenue or Covent Garden, but in gritty Rafah, it is conventional thinking.

As human rights activist Ayaan Hirsi Ali has repeatedly explained to Westerners left shaking their heads in abject disbelief, "What is unique to Islam is the tradition of murderous martyrdom, in which the individual martyr simultaneously commits suicide and kills others for religious reasons."[7]

Surely Hamas forces some Gazans to lose their lives against their will. But is Israel responsible for those deaths? The global consensus suggests that Israel is, indeed, responsible. Provoking the revulsion of the West obviously works. But is Israel truly responsible, legally?

Even after initiating senseless wars that leave Gaza in ruins, result in displacing nearly the entire Palestinian population and cause the deaths of thousands, Hamas remains wildly popular. In Gaza, Hamas terrorists are heroes—even though its senior leadership are now all dead. A new generation always seems ready to answer the call. The people refuse to turn away from terror. This was not immediately true in Germany and Japan. It's not even true in Lebanon today. The Lebanese have always regarded Hezbollah as interlopers. But for Gazans, the destruction of Israel, and the death of Jews, remain as ceaseless, overarching objectives. Nor have they lost faith in suicide as a religious rite of passage.

This is the reality that Israel faces, and it is the same reality that much of the world either refuses to appreciate or rejects outright. The presence of civilians willing to die is no excuse for killing them. They remain innocent and blameless as though utterly lacking in agency. The hands of the Israeli military must be tied. Living in densely crowded urban areas, with Hamas hiding among them, is tantamount to a Palestinian version of the Iron Dome.

The canards and falsehoods about Jews intentionally killing Palestinians is simply too irresistible not to exploit. This is where the medieval Christian blood libel against Jews has been resurrected, and where it receives a geographic makeover, too.

Middle East Arabs are being substituted for the European Christians of the Dark Ages.

The libel looks like this: Despite the vast amount of biblical and archeological evidence to the contrary, we are told that Jews never had any historical connection to these Arab lands. In this wholly revisionist and fictitious account of the Jewish presence in Israel, Jews from Europe, and then America, forcibly colonized the entire region, overwhelming Arabs with Jewish money and Western armaments. They stole the land and disenfranchised and brutalized the Palestinians with apartheid policies and ethnic cleansing. Such settler-colonialism, we are told, is as bad if not worse than what imperialist Europeans did to marginalized, defenseless people around the world.

Actually, Israel's creation wasn't anything like that. For starters, there has never *not* been a continuous presence of Jews in their ancestral homeland—going as far back as biblical days and the Kingdom of Judah. After centuries of forced exile, Jews started to return to these lands in the nineteenth century and began purchasing parcels of property—from the Ottomans, who occupied Israel at that time. No colonial power from the West sent them—like the Dutch in South Africa, the Belgians in Congo, the French in Algeria, and the British in Egypt. Jews traveled on their own dime, racing back to live on the land of their forefathers and foremothers. As for a land-grab aided by Europeans or Americans, Jews fought their own battles with a ragtag military outfit—many of whom were recent Holocaust survivors—during its War of Independence, using fully purchased secondhand weapons from Czechoslovakia. Nothing was given to them, and they took nothing that didn't already belong to them.

Nonetheless, this new blood libel is what students on college campuses, the readers of the *Washington Post*, and viewers of MSNBC are spoon-fed, and what they quite naively believe. Truthful information about the Middle East, and the legitimacy of Jewish claims to Israel and the disputed territories where Palestinians now live, is readily available—but you have to look for it. It won't be discussed in American classrooms, or found on Wikipedia, or in intellectual magazines or mainstream media. Algorithms are written to bury the truth about Israel and to ennoble the story of the Palestinian people. The truth requires a few keystrokes and a bit of intellectual bullying at school—because an alternative version of that complex history is not tolerated in our culture. The simplistic fable about Palestinian victimhood is taken on faith.

It was here that I once, years ago, entered the debate in defense of Israel. During Israel's 2014 war against Hamas, I wrote an op-ed for the *Wall Street Journal*, "About Those 'Innocent' Palestinian Civilians: Gazans Shelter Terrorists and Their Weapons in Their Homes, Right Beside Sofas and Dirty Diapers."[8] The essay appeared in both the European and American editions. For the next few days, many people around the world had concluded that I must be a monster. I was accused of justifying the murder of Palestinian children and declaring that there is no such thing as a Palestinian civilian.

I never wrote anything of the kind. I invite you all to read the essay and decide for yourselves. Because the essay was, and remains, behind a paywall, most people who denounced it never actually read it. What they read was the online chatter in the form of shrill denunciations simply because in the essay, Israel was being defended and some Palestinians blamed.

Here's what I did say: Most Gazans are aiding and abetting Hamas. They are willing accomplices. They lend material support. They sacrifice themselves in shielding weapons and militants. They might qualify as civilians, but they are not innocent of any involvement in killing Israelis, and in many cases, they are complicit in their own deaths. Under international law, when innocence is lost, so too is the protected status that civilians would otherwise enjoy.

I know this is difficult to accept. People in the West and not born Muslim—in say, Wisconsin, Vancouver, Kraków, Luxemburg—or if Muslim, not committed to a strict adherence to Sharia law, would never do such a thing. But it is commonplace in Gaza, a pledge of loyalty to the Muslim Brotherhood, no different from the true believers of ISIS, al-Qaeda, the Taliban, and Boko Haram.

That doesn't mean innocent Palestinian civilians don't exist in Gaza. There are those who take no part in the barbarism of Hamas and curse the day that Hamas ever came into their lives. But the vast majority adore Hamas, endorse their methods, and revel in their madness. And that's why there are few "innocent" civilians in Gaza. In electing a terrorist organization in 2007, a malevolent outfit committed to a Charter that calls for the killing of all Jews no matter where they reside, they knowingly placed themselves at risk. By opening their homes and allowing them to serve as command centers and for the warehousing of weapons, they have, under any fair reading of international law, joined the fight.

Palestinian children, of course, have made no decisions of their own. They are truly the victims of their demented parents. In the United States, for far less parental neglect—like locking a child inside a car during the summer heat—social workers are summoned to take custody over the children. In Gaza, parents who are the proximate cause of their child's death are rewarded with cable news screen time. Instead of condemning Palestinian parents, where the blame belongs, the world points its finger at the country that is simply trying to protect its own children from barbarous next-door neighbors.

Aside from the children, innocence in Gaza is very much in short supply. Life expectancy is abysmally short. Little priority is being given to preserve life. Palestinian death is too valuable for Hamas to forfeit. They view themselves not as devoted caretakers, but as strategic undertakers. Humanitarian aid is stolen by Hamas for its own use (and sells what it doesn't need on the black market) and not distributed to relieve the suffering of their people.[9] Hamas is playing the long game. An all-out death strategy. Despicably involving the people they refuse to protect.

It was the Gazans that granted terrorists such power. It was their choice in democratically electing known killers to represent them. Hamas didn't seize control. Once in office, nothing but havoc followed. The aftermath was a foregone conclusion. Gazans installed into office not civic leaders or land-use planners or even bureaucratic technocrats. They chose, instead, terror tycoons. Not bridge builders but bomb makers. The children, brainwashed since birth to hate Jews, are tragic innocents. Their parents sealed their fate. Disastrous decision making set Gazans on an unavoidable course toward disproportionate death.

CHAPTER 2

A War of Moral Confusion: Casualties of War Are Not Victims of Genocide

Bob Simon had an illustrious forty-seven-year career in broadcast journalism, all of it for *CBS News*. He is most remembered for his nearly twenty years on *60 Minutes*, but earlier in his career he was the network's chief Middle Eastern correspondent. In an earlier period, he reported on the events in the region from *CBS*' Tel Aviv bureau. Audiences saw him often embedded in hot spots such as Vietnam, Northern Island, Grenada, Haiti, Somalia, and Egypt during the uprising known as Arab Spring. He covered the war between Israel and Hezbollah in 2006.

Simon obviously knew a lot about global warfare having seen so much of it up close—especially in the Middle East. He witnessed first-hand how battle scars inflicted by armies directly damaged the local population.

Bob was also my friend. During the Israel-Hamas War in 2014, I wrote essays defending Israel, aside from that widely criticized op-ed in the *Wall Street Journal*. Throughout the six weeks of the war, I wrote for the *Daily Beast*, *Haaretz*, and *The Times of Israel*. Each one in various ways called attention to the impossible moral dilemma Israel was placed in, given such unprecedented surroundings—an urban battlefield where terrorists and civilians were indistinguishable, and where a terrorist group adopted a civilian death strategy as a deliberate war aim. Civilian death became the bane of Israel's global standing.

I realize that even contemplating a civilian death strategy sounds preposterous. Such a thing cannot exist—even in war! Sure, kill Israeli soldiers. Perhaps aim for Israeli civilians, too. The history of the Middle East is one long march toward eliminating the Jewish presence. But a war strategy where success is measured in the death of your own civilians, and most don't seem to mind?

Either your people are innocent civilians or bloodthirsty, death-wish civilians. It's impossible to be both.

Bob and I ran into one another on Broadway near Lincoln Center when the war was nearly over. He looked uncomfortable. Apparently, I was the last person he wanted to see.

After we embraced, he said, "Thane, I've been reading your writings these past several weeks, but I have chosen not to comment."

"That's okay, Bob, there's no need to ever respond," I said, knowing quite well what his response might involve.

"You must know I largely disagree with you."

"I assumed that much," I answered.

"I have one rule," he interjected emphatically.

"What's that, Bob?"

"You can't kill children."

I instantly replied, "I agree with that rule. Who would be against such a rule? But, Bob, what is Israel supposed to do about those ten thousand rockets fired from Hamas and Islamic Jihad at Israeli cities, intended to kill Israelis, including Israeli children?"

He paused, let out a sigh, and conceded, "I haven't figured that out yet."

We both stood there as pedestrians crisscrossed the clogged New York City streets with their usual brusqueness. The midtown traffic snarled. After some mutual fidgeting, Bob broke the silence, "I guess Israel could establish a safe zone on its southern border with Gaza. Make an encampment. Take responsibility for the women and children of Gaza." (A pretty original idea, one that Israel actually adopted in the war that commenced on October 7, 2023, although these civilian corridors were located within Gaza.)

Bob could not have imagined that nearly a decade later, four thousand elite Hamas terrorists and two thousand two hundred Gazan civilians would surge through an inexplicably unsecured border with Israel. Some invaded with paragliders. As many as four thousand six hundred rockets were fired into Israel simultaneously. Hamas and its henchmen infiltrated twenty-one communities, ransacking homes in villages and *kibbutzim*, murdering 1,200 Israelis and torching, butchering, and gang raping with abandon. There were 250 taken hostage. Over eighteen months later, the whereabouts of the remaining fifty-nine hostages were unknown, with thirty-five presumed dead, and, pursuant to a ceasefire that coincided with the return of Donald Trump to the White House, some of the living hostages and the remains of the dead ones were returned over a forty-two-day period.

Obviously, I couldn't have conceived of anything like this ever happening, either. Israel's sovereignty had never before been breached. But it did cause me to wonder at the time. So, I asked Bob, "If Israel had done as you suggest and created safe zones, would Gazans actually leave their homes to save their families, forcing Hamas to fight without human shields?"

"I don't know," he conceded. But I think we both knew the answer.

That short conversation sums up the dilemma quite well. No one wants to see dead Palestinian children; but to protect them, Israel would have to choose not to defend its own children. I know of no moral principle where a nation is expected to favor the lives of the children of its mortal enemies over its own—or its own soldiers, for that matter. What complicates these issues even further is that Palestinian parents don't seem all that interested in sparing the lives of their children. They are essentially telling Israelis who are warning them to evacuate: "Thanks, but no thanks. We're fine with being in harm's way."

Israel is being asked to become its demented brother's keeper.

In 2010, the longtime publisher of *The New Republic*, Martin Peretz, caused a stir by saying, "Frankly, Muslim life is cheap, especially for Muslims." The fallout from his statement was not inconsequential (an award he was set to receive from Harvard was withheld). He eventually apologized. But why should he have had to? His observation was demonstrably true. These were not his calculations or his own valuations. Muslims around the world have been responsible for cheapening their own lives—with civil wars in Syria and Yemen, the Kurdish portion of Iraq, Western Sahara, Sudan, a ten-year war between Iran and Iraq. Millions have been slaughtered in sectarian warfare. And, yet there has not been a peep of protest from Muslims around the world, and there's silence from the press.

Muslims often mock the West for valuing earthly human life over the glories of the afterlife. From Denmark to Dearborn, we are told that nonbelievers of the Prophet have no idea what they are missing: how spiritually empty and miserable this life is, and what awaits believers beyond this realm. Westerners do not glorify death. And, in doing so, they are forfeiting the seven blessings from Allah pledged to martyrs. In Western imaginations, however, those bounties aren't likely to catch on anytime soon. For the time being, Americans are passing on the suicide vests.

The truth is that not all cultures value life in the same way. Human beings all have preferences in what we value. When it comes right down to it, most Westerners prefer themselves, their children, neighbors, and countrymen to the lives of strangers and foreigners. Indeed, it is the mark of democratic Western nations that we place a higher value on the lives of our own citizens—and grant them more human rights—than most societies have done throughout history.

In 2011, Israel released one thousand Palestinians, many of them hardcore terrorists, in exchange for Israeli soldier Gilad Shalit, who had been kidnapped in 2008. Does that mean that one Israeli life is worth one thousand Palestinians? (One of them was Yahya Sinwar, the mastermind behind the October 7 massacre. Leave him in jail, and October 7 may have never happened.) The exchange doesn't suggest that Arabs and Israelis are of equal value. Hamas understands that it doesn't have to kidnap one thousand Israelis to reclaim one thousand of their own. They have accepted these distorted valuations and don't seem insulted by what they imply.

This kind of devaluation of Muslim lives is surely not limited to Gaza. Another terrorist group, the Houthis from Yemen, like Hezbollah in Lebanon, took the war in Gaza as an occasion to cause its own mischief and murder of Israelis. The Houthis' mottos include, "death to Israel," "death to America" and "damn the Jews." Israel stepped up its counterattacks in response to Houthi missile fire, which failed to circumvent Israel's air-defense systems. Israel's aerial response, predictably, was severe. Israeli officials issued a strong message that unless they halt their aggression, the Houthis would soon face the same fate as Hamas and Hezbollah.

A senior researcher at the Sana'a Center for Strategic Studies, Abdulghani al-Iryani, said that threatening the Houthis will do no good. The usual rules of military deterrence simply do not apply to Islamist states.

"I don't think they'll stop because of the punishment the people are getting from the Israelis and from everyone else," he said. "To them, the loss of life among civilians is totally irrelevant. They don't care."[10]

Here's another way to look at it. Israel knows bombing buildings in Gaza, no matter how pinpoint the operation and precise the fighter pilot's aim, will result in more civilian casualties than if IDF commandos invade Gaza and fight Hamas house-to-house. Choosing that approach saves the lives of Palestinian civilians but jeopardizes the lives of IDF soldiers who may be killed in action. Since Israel possesses all the air power it needs to flatten Gaza in an hour's time, the genocide charge is bogus for that reason alone.

Should a Palestinian child be valued as much or more than a teenage Israeli soldier? Under what moral principle is that the case? International humanitarian law specifies that sparing the lives of soldiers—what is known as "force protection"—is not supposed to be favored over the lives of civilians. That rule is not generally enforced by military commanders, however. Military officers believe they owe a duty to their soldiers not to place them in deathtraps just to spare civilian life. Military doctrine might suggest otherwise (so would Michael Walzer), but try convincing army commanders that troops are expendable to save the lives of noncombatants. Military experts Asa Kasher and Amos Yadlin believe that soldiers' lives should actually receive greater priority over civilians, otherwise terrorists will believe that their proximity to civilians makes them immune from risk averse artillery fire.[11]

Moreover, what mother would be convinced that ground troops are morally superior to airstrikes if it means the certain death of her grown child? Years ago, the parents of IDF soldiers killed in an attack on the Jenin refugee camp in the West Bank wanted an explanation from the IDF chief of staff why he didn't just order the bombing of the camp with F-16 aircraft.[12]

In Western societies, children are objects of extreme parental investment; in Gaza, children have value mainly in relation to how they advance the Palestinian cause (or whether their deaths grant them lifetime stipends from Hamas or the Palestinian Authority). Gazan parents accept financial compensation directly from the Palestinian Authority's budget for their martyred children. Streets and parks are named for martyrs. Perversely, the reward structure that Hamas has set in place makes these children more valuable dead than alive—to their families, and certainly to Hamas itself.

This kind of calculation seems insane from the perspective of an American helicopter mom, but in Gaza, dead children have their own special currency. The average Gazan today apparently believes this strategy to be working and that the family's sacrifice serves a positive end. Yes, I understand, if you don't do much reading about political Islam, or you eschew the conservative press, this sounds like a fantasy from the *Arabian Nights*.

But it's real, I assure you. Dismiss the realities of civilian human shields, and you have just become a stooge for terrorists who are laughing at your Western spine and infidel's gullibility, as they mark yet another notch on their propagandist's toolbelt.

Given such a psychotic state of affairs, in order to win the world's favor, Israel must prove itself to be the morally superior nation and serve as legal guardians for Gazan children—essentially, play the role of Gazan parents in absentia. IDF soldiers suddenly recommissioned as babysitters. If there is zero tolerance for dead Palestinian children, then what other choice would Israel have—stop the shelling, mortar attacks, and airstrikes and turn the ground troops around? Pack up the weapons and go home? Wait for Hamas, or some other terrorist entity, to reconstitute themselves? All military actions undertaken by Israel in its self-defense present enormous risk to Palestinian families who refuse to help themselves.

Let's remember: Israel builds bunkers to give their children a place to hide when sirens sound. Jewish children are never shields. Incoming rocket barrages are destroyed in the sky, land harmlessly, or damage property, but they do not cause loss of life. Yes, occasionally one breaks through the Iron Dome and injures a civilian. But that's largely it. Israel refuses to give antisemites the satisfaction of seeing dead Jewish bodies piled up like in the Holocaust.

It's not as if Gazans have nowhere to hide. Hamas built an elaborate network of tunnels, dug deep into the ground, traversing over 310 miles of the Gaza Strip, and reinforced with steel. These tunnels are equipped with internet access and air-conditioning. But the Palestinian people are granted no entry into these tunnels, which could easily serve as underground bunkers. That's because the tunnels were built to protect terrorists, stockpile weapons, and hide Israeli hostages. Hamas safeguards what it values most. Saving the lives of civilians is a nonexistent priority.

Everyone has strong opinions about what Israel absolutely may not do to defend itself from terrorizing Gazans. Bob Simon, with all his many years observing the Middle East (he was also once a hostage of Saddam Hussein), held a strong view of his own: children must always be spared.

Yes, agreed. But how can that be done without forcing Israel to live in a state of perpetual surrender and maximum vulnerability?

When you ask these same people of similarly aligned conviction what Israel *can*, and should, be allowed to do in defending itself, suddenly they need to make a phone call or are conveniently summoned elsewhere, or become plainly flummoxed. Bob Simon, who knew the region as well as anyone who had ever chronicled the dog days of war, answered honestly: "I simply don't know."

Nearly a decade later, on October 7, a ceasefire broken by Hamas, culminated in the worst attack against the Jewish people since the Holocaust. And we're right back where we always seem to start. A terrorist organization commences a war with a state. The state retaliates in self-defense, as it has a right to do under international law, and an obligation to its people. Terrorists launch attacks from within a civilian population. Terrorists, and some civilians, get killed. Terrorists cry foul, complain to the global community, and demand a ceasefire—ostensibly to save civilians but ultimately to enable the terrorists to regroup and fight another day.

Since when is the initiator of hostilities—the party that launched a war of aggression—in a position to complain of collateral damage and demand a ceasefire? Especially when the initiator is an adversary that committed unspeakable acts to civilians and is still holding hostages they refuse to release.

The question remains: What is Israel to do? To do nothing rewards Hamas for being willing to sacrifice its own people, and grants them a license to kill Israelis. In what universe would the United States allow Mexican or Canadian terrorists to slaughter Americans from the "ocean to the ocean," and not take any defensive measures to avoid further acts of mass murder?

Israeli novelist Amos Oz happened to be in Germany promoting a book during the 2014 war between Israel and Hamas. In addition to being a celebrated Israeli writer, he was also one of the founders of the Peace Now movement. Ideologically, he was opposed to the West Bank settlements and in favor of a two-state solution.

Peace Now activists were generally amenable to almost any concession if it could result in a peaceful resolution to the Middle East conflict. Their movement openly declared, as the organization's name intimated, that peace was what they most wanted—either right *now*, or as soon as possible. Their progressive agenda lent credence to a complete reframing of Israel's negotiating strategy with the Arabs in the disputed territories: Palestinians need to be seen as partners in peace, not as enemies in war.

Having Oz available for a sit-down interview with *Deutsche Welle* while a war in Gaza raged was seen by both German media and Palestinian sympathizers as a real coup. It was nothing short of hitting the Israel-bashing jackpot. Someone of Oz's stature, who had a human rights background and was a frequent critic of Israel's more nationalistic and tribalistic governments, could speak directly to the disproportionate death toll in Gaza and how it has eroded the Jewish soul and damaged Israel's standing on the global stage.

Deutsche Welle was in for a surprise. As soon as he was asked about IDF airstrikes that resulted in the death of Palestinian children, and whether Israel's actions had been excessive, Oz wrote an entirely different script for how this interview would proceed. He said he would like to begin by asking Germany's citizens two questions of his own:

"Question 1: What would you do if your neighbor across the street sits down on the balcony, puts his little boy on his lap, and starts shooting machine gun fire into your nursery?

Question 2: What would you do if your neighbor across the street digs a tunnel from his nursery to your nursery in order to blow up your home or in order to kidnap your family?

. . .

I am afraid that there can be no way in the world to avoid civilian casualties among the Palestinians as long as the neighbor puts his child on the lap while shooting into your nursery."

Complete silence all over Germany—so appropriate given its role in Jewish mass murder. And that was the response from a founder of Peace Now! What does that tell you about the capacity for peaceful coexistence between Israelis and Palestinians? Imagine what it took to shatter Oz's confidence in the possibilities for peace. He gave Germans a hard-bitten assessment of the neighborhood in which Israelis live. The unimaginable choices they are left with in order to safeguard their own children's nurseries. What Israel is forced to do; what they simply cannot avoid doing.

If Gazans refuse to remove their children from their laps while targeting Israeli children, then the Jewish state is compelled to play right into the hands of Hamas and give them the optics they seek: dead Palestinian children. Until Gazans disengage themselves from the terrorists who terrorize them too, their children will remain at grave risk, and the world will recoil at the outcome.

But there is one disquieting takeaway from Oz's interview, a true achievement Hamas can take credit for: after years of terror, they wore down one of Israel's leading doves. As one of Israel's greatest novelists, he was quite familiar with inventing imaginary worlds. But fiction writers are not doomed to live in the realm of make-believe—especially not coarsened Israelis who, like Oz, have lived through nearly all of its wars. Israel's mandatory military service means that even an artist was once a warrior.

Oz was a man of his time and a realist when it came to the Middle East. He wanted peace, but, unlike so many Jewish-American progressives who have been insulated from what battle-tested Israelis experience in the ordinary course, Oz instantly recognized the warning signs of living beside Jew-hating religious fanatics. Implicitly, he was insinuating what international lawyers and human rights groups dare not admit: perhaps law-abiding states are not obliged to faithfully adhere to the laws of war when its enemies are under no such obligation.

There is a saying in Israel: "We can't allow the Arabs to out crazy us." What does it mean? The translation goes something like this: "The Arabs know no bounds, feel no compunctions, and recognize no moral limits. They possess a much higher threshold for violence. They answer to no agreed-upon rules. They predictably break their word. The long history of breached ceasefires always starts with them. We will get slaughtered if we believe they will abide by the rules of warfare. No courtesies will be reciprocated. We must at all times imagine that anything is possible."

The massacre on October 7 was a tragic example of what can happen if Israel is out-crazied. The nation is still coming to terms with the reality of such a colossal intelligence failure. Its sovereignty breached and taken by surprise. Hamas terrorists and Gazan civilians infiltrated Israel from every direction—by motorcycles, pickup trucks, speed boats, and paragliders. Felonious civilians dashed through the security fence on foot and bicycles. They headed hurriedly for Israeli villages and *kibbutzim*, knowing exactly where they were going and what to do when they arrived.

The sheer amount of savagery that took place once the invaders reached the campgrounds of the Nova Music Festival surprised even the military commander of Hamas, Yahya Sinwar.

His men, and their civilian henchmen, took part in an orgiastic, blood-curdling murder spree. In text messages after the massacre, Sinwar wrote that the brutality exceeded his expectations. He didn't realize that Gaza's civilians would rise to the occasion. "Things went out of control," he wrote, specifically, about the civilian gangs that raped Israeli women, mutilated bodies, and took hostages. "People got caught up in this, and that should not have happened."[13]

It's doubtful that Sinwar was really that surprised. He knows the Islamist mindset toward the West, and the Muslim Brotherhood, his sect within Islam, are comprised of devout followers of Muhammad as wartime general. Following him as the Prophet is far less interesting. Savage attacks have become common occurrences all throughout Europe, Australia, and Canada. Each of these nations opened their doors to Islamists not realizing that, asylum aside, these immigrants wanted nothing more than to import Islam to Europe. Toppling democracies would be nice, too.

While Israel battled Hamas, the Western world was embroiled with its own similarly inclined adversaries. The only difference was that Europe and Canada were largely capitulating to and making excuses for Islam. No one seemed to be paying attention to the heightened ambitions of these new home-grown enemies. Israel knew better.

France was in the throes of crime-infested no-go zones. Nations were surrendering huge swaths of public spaces for religious calls to prayer. Flag burnings became public rituals. Muslim mobs chanted "Death to" whatever it was that offended them that morning. Cartoonists were killed for mocking the Prophet. Jews were tormented, and, in some cases, tortured for being Jews. Western nations found themselves afraid to even acknowledge the serious problem their lax immigration laws—and pretentious talk of inclusivity—had brought them.

Integrating large numbers of Muslim arrivals into pluralistic, liberal democracies was not going to be an easy lift. Far too many Muslims resisted the allure of a multicultural utopia. Europeans stood stupefied, unsure of what else to offer them. Sharia law, soccer, and violent demonstrations pretty much defined their tastes—and not always in that order. Ironically, Europeans ceded their continent to the very same people with whom they fought wars during the Crusades, the Middle Ages, and World War I. This time, however, Europe simply opened its doors without bothering to raise a sword.

Perhaps Amos Oz, back in 2014 when he visited Germany, was not only defending Israel against charges of war crimes. He was also delivering an omen. The Syrian Civil War was already hemorrhaging refugees. Germany would soon become the most welcoming country to accept fleeing Muslims. The Islamic madness that Oz was trying to describe would soon infect Germany. Difficult choices would have to be made. The Germans were perhaps being advised not to judge the Jewish state too harshly.

In late August 2024, five Muslim teenagers in Germany were arrested for plotting an "Islamist-motivated terror attack." One Syrian migrant, with ties to ISIS, wielding a knife, killed three people at a German music festival. When captured, the terrorist explained that he lurched at the necks of his victims, intending to sever their heads.[14]

No one in Germany finds any of this shocking anymore. They know the government was slow to acknowledge certain truths about asylum-seekers—the extracurricular activities and murderous prejudices they brought with them and incorporated into their new lives in Germany.

On New Year's Eve in 2016, 1,200 women were sexually assaulted in various German cities by over two thousand Muslim men in what appeared to be a coordinated celebration of the "infidels' holiday."[15] Nothing in the Koran apparently prohibits such cruelties against non-Muslim women. The vast majority of Muslims living in Germany who played no role in this ghastly exhibition of ingratitude failed to condemn the acts of their co-religionists.

It took months for the German government and independent press to finally reveal the extent of these nationwide New Year's crimes. With so many Germans already critical of the vast number of new immigrants being uneasily absorbed into the country, failing to report the story truthfully—to reveal just how nightmarish it was for those 1,200 women—was nothing less than a betrayal. Worse still, many of those arrested received suspended sentences.

Germany was not alone. *The Free Press* published a litany of stabbings by knife-wielding Muslims in the West and wondered why so many nations and law enforcement bodies chose to overlook these acts of violence,[16] pretending they were some Middle East mirage rather than a very real global menace—resulting in murder, mutilation, and real threats to public safety. In April 2024, a bishop and priest were stabbed during services in Australia. The attacker, a teenager, was videoed shouting: "Allahu Akbar." In March 2024, four violent Islamists were arrested in Stockholm. A member of the British Parliament, Mike Freer, resigned in January 2024, fearing that if he remained in public office, he would be assassinated for having supported the bombing of Syria to stop Bashar al-Assad from killing his own people.

And the list goes on. A teacher killed in France, two Swedish nationals murdered by gunfire in Belgium, a German tourist murdered in Paris—all taking place in the aftermath of the

October 7 massacre, and all unsparing in the same graphically violent details. Muslim teenagers in southern France announcing, "We're here to kill whites," went on a mass stabbing, killing one sixteen-year-old boy and wounding several others. In June 2022, a mass shooting in Oslo, left two dead and twenty-one wounded.

Two gay men in Ireland were tortured and decapitated in April 2022. The alleged assailant, born in Iraq, explained his motive: homosexuality was "a sin" and "you won't find many Muslims gay and religious." That's true, something of which queer college-campus, pro-Hamas protesters don't seem to be aware: the short lifespans of homosexuals and lesbians in Muslim societies.

And let's not forget how Islamic extremists have declared war on the creators of Western culture itself. After decades of living in strategic incognito, largely under the protection of the British government, novelist Salman Rushdie decided it was finally time to ignore an Iranian *fatwa* placed on his head—and that had never been retracted. He moved to America and ventured back into the world as a free man, four decades after his "blasphemous" novel, *The Satanic Verses*, piqued the ire of humorless ayatollahs. Big mistake. The time horizon for a murderous Islamist is infinite. While speaking at a literary festival in upstate New York, Rushdie was attacked onstage.[17] He survived but lost an eye and the use of one of his arms.

Taylor Swift's worldwide Eras Tour was the biggest cultural event of 2023 through the first half of 2024. Jet-set "Swifties" flew around the world to catch the blockbuster show. Each global city hosted several nights of the concert. And every concert was sold-out at the largest stadiums. Obviously, anti-Western Islamists have different tastes in music. Offense is easily taken, and a bomb is usually the best way to register disapproval.

Who knows how the Prophet Muhammad would view Taylor Swift's music, outfits, or choice in boyfriends? Apparently, unfavorably. The Eras Tour provided a spectacular opportunity to murder as many infidels as possible in a single location. That's just what ISIS operatives had planned to do in Vienna. All three of Swift's shows were cancelled when the CIA informed Austrian authorities of the plot.[18] The co-conspirators acknowledged that the plan was to murder "tens of thousands [of] Americans who were scheduled to be in Vienna."

With the entire world watching and Western tourists jam-packed into one of Europe's most iconic cities, the 2024 Paris Olympics would have provided Islamic terrorists with the ultimate trophy target. Fortunately, there was no incident, but we don't know how many terror threats the French government received and averted. More than any other country in Europe, France has devoted countless resources to counterterrorism. Islam has been in France longer than other Western nations, largely because an earlier generation of immigrants arrived in France from its former North African colonies. That, along with liberal immigration policies, gave France Europe's highest Muslim population. France also happens to possess Europe's largest Jewish population. Bad combination. The French, and especially its Jews, have become Islam's go-to victims. The opening ceremony of the Olympics, which was lavishly produced along the Seine, apparently, was scaled back from its original production due to security concerns.

On top of all this—from London to Amsterdam to Berlin—violent pro-Hamas demonstrators have convulsed in rapturous celebration of the butchering and raping of Jews. Amsterdam, in fact, was the scene of an especially ugly incident—a modern-day pogrom as a double feature following a soccer match between Maccabi Tel Aviv and Ajax, the local Dutch team that is often nicknamed, "The Jews." Three thousand Jewish and Israeli soccer fans traveled to Amsterdam for the match. The real show came after regulation time, however, with gangs of masked Muslims armed with knives, clubs, and even cars, attacking and chasing Jews through the streets.[19]

This is the new normal for those living in Western nations, and especially for their Jewish population. The old normal in the Middle East has resulted in improved relations between Israel and its Arab neighbors, but the enmity with Palestinians has gotten worse. Muslims living in the West are more hostile to Israel, and, paradoxically, against Western values, than those in the Middle East. That's a bad sign for everyone. Israel's wars against terrorism actually involve everyone. The Jewish state is owed a debt of gratitude. Those cheering on Hamas are, knowingly or unwittingly, rooting for the wrong team—unless one wishes to see the demise of Western civilization.

Given this grim state of affairs, why should Israel care one bit how others judge the methods by which it secures the safety of its people? And before judging Israel at all, one should first consider saying, "There but for the grace of God, go I." Israel's problem is your problem. Will you be willing to accept the world's criticism on how you choose to rid your nation of Islamic terrorism? Because if you are not so amenable, have the humility to keep your mouth shut.

It has become increasingly difficult to speak honestly about Islamic extremism. Only a handful of nations have been spared the continuous threats of violence, and intrusions on personal liberty, that seems to accompany Islam wherever it goes. Some have been more successful preserving their values and ways of life, but this required the politically incorrect maintenance of closed borders. Germany and Poland are two European nations going in opposite directions. Germany's dominance has suffered from Islam's presence; Poland's mediocrity is less of a liability when it can assure its citizens that its subways won't explode.

How soon we forgot the aftermath of 9/11. Less catastrophic acts of Islamic terror were perpetrated in London, Paris, Nice, Madrid, Brussels, Manchester, Bali, Boston, and Los Angeles—all from the same sworn enemy of the West. Try having a frank conversation about Islam, and risk arousing the world's woke consciousness. Challenge progressive protocols about multi-culturalism and object to illegal immigration, and charges of racism and Islamophobia immediately fly. The Islam practiced by extremists, and that has permeated large Western cities, demands all other religions and cultures become subservient to the only one true religion, and the only Prophet. Western liberal ideals must be subordinated to Sharia law. Fantasies of a modern-day caliphate abound. Its defies belief when Western nations make it so easy to shout "Allahu Akbar" right before an Islamist takes another infidel's life.

When Israelis look outside their windows, that's what they see.

Europe fought against the spread of Islam for centuries. Long before political correctness, Islam was depicted in popular culture with savage imagery alone. Two iconic feature films from sixty years ago addressed the matter of Arab violence in a historical context—without added softeners. *Lawrence of Arabia* (1962), widely considered one of the greatest motion pictures ever produced, received multiple Oscar nominations. *Exodus* (1960) was critically acclaimed, as well. Both delved into the politics of the Middle East and the casual acceptance of Muslim violence.

Lawrence of Arabia depicts the Arab Revolt against the Ottoman Empire during World War I. Tribal Arabs throughout the Middle East joined forces with the British in an effort to defeat the Turks. Most of the countries that presently make up North Africa, the Middle East and the Persian Gulf didn't even exist at the time. But bands of Arabs did not need much persuading from Major T. E. Lawrence to wage war while resorting to savage means—swords and machetes galore.

Exodus picks up thirty years later. The British had taken control of Palestine, but the newly formed League of Nations required the colonial powers to eventually withdraw from Africa and the Middle East. This British Mandate left the United Kingdom in a custodial role. The land would ultimately be returned to the Jews and Arabs. (Yes, for those walking around with incorrect facts, Israel, the West Bank, and Gaza Strip were all "occupied" by the British; after that, the West Bank and Gaza were occupied by Jordan and Egypt, respectively.)

By the end of World War II and in the aftermath of the Holocaust, world Jewry thought it was time for England to dismantle its protectorate and leave the region, allowing the dreams of Zionism—Jewish self-determination—to finally flourish. Diasporic Jews would then return to their ancestral homeland, and a new nation would be born.

The British weren't ready to relinquish control. They even blocked the exodus of Holocaust survivors to Palestine. Many had nowhere else to go. *Exodus* tells the story of the United Nations' vote to partition the land into separate Jewish and Arab nations. The Jews accepted; Palestinians refused to divide the land. And the Middle East Crisis began.

The film is unsparing in what Arab rejectionism meant. Near the end of the film, Arabs are so enraged by the Jewish presence in Palestine, they raided villages and *kibbutzim*, seeking women and children to slaughter. Sound familiar? Yes, in 1960, if you exited a movie theater having just seen *Exodus*, you would come to learn what Israel faces. These were no ordinary enemies. To them, Jewish women and children were legitimate targets. One would be left to wonder: "Are these Arabs even capable of having a state of their own?"

The ghastly events on October 7, 2023, may have been shocking, but it was no aberration. What happened in southern Israel has happened throughout the Muslim world, an entire region awash in horrific and bloody storylines. Algerians and Iraqis slicing babies. Syrian dictators showering their political rivals in acid. Wives raped in front of spouses and parents. Chemical weapons from Syria aimed at children. Boko Haram in Nigeria hacking Christians to death with machetes.

This is the world that Israel has the misfortune to inhabit. Consider this before leaving your gated fortresses in Beverly Hills, Boca Raton, Scarsdale, or Shaker Heights. It must be nice feeling reassured that your neighbors are not planning to slit the throats of your children while you're away.

Listen to Amos Oz. This was the point he was trying to make back in 2014. Aside from deluding yourself and demonizing a democratic country that's trying to make the best of a bad neighborhood, you are doing Islam no favors pretending that Muslims are adapting well to Western societies. They are not. Sharia law is fundamentally incompatible with liberalism, pluralism, the rule of law, and mutual tolerance. Far too many Muslims see all the world's problems solved by Islamic supremacy. They enjoy the benefits of the European Enlightenment while longing for the Dark Ages.

This is what the West is placating and allowing to fester.

CHAPTER 3

Listen to What They Say and Watch What They Do: When A Nation's Enemy Is Committed to Eternal Warfare

Less than forty-eight hours after the October 7 atrocity, a female student of slight build at the University of Toronto, wearing both a hijab and keffiyeh, held a sign that read: "You Don't Get to Choose How We Resist."

At this point, not a single Israeli soldier had entered Gaza, nor had a single bomb been dropped. There were very few Palestinian deaths, only those marauding terrorists and Gazans who never managed to get back across the border. They had been cornered and killed by the late arriving IDF. And they most assuredly deserved to lose their lives.

All the world knew was that well over one thousand Israelis had been gruesomely murdered. Most of the victims were peacenik civilians and *kibbutzniks*. Most were teenagers who attended the Nova Music Festival, and women, children, and the elderly from neighboring villages. Police reports, eye-witness accounts, and forensic evidence that had been gathered at multiple crime scenes had already concluded that teenage girls were gang raped and babies were cut out of their mothers' wombs, or set on fire.

Decapitations occurred that would have shocked and terrified even the Nazis.

Female victims were discovered with their pelvises broken, hips torn apart, breasts slashed off with knives, vaginas blown apart with guns. Some of the victims continued to be raped after death. When finished, terrorists sat down and consumed the uneaten breakfasts they had interrupted. Before taking grandmothers and children hostage, Hamas operatives and ordinary civilians ransacked the homes of Israelis before setting them on fire—often with the Israelis still locked in their saferooms.

And yet, a Muslim female Canadian college student was already cheering on the terrorists, making it plain that to her, these were acts of justified "resistance."

Is it possible she could be right? Resistance, in any form, does not have to be measured. It can be completely unrestrained. Delivered with varied brutality. If the resistance is deserved, if the cause is just, there are no limits to what a resistance movement can do to its real or perceived enemies—regardless of whether the targets are women, the elderly, or children—directed entirely against civilians and not soldiers.

What could possibly justify what occurred on October 7? What could the nation-state of Israel and its people have possibly done to warrant such an assault? The world appeared to downplay and excuse the actions of Hamas and its civilian assistants almost instantly, and deflected the focus entirely onto Israel's anticipated response, as if the Jewish state had no actual right to self-defense.

The Canadian co-ed was far from alone. On campuses around the Western world, but especially in the United States, faculty and students emphatically believed that the October 7 massacre was justified and appropriate, and any sympathy directed toward Israel was misguided and immoral. How else to explain tearing down the posters of Israeli hostages? Pictures of young children and the elderly defaced. The Israeli hostages were deemed wrongful distractions. No grief can be expended on them. The crimes committed against the Palestinians are special and cannot be diluted by redirecting sympathy onto the people responsible for those crimes.

But what exactly are those crimes, and is there any truth to them? Palestinians and their entourage of political progressives believe they are engaged in a righteous anti-colonial crusade against an illegal occupying army of Jews. They believe they are waging a just war against a rogue Jewish state. These Jews have no claim to the land they have stolen. Since 1948, Jewish invaders have persecuted the Palestinian people, depriving them of their land, their rights, and expelling them from their homes. For nearly eighty years, Israel has governed Palestine like a settler-colonial occupier and apartheid regime that has engaged in systematic ethnic cleanings of indigenous Arabs—in addition to unjust imprisonments, home demolitions, deprivation of essential services like water and electricity, economic deprivations, restriction of access to health care, starvation, and arbitrary killings. Such is the plight of second-class status in Israeli-occupied Palestine.

Occasionally, there are allegations that IDF soldiers rape Palestinian women. They are, however, unverified and unproven allegations, nearly always. But even if true, Israeli society has shown time and again that when soldiers conduct themselves dishonorably, they are prosecuted and punished.[20] The Israeli Supreme Court has been a stern taskmaster over the IDF. The proposal to strip the court of such oversight, among other judicial reforms, was the reason for mass weekly protests throughout nearly all of 2023—ending with Hamas' massacre on October 7.

Just how would a Palestinian be treated in Gaza for raping an Israeli woman? He would be rewarded by having a park named after him.

But let's address the two primary justifications for this incessant anti-Zionism: land-theft and apartheid. The same passions that galvanized the global revulsion against Apartheid in South Africa and British colonialism in India, we are told and far too many believe, must be showered on the poor indigenous Arabs of Palestine.

That this argument serves as a justification for unimaginably savage violence is patently absurd. Its widespread dissemination and belief are a combination of ignorance and antisemitism, because there is no truth to it. Israel has absolutely nothing in common with the British presence in India or the Dutch, French, and German Afrikaners in South Africa.

Let's start with colonialism. Israel's haters have this backwards. The political movement known as Zionism and the resulting creation of the State of Israel is perhaps the first, and most successful, anti-colonial success story ever achieved on behalf of an indigenous people—that being, the Jews! England had no territorial claim to India, nor did the French in Algeria or Belgium in Congo. Those are unambiguous examples of Western colonialism. But the Jewish people are integral to the land of Israel. It is their ancestral homeland, the origin of their nationhood—the Kingdom of Judah, which preceded the Ancient Greeks, existed nearly one thousand years *before* the founding of Islam. Does Israel's defense require a tutorial on the Old Testament? Are we in utter denial that there ever was a King David and King Solomon?

Israel was occupied for two thousand years until the Jewish people reclaimed their ancestral homeland with the creation of the Jewish state. Israel is not the embodiment of colonialism; it is its antidote, the national liberation and self-determination of the Jewish people. Nothing was stolen from the Arabs, and—unlike the British in India or any other colonialist project—no Jewish state sent Jews to settle in a foreign country. Jews started returning to Ottoman- and then British-occupied Palestine on their own. They are not settlers from a foreign power; they simply returned to their ancestral home.

Moreover, unlike South Africa, Israel is not and has never been an "apartheid" state, which is defined as forcible separation, or setting *apart*, on racial grounds. First, Muslims are a religion and not a race. But more importantly, over twenty percent of Israel's population is comprised of Muslims, and they enjoy the full assemblage of civil rights as any other person living in democratic Israel. Unlike in Apartheid South Africa, in Israel, Muslims ride the same public transports, attend the same schools, eat in the same restaurants, attend the same concerts, serve in the legislature, are appointed to Israel's Supreme Court, and are permitted to date and marry whomever they wish.

In what way does such a society have anything in common with Apartheid in South Africa? An Ethiopian Jew was crowned Miss Israel not too long ago. Enough said.

The movement to proclaim the self-determination of the Palestinian people started in the mid-1960s, before any Israeli lived in Gaza or the West Bank. The Palestinian Liberation Organization (PLO) was a secular entity. Today the movement is largely Islamic, affiliated with the Muslim Brotherhood, and is known as Hamas and Islamic Jihad. (Hezbollah, in Lebanon, are Shiite Muslims.) This explains Gaza's relationship with Iran, which is the chief sponsor of Islamic terrorism around the world.

And that's really the point: these are terrorist entities passing as political liberation movements. Statehood is not their primary mission; wiping Israel from the map is.

Israelis and Palestinians are locked in a territorial dispute, not a colonial one. Both peoples have legal and factual claims to the West Bank and Gaza. But the Israelis have time and again acceded to a Palestinian homeland in those territories. It is the Palestinians who have rejected statehood and peace with Israel, instead favoring terrorism and the elimination of any trace of Jewish life in Israel.

There is no Jewish life in Gaza. Israel ceded the territory in 2005. The only reason for the naval and air blockade that Israel has imposed on Gaza is to stem the tide of terrorism. Gazans prefer a terror state over a true nation along the Mediterranean Sea. If Gaza was importing supplies for hotels and hospitals rather than rockets and munitions, Israel would not be imposing blockades, and neither would Egypt on its border with Gaza. Israelis would be helping Palestinians unload cargo.

The only reason Gaza is referred to as an "open-air prison" is to disguise the fact that Gaza isn't being occupied at all, that nothing is stopping them from building their own state. Instead of nation-building, Hamas planned October 7. And what they did—what they managed to accomplish—was not a secret or an IDF propaganda operation. Wearing GoPro cameras on helmets and armed with knives and guns, the terrorists filmed their own barbarism and blood-soaked exploits for the whole world to see. In some cases, their handiwork was captured on the iPhone cameras of their victims. The images were then loaded onto social media feeds, making sure that friends and relatives of the victims witnessed what had happened to them in real time.

Within days, terrorist-sympathizers gallingly denied that anything so barbaric had happened. How do you explain all that physical evidence of dead bodies, blood on the clothes, and all that graphic video footage? A simple explanation: IDF soldiers raped and dismembered their fellow Israelis as a pretext for a genocide of Palestinians.

Vulgar signage soon sprang up on campuses around the United States with calls to "Free Palestine!" and "Globalize the Intifada!"

This is what Israel was fighting, and what Zionists living in the West were going to hear from friends, neighbors, and colleagues. Everything we knew had been turned on its head in an instant. No intellectual, common-sense honesty about Palestinians and their love affair with death. Recycled platitudes about a "Two-State Solution." Really? There has been so much success with that in the past. Palestinians do not wish to live in a state that borders a Jewish one. Even *they* are not calling for two states anymore. Palestinians are not satisfied with operational control over Gaza, Ramallah, Nablus, and Jenin—Arab cities where no Jews presently live. They demand a nation that includes Tel Aviv, Haifa, Jaffa, and all of Jerusalem.

Since 1947, Palestinian leaders have rejected five separate proposals for statehood that would have granted them 97 percent of the territory they claim they needed to build a nation.[21] There must be a reason why they never take "yes" for an answer, why they ultimately rejected these deals and defaulted to violence. The building of a Palestinian nation is of far less interest to them than the destruction of the Jewish one.

When people tell you who they are and what they plan to do, it's probably a good idea to take them seriously. That was true of Adolf Hitler, the ayatollahs of Iran, and the Palestinians of the Middle East. If you listen to what Palestinians actually say—not simply reading between the lines, trying to decipher alternate meanings, giving them the benefit of the doubt—but the actual words they use, the truth is instantly revealed: Israel has no partner in peace. What they have is the misery of being consigned to a permanent condition of self-defense.

What more does the world need to know to possess complete knowledge of Palestinian intentions. Nawaf Moussawi, a Hezbollah leader shamelessly bragged: "We are lovers of war. After all, fighting is what we do." Hyperbole? Trash talk? Just look to Article 13 of the Hamas Charter: "There is no solution for the Palestinian question except through Jihad." Article 7 reads:

"Israel will exist…until Islam will obliterate it, just as it obliterated others before it. The Day of Judgement will not come about until Moslems fight the Jews (killing the Jews), when the Jew will hide behind stones and trees."

Pretty declarative statements. Those who recite such words are not the type of whom it can be said cooler heads will prevail. Bloodlust seems to override all other considerations. The loose lips of its leaders, and the group's founding documents, tell the whole story.

What about the people themselves? More than two-thirds of Palestinians support Hamas' surprise, murderous attack in southern Israel, according to a poll conducted by the Palestinian Center for Policy and Survey Research, dated June 12, 2024.[22] That's a full eight months *after* the massacre. The majority of Palestinians, apparently, have no regrets.

According to a poll conducted by Shikaki in March 2024, 90 percent of Palestinians, whether they live in Gaza or the West Bank, entirely dismiss the idea that Hamas committed war crimes on October 7, with the same percentage claiming to have no knowledge of what exactly Hamas did on that day. The vast majority, 75 percent, are satisfied with Hamas' leadership in Gaza, with the architect of the slaughter of Jews—Hamas' military chief, Yahya Sinwar (since then, assassinated)—having received a 65 percent approval rating.

The Gazan love affair with Hamas has held steady between wars—meaning, after being defeated by Israel in 2014, which left the enclave decimated, Gazans didn't hold Hamas, their heroes, responsible. One month after the ceasefire that brought hostilities to an end, a poll taken in Gaza showed that 70 percent believed Hamas had won the war, 94 percent reported that they were satisfied with Hamas' performance in the war, 78 percent were pleased with Hamas' defense of its own civilian population, and 86 percent approved of Hamas continuing to mount rocket attacks against Israel.[23] All this despite over two thousand dead and the near flattening of their homes and lives.

By contrast, hardly anyone in Gaza today, just 10 percent, is satisfied with the leadership of Palestinian Authority President, Mahmoud Abbas, who is based in the West Bank. The Biden administration proposed that the Palestinian Authority should govern Gaza once this war is over. Good luck with that. As for the prospects for peace, 65 percent categorically oppose a two-state solution, while 63 percent support a continuing armed intifada.[24] Over 80 percent of West Bank Palestinians support what Hamas did on October 7.[25]

Here's an actual exchange on the morning of October 7 between a young Gazan male, a civilian, using the phone of his victim to call home to speak with his parents. If you thought he was excitedly calling to inform them of a stellar report card he received in school, you would be mistaken. Palestinian children are photographed wearing suicide vests. They are taught to use knives for the slitting of Jewish necks and AK-47s for more elaborate life-taking. They are indoctrinated with twisted ideas about the Nakba and how Palestinians must avenge the catastrophe and the displacement it caused.[26]

That is what was on the mind of the young man using a dead Israeli's phone to call his parents. He wanted to make them proud sharing in his jubilation of murdering ten Jews.

"Look how many I killed with my own hands! Your son killed Jews!" he says, according to an English translation.

"Mom, your son is a hero," he later adds.[27]

He ends the call by promising that he will use WhatsApp to give them further details.

His parents are not appalled; instead, they applaud his achievement. Beaming with pride, his mother says, "I wish I was with you."

Surreal, but no surprise. Gazans live in a constant state of murderous passion towards Jews. The IDF located tunnels beneath the Al-Maghazi Boys Preparatory School B and Al-Zaytun Boys Preparatory School A. The textbooks these children read, created by UNRWA, the United Nations relief organization designated exclusively for the caretaking of Palestinians, is filled with math problem-solving that has the dual purpose of subtracting Jews—by killing them! The maps used for geography exclude Israel from the Middle East. The life histories of terrorists are glorified. UNRWA teachers made sure to impart that what Hamas and Islamic Jihad accomplished on October 7 was a "splendid spectacle," "a real victory for the liberation of Palestine," and "an unforgettable and glorious morning."[28]

A report that examined the staffing and curricula of UNRWA-run schools provides disturbing evidence that the funding earmarked to aid Palestinians is really inciting violence against Israelis. These are United Nations' employees teaching Gazan children to hate and kill Jews. Israel believes that more than one hundred UNRWA employees fought alongside Hamas on October 7, and over 1,200 have official roles within terrorist groups. More than 10 percent of UNRWA's school principals and senior education staff are members of terrorist groups.[29] One of the employees was recorded on October 7, announcing, "I'm inside, I'm inside with the Jews" and "We have female hostages, I captured one."[30]

At least one school principal and a school counselor were among the fighting hordes. These teachers were not content with merely praising and entreating murder in the classroom. They wanted to partake in the real thing.[31] Ten UNRWA employees discovered to have played a role in the atrocities were fired.

The Secretary-General of the United Nations, António Guterres, conveyed his public sympathy for Mohammad Abu Itiwi, who was both an UNRWA employee and a known Hamas operative, after he was pronounced dead in an Israeli airstrike. How was such a man—a commander in Hamas' notorious Nukhba unit, who actually took part in planning the massacre at the Nova Music Festival—on the secretary-general's payroll? And what does it say about where the Secretary-General's sympathy actually lies?

Matthias Schmale, who now serves as a United Nations humanitarian coordinator, headed-up UNRWA's Gaza office from 2017 until 2021. At the end of his tenure, during an interview with Israeli cable news, he acknowledged that, "Would I be totally surprised if at the end of the day there is proof that 2,000 UNRWA staff are members of Hamas? No, I wouldn't be."

UNRWA controls the educational content of what Palestinian children—the next generation—learn and know about the historical relationship between Jews and Arabs in the Middle East. The curricula and lesson plans lead Palestinian children to believe that Jews are without any history at all in the region—they are nothing but usurpers.

The CEO of the entity that produced the report, Marcus Sheff, said, "UNRWA has repeatedly failed to act despite mounting evidence and repeated warnings of the deep influence of terror groups on UNRWA's schools. This is not just about accountability but about protecting young minds from an education that fuels hatred and extremism."[32]

One of the UNRWA-created exam materials had this as a correct answer: "Liberating the Al-Aqsa Mosque and making sacrifices for it is a duty for all Muslims." The Al-Maghazi School handed out materials that celebrated violence and referred to the firebombing of an Israeli bus as a "barbecue party."

To this day, almost nothing has been done to recreate lesson plans and rectify the murderous prejudice against Israel that these teaching materials evoke. And the incitement to violence among school-age Palestinians has not abated, either. Yet another generation of Palestinians are being groomed to hate Jews and commit themselves to the destruction of Israel.

The Biden administration was aware of the link between UNRWA-operated schools and the creation of *jihadist* educational materials—and covered it up. The State Department felt compelled to resume supplying UNRWA with tens of millions of dollars in funding. An internal memo was discovered showing that teaching materials included "references to jihad in and violence in Arabic language lessons for grades 6 and 9," as well as accusing Israel of "deliberately dumping radioactive and toxic waste in the West Bank."

The State Department dismissed the language in these textbooks as "in line with U.N. principles" and only "viewed as inappropriate by some other audiences."

Michael Chamberlain, the director of Protect the Public's Trust, said that the State Department "tried to sell a wholly unrealistic version of UNRWA to Congress. Even with all they knew, they shrugged and wrote the checks anyway."[33]

These schools are operated under the auspices of the United Nations, ostensibly a global body dedicated to the pursuit of peaceful coexistence. Teachers who draw salaries from the United Nations are teaching Palestinian children to hate Jews and erase Israel—as if the Jewish state existed only on a chalk board. How, under these circumstances, can the United Nations possibly present itself as an honest broker when it comes to any issue related to Israel, most especially the charges brought against it before the International Court of Justice?

Of course, why should we expect more from teachers when no Palestinian officials have ever rejected terrorism, abhorred violence, and acknowledged the existence of the Jewish state. In nearly eighty years, why has not a single leader with the moral rigor of a Mahatma Gandhi or Martin Luther King Jr. emerged to represent the Palestinian people? The concept of passive nonviolent resistance was always available throughout this conflict. Nelson Mandela proved its viability in the struggle against South African Apartheid. Yet, no Palestinian leader has ever said: "It worked in India with the British, and in the Deep South in America. Let's show a different side to the Palestinian temperament, and our capacity for peaceful solutions to a conflict."

Instead, the Palestinians have always been drawn to terrorism—even before the Palestinian liberation movement began in the mid-1960s, and before there was a state of Israel in 1948. In 1929, before anyone referred to Arabs living in British-occupied Palestine as Palestinians; before Jews could be accused of an "occupation," "apartheid," and "ethnic cleansing"; before there were settlements; before fanatical Islamists became such an attraction to young male Muslims—the eight hundred Jews living in the biblical city of Hebron (in the West Bank), literally the place where Abraham, the father of both Judaism and Islam, once walked, were attacked by three thousand Muslims bearing swords, clubs, axes, and daggers. They murdered, raped, and torched what was already a small Jewish community—leaving sixty-seven dead. Children watched their parents being butchered; babies were slaughtered in the arms of their mothers.[34]

This horrific event foreshadowed the region's future. In the first few decades of the secular Palestinian Liberation Organization (PLO), before there ever was an Islamist Hamas, through airplane and cruise ship hijackings, midnight raids, explosions, murdering the entire Israeli Olympic team, and then the suicide bombings of the Second Intifada, violence was the Palestinian's signature brand of diplomacy. That's why security fences were erected in both Gaza and the West Bank; that's the reason for the checkpoints, long lines, and curfews. No Second Intifada with bus, hotel, pizza shop, and suicide bombings, then no need for security fences. It's that simple. But it seems that without violence against Jews, Palestinian nationalism has no meaningful purpose. When Palestinians want to get the world's attention, the language of terrorism is how they speak. Seeing no common language that involved diplomacy, Israel has been forced to always react with counterterrorism.

Take the founding Chairman of the PLO, the terrorist arm of the Palestinian people, Yasser Arafat. He ultimately received a joint share of a Nobel Peace Prize for agreeing to the Oslo Accords, in principle. Soon thereafter, in lieu of further negotiations, he initiated the Second Intifada. A corrupt man who confiscated hundreds of millions of dollars set aside for the Palestinian people, and never far from a handgun, he was a far cry from a diplomat or peacemaker.

Pro-Hamas protesters are wholly ignorant of the history of Palestinian rejectionism and violence. In addition to the written Charters of both the PLO and Hamas, which clearly spell out the game plan for the Palestinian people—drive the Jews into the Mediterranean Sea—Arafat was never shy about publicly stating the direction his leadership was taking the Palestinians, and what he had in store for the Jews. In 1972, the same year the PLO, and its Black September offshoot, orchestrated the assassination of the Israeli Olympic team in Munich, Arafat said, "Peace for us means the destruction of Israel. We are preparing for an all-out war, a war that will last for generations."[35]

Israeli historian Benny Morris, who is no friend of ultranationalist Zionists, noted Arafat's bad faith as a peace negotiator and his longstanding hatred of Jews. While at Camp David back in 2000, Arafat reportedly said, "There was no connection of the Jews to the Holy Land at all.... [W]hen President Bill Clinton mentioned the ancient Jewish temple at Camp David, Arafat said, 'What temple?'"[36]

One doesn't need to eavesdrop on encrypted internet chatter among Palestinians to know of their genocidal intentions for the Jews. They have been pretty transparent about it. Who among them has expressed shame and remorse for what occurred on October 7? Who among Muslims anywhere, for that matter? Soon after the massacre, when Israel had just commenced its military operations, Hamas released this official statement:

"We will repeat the October 7th massacre *again and again* until Israel is destroyed.... We are a nation of martyrs and are proud of it. We'll sacrifice as many Palestinian lives as it takes."[37]

The official statement had many official backers, just in case anyone blindly interpreted the statement as a peace offering or public apology. "We would do it again!" said a former Hamas official, Ahmad Abd Al-Hadi, in the Lebanese newspaper *An-Nahar*. "If we could go back in time, we would do it again, because the justifications still exist." Ghazi Hamad, a member of Hamas' political bureau, in Arabic, proudly informed Lebanon's LBCI

TV in October 24 that Israel "must be finished.... We must teach Israel a lesson, and we will do this again and again. [The Oct. 7 massacre] is just the first time and there will be a second, a third, a fourth...the occupation must come to an end." When he was asked to clarify the meaning of "occupation," given that no Jews or Israelis have actually lived in Gaza since 2005, he replied, "Yes, of course," he meant the "annihilation" of Israel.[38]

This eliminationist impulse has never dissipated over the years. It was always there. October 7 was just a shocking manifestation of this deeply rooted hatred that only intensifies in militancy. "Israel is a country that has no place on our land," said Ghazi Hamad, continued in his interview on Lebanese cable news. "We must remove that country, because it constitutes a security, military, and political catastrophe to the Arab and Islamic nation...We are not ashamed to say this, with full force.... [W]e have the determination, the resolve, and the capabilities to fight."

Khaled Barakat, once a senior member of the Popular Front for the Liberation of Palestine, wrote in *Al-Akhbar*, a Lebanese newspaper, "The extinction of the Zionist project is only a matter of time thanks to armed struggle, Jihad in Palestine, Lebanon and Yemen."[39] Jibril Rajoub, the secretary-general of Fatah, the political party in the West Bank that runs the Palestinian Authority, justified the October 7 massacre, describing it as an "defensive operation," boasting that it was necessary because it "thwarted attempts to liquidate the Palestinian issue, as well as efforts to achieve normalization [between Israel and Saudi Arabia]."[40]

The architect of Nova Music Festival terrorist strike, Sinwar himself, trivialized the loss of Palestinian lives as "necessary sacrifices.... We make the headlines only with blood.... No blood, no news." He had long spoken favorably about the greater the number of Palestinian civilian casualties, the more pressure is placed on Israel.[41]

Even as the October 7 War reached its first true ceasefire, on January 15, 2025, after fifteen months of fighting and forty-four thousand dead Gazans, the default leader of Hamas—the only one still left standing—Khalil al-Hayya, triumphantly announced from the safety of Qatar that the October 7 attack "will forever be a source of pride for our people."

No remorse or words of regret. No acknowledgment of all the destruction, death, and suffering. He was unrepentant and elated. Indeed, he promised another October 7! "Our people will expel the occupation from our lands and from Jerusalem in the earliest time possible."

When world leaders, student activists, and nefarious Islamists called for a permanent ceasefire in Gaza, and a Boycott, Divestment and Sanctions (BDS) arms embargo imposed against the Jewish state, what outcome do they foresee? Did they anticipate the return of the hostages as a goodwill gesture? Did they imagine Palestinians laying down their weapons and renouncing violence? Did they predict a serene Middle East, an expansion of the Abraham Accords, or even the mutually respectful relationship that Israeli Jews have with Israeli Arabs, who comprise 20 percent of Israel's population? So few of the pro-Hamas protestors are even aware of that relationship and how it puts the lie to any bogus apartheid charge.

None of those developments actually happened when a ceasefire was declared in mid-January 2025. Long-suffering Israelis see none of those eventualities, and they have no reason to imagine it getting better. All these many decades and Palestinians simply never tire of terrorism.

I don't credit Israel's critics with desiring a fuller picture of the landscape that Israelis see before them. All that seems to matter to them is that Israel stop defending itself.

Israel's existential dilemma, ignored. The fate of the hostages, forgotten. The certainty that Hamas and Islamic Jihad will continue to launch rockets at Israeli population centers, not our problem. The futility of "de-escalating" the situation on the ground in Gaza, let's see what happens. The real concern of unrelenting violence is irrelevant because even the well-intentioned refuse to hear what the Palestinians are actually saying.

Only the Israelis are paying attention, and for good reason. Proximity to violence gets a nation's guard up.

Israel's primary problem is that it must live with Islamic terror up close and far too personal for any nation's comfort. And it requires a perpetual state of high alert. Israelis live in a constant state of emergency preparedness and military readiness. How can any other Western, democratic nation possibly understand or appreciate this unless *this* is your daily reality?

Especially when the other side is completely unaccountable. Western countries, the United Nations, and human rights groups treat Palestinians like children too young to know the difference between right and wrong, who petulantly throw harmless tantrums. Better to simply tune out Palestinian leaders and Hamas commanders. Trivialize their threats. Dismiss the words they use. Gary Lineker, a *BBC* broadcaster, while on the air referred to what happened on October 7 as "the Hamas thing."

Taking Hamas seriously—appreciating that there are such people who traffic in terror—lends credence to Israel's universally recognized right to self-defense. Better to focus on the power imbalance: a thriving state against nonstate resistance fighters, a "settler colonial enterprise" against a people dispossessed of their land, white privilege against the presumptive innocence of anyone with darker skin, and the disproportionate body counts whenever Israel is forced to retaliate against the terrorists who plague them.

Given what Palestinians say and have always said—including the immediate aftermath of October 7—what choice does Israel really have other than to fight until every last terrorist is dead and no longer a threat? The reality of Palestinian intentions informs Israel's military response, as it should. That's the natural consequence of perpetually demanding the end of days for the Jewish state.

Perhaps even more important than what they *say* is what Gazans and Hamas actually *did* on October 7. Nothing speaks louder; it's the most straightforward act of communication imaginable. After October 7, how can anyone not see the Oslo Accords, signed in 1995, as anything but a delusion? What sounded at the time like a massive peacemaking breakthrough in the longstanding Middle East impasse, ultimately meant nothing to the Palestinians, who have always been clear that only one state interests them—the one presently called Israel. When it came time to implement the "Two-State Solution," the Palestinian contingent was too busy planning the Second Intifada.

Once again, terrorism was preferred over nation-building.

The "Two-State Solution" is by now an impractical joke, spoken by simpletons who haven't picked up a newspaper in decades.[42] "Land for peace" is a pipedream. "Palestinians simply want what everyone wants: a country of their own," a common refrain, is simply not true. The events of October 7 shattered all those illusions. After all these years of indefatigable violence, Israel has no reason to trust anything other than more acts of terror unless the terrorists are finally and decisively stopped. Another October 7-like ambush is far likelier than some mind-blowing gesture of peace from the Palestinians.

What took place on October 7, savage though it was, was not unimaginable. Israelis were left shaken, but not entirely shocked. Having low expectations about their neighbors is an Israeli's rite of passage. Gaza is an enclave populated by terrorists, and a great many who comprise a civilian army. The civilians are not unaware of what is happening in the tunnels underneath homes, hospitals, and mosques.[43] Many are actively assisting Hamas.

Dr. Muhammed Abu Salmiya, a pediatrician and the head of Al Shifa Hospital, allowed his medical facility to serve as a Hamas command center. Tunnels run underneath the hospital where hostages were held, including the dead body of nineteen-year-old teenager, Noa Marciano.[44]

The IDF has discovered weapons stored in far too many Gazan homes—even under the beds of children—for anyone to plausibly claim that civilians are just watching the war from a distance.[45]

Because Hamas masked operatives are not suit-wearing statesmen, the tendency is to over-scrutinize the country that is in uniform and conducting itself according to the laws of armed conflict.

It's a combination of indifference and detached disbelief. The barbaric crime scene that Gazans indelibly left behind on October 7 will never be forgotten by Israelis, but it will also never be entirely believed by an already antisemitic mainstream media. So appalling and foreign to Western sensibilities, even the GoPro video footage becomes unwatchable to the very people tasked with reporting the news of the day and the truths that need to be told.

The world must come to terms with these truths that have been ignored, excused, and wished away for decades. Magical thinking in the Middle East always results in dead Jews.

The historical record of Arab animus toward Jews is best demonstrated by the Jewish flight from Arab nations after 1948. How many Jews presently live in Iraq, Iran, Egypt, Jordan, Syria, Lebanon, Algeria, Yemen, Libya, Morocco—and, of course, Gaza, Ramallah, Nablus, and Jenin? Nearly a million Jews once did. Now fewer than two hundred live in *all* of these countries and territories combined. Most fled to the new state of Israel, others to France and several other European countries, and the rest to America and Canada.

Without an Israel that can defend itself and will reliably retaliate to establish deterrence, the Middle East will remain toxic and lethal for a people who have always lived there and endured its singular persecutions.

If Israel won't defend itself, we know that the world has a terrible track record when it comes to rescuing Jews. At the same time, as we have discovered throughout history, the world is not all that keen on Jews defending themselves, either. The image of the Jew as perpetual victims and rootless cosmopolitans is more in line with how the world imagines the Jewish people. Dara Horn's provocative book, *People Love Dead Jews*, got it right. Jews are most appreciated as object lessons, universal allegories, cautionary tales, artifacts of defeated lands—but not as real people who can be accepted on their own terms with empathy and mutual respect.

The image of Israel as intrepid defender of the Jewish people, "Start-up" and first-responder nation, high- and bio-tech innovators, agricultural magicians, de-salination wizards, agile warriors, and pluralistic culture czars, isn't exactly the downer that matches the world's perceptions of Jews. But if Jews can so easily be made to disappear, then what's all this we hear about an invincibly powerful, white-privileged people.

Jewish vulnerability as a visible minority has spanned all of recorded history. Jews have always been at the mercy of a mostly unwelcoming majority. October 7 demonstrated that even a stateless minority—in this case, the Palestinians of Gaza—could not contain their grand designs for dead Jews.

It's important to note that I am referring here to neighbors, not terrorists. Ordinary people living in the adjoining land. Not cold professional killers. Hamas militants landing in Israel on paragliders is one thing. Civilians surging through the Israeli border to claim a Jewish trophy of some sort is something else altogether. This is the scenario that connects October 7 to the massacre in Hebron in 1929, and the depiction of ordinary Arabs in *Lawrence of Arabia* and *Exodus*. It is the attitude and animus toward Jews held by civilians in Gaza that is even more nightmarish than Hamas.

And it is the reason why those who live in southern Israel will never have faith in a peace process again. Their neighbors saw to that. Civilians played an active role in Hamas' atrocities on October 7, and the days and months thereafter. If a Gazan crossed Israel's southern border by foot, car, or motorbike and stopped at a town or *kibbutz* to rampage, ravage, and kidnap Israeli civilians, it matters little whether they are card-carrying members of Hamas.

Hamas and Islamic Jihad have not cornered the market on Palestinian thirst for Jewish blood. Amateur terrorists proved to be very good at it, as well. Not all the hostages were kept in dark tunnels, subject to torture and sexual abuse at the hands of Hamas. Many Gazans volunteered to guard hostages in their own homes.

The direct involvement of ordinary civilians in the October 7 massacre is truly staggering. A report issued by the IDF estimated that six thousand Gazans infiltrated Israel. As many as 2,200 civilians can be seen in the extensive video that was captured on that day, looting homes and participating in the ambush.[46] It is estimated that as many as seven hundred Gazans laid siege to *kibbutz* Nir Oz, one of the residential communities closest to the Gaza border. Of that number, as many as 550 were unarmed civilians. This was a joy ride for them, something to check off on their bucket list.

In an expose in *Tablet* magazine on the ugly face of this pogrom, Deborah Danan wrote, "Some of those civilians carried out wholesale acts of terror themselves, including rape and abduction—and in some cases, the eventual sale of hostages to Hamas—while others abetted the terrorists."[47]

The level of barbarism of ordinary Gazans is difficult to comprehend when one considers who the victims were. Yes, they were Israelis, but what were their beliefs and political inclinations? Did they possess any special feelings of hatred for Palestinians?

Not that anyone deserves what happened on October 7, but it's worth knowing just who Hamas had picked to be the targets of their barbaric attack. They weren't ultra-religious or nationalistic settlers from the West Bank. Southern Israel, which borders Gaza, is not disputed territory—except in the minds of most Palestinians who feel that all of Israel belongs to Arabs. But it just so happens that the Israelis who live in the south, by and large, are left-wing peaceniks. Why else would the Nova Music Festival have selected that location? Holding the concert in the more religiously biblical West Bank would have had far less popular appeal.

Instead, thousands of young people attended the Nova Festival on *Shabbat* (Saturday) and on *Simchat Torah*, to boot—knowingly *not* spending the holiday in synagogue. They slept under the stars, inside tents and sleeping bags, after having enjoyed the music, blithely unaware that soon they would experience the worst moment of their lives. For many, life would come to an end in the morning. If you can endure the horror—the shuddering jolt that such promising lives were mutilated and murdered—just look at their faces on Instagram. Many had long hair, nose and ear piercings, and tattoos.

These were the people Hamas wanted to eliminate next door.

Here's a question the world should have demanded an answer from Hamas. Why would Gazans storm Israel and head straight for teenagers to murder, mutilate, behead and gang rape—not on account of something they had done, or what they believed in, but solely because the vast majority were Jews and Israelis?

A female photographer was planning a joint exhibit with a photographer from Gaza. Both were artists, and, as she was led to believe, friends. They wanted to showcase the photos they had taken of their respective peoples, glimpses of adjoining neighborhoods, separated by a security fence, caught in intractable wars but with common links to the land. While working on the show, she invited him to take photos of her local streets.

On the morning of October 7, before Hamas had breached the border, she received a nervous call from her Palestinian friend. He asked her to look out her window to see whether there were any Israeli soldiers. Why was he calling with such a question?

He wanted to know whether the coast was clear.

Apparently, all that time when he was taking photographs, her Palestinian friend had mixed motives. He shared his photographs with Hamas operatives. They needed the lay of the land so that the siege on southern Israel would succeed with maximum efficiency.[48]

"Whoever says there are people there who are uninvolved, here is the proof," she said, lamenting his betrayal of friendship and her role in assisting Hamas. "They are all involved. They are all Hamas."

Her experience was no aberration. Soon we would all come to learn the full extent of murderous involvement from the civilian "noncombatants" of Gaza. Israeli Special Forces conducted an operation in central Gaza in early June 2024 where they rescued four hostages held captive in two different apartment buildings.[49] Their captors were "civilians," one being a "journalist" with *Al Jazeera*. The journalist's entire family all shared guard duty. He may have also been a Hamas operative. The fact that he also had a press pass does not make him an innocent civilian.

No Hamas terrorists lived in either of those buildings. The hostage keepers were *all* civilians. One of the hostages released earlier in the conflict, Mia Schem, said that she was held by a Palestinian family. "Entire families are in the service of Hamas."[50]

Investigative journalist David Collier defrocked the *BBC*'s notorious, laughably deceitful storylines depicting Israel as irredeemable aggressor and the Palestinians as blameless innocents. The network neglected to disclose that the subject and narrator of a recent documentary was not himself untainted by terrorism. He was, in fact, the son of a high-ranking Hamas official.

"They pretend that Hamas and the Palestinians are two completely separated entities—as if Hamas is some alien invasion power that dropped from the sky, nothing to do with Palestinians," Collier said.[51]

Quite often, the terrorists and civilians of Gaza are difficult to tell apart. Roni Krivoi was recaptured by civilians after he successfully escaped from Hamas. The civilians dutifully returned him. "There are no innocent civilians," he said. "Not one. They don't exist. All of them are terrorists."[52]

Are such people actual civilians or quasi-terrorists? It makes a difference. If they are associated with Hamas to any degree, international humanitarian law does not offer them any special protections. They would be treated the same as military personnel—because that's what they are.

How about the people who tagged along with Hamas once Israel's security fence was flung wide open? They most certainly participated in the siege of southern Israel. They may have acted alone, but not in opposition to Hamas' interests. Henchmen is probably how they would best be described.

In a legal and moral sense, that makes them not that much different from Hamas at all. Some "civilians" committed the most heinous of crimes. When it came to that fateful morning of grotesque wilding, the civilians may have actually outperformed the terrorists.

What does that tell you about who bears responsibility for the war that followed, and who can rightfully claim innocent civilian status?

There is the unforgettable image of Shani Louk that went viral on October 7. She was an Israeli German bloodied, half-naked, and paraded through the streets of Gaza in the back of a pickup truck. Ordinary citizens were cheering in appreciation of this great conquest, spitting on her and shouting, "Allahu Akbar!"

Only on a psychotic day like October 7 might a child be fortunate to be kidnapped and taken to Gaza. The alternative would have been decapitation or cremation. Of course, as we tragically came to learn in February 2025, the two Bibas brothers who were abducted when one was four-years old and the other nine months, ended up brutally murdered by their captors anyway.[53]

Irit Lahav, an avowed peace activist who regularly volunteered to drive Gazans suffering from cancer into Israel for their treatments, spoke of the devastating damage October 7 did to her worldview of Palestinians. "It broke my heart. How can we ever get over this sense of betrayal? The Palestinian public simply hate us."[54]

What other conclusion could Israelis, or anyone for that matter, draw? A seventeen-year-old hostage, Agam Goldstein-Almog, said, "If we previously believed that there was a chance for peace, we've lost all faith in these people, especially after we were there and among the population."[55]

It got worse, even more gruesome, involving the otherworldly experience of an Israeli father whose son, IDF Sergeant Adir Tahar, was murdered and decapitated while stationed at his post near the border with Gaza. He was among the first to fall when the siege commenced. His father, David, was horrified that he was forced to bury his son with his head missing. Israel's internal police, Shin Bet, learned from a source that a Gazan civilian had possession of Adir's head. The Gazan owned an ice cream parlor and stored the head in his freezer. He hoped to sell it to Hamas. He was no terrorist, just an ordinary Gazan businessman, fortunate to be in possession of the head of a dead Israeli soldier, stored away for safe keeping.[56]

Such displays of jaw-dropping barbarism can break the spirit even of those known to have an unlimited capacity for compassion and mutual understanding. The strangling of the Bibas brothers proved to be too much for one senior Reform rabbi who delivered a sermon to his congregation of utter defeat.

"[W]e must cease deluding ourselves," Rabbi Ammiel Hirsch said. "The polite lie that we tell ourselves over and over again is that Hamas does not represent the Palestinians. It is simply not true. We recite this like a mantra so that we do not have to face the terrible truth that Hamas is the Palestinians.... [T]here were wild celebrations on the streets of Gaza as hostages were enslaved and corpses defiled.... No one objected. No one helped the hostages escape."[57]

The Israelis, even those on the far left, have given up all hope. Even if Hamas can be completely routed and made to disappear, won't the Gazans anoint a new terrorist group to take its place? One fears that the presumptions are in reverse. Despicable though they may be, Hamas are not the dictators of Gaza. The marching orders come directly from Gaza's civilians—the collective solidarity of the terrorist's creed.

Israel's president, Isaac Herzog, normally more dovish on such matters and no real compatriot of Prime Minister Benjamin Netanyahu, resignedly said, "It is the entire nation out there that is responsible. It is not true this rhetoric about civilians not being aware, not involved. It's absolutely not true. They could have risen up. They could have fought against that evil regime which took over Gaza in a *coup d'etat*."[58]

He's right. The world can engage in all manner of unhinged shrieking about "innocent civilians," but it won't alter the reality that Gazans adore Hamas, hate Jews more than they love themselves, and would sacrifice anything to become martyrs for their barbaric cause.

If there ever was innocence among the civilians of Gaza—not counting the children, of course—October 7 and its aftermath convincingly shows that it has been lost.

It wasn't just Palestinians who celebrated October 7 as some wonderful win for Islam. Turkish President Recep Tayyip Erdoğan openly denied that Hamas is a terrorist organization. But he was quite certain that Israel was committing war crimes—this from a nation that continues to deny the Armenian genocide that it once perpetrated and has never acknowledged. There was dancing in the streets of Kabul and Islamabad when news first reached Iraq and Pakistan, respectively. The Lebanese people waved Palestinian flags. There were fireworks in Iran. And pro-Hamas rallies in Yemen.[59]

The good news: the nations that signed the Abraham Accords and normalized relations with Israel did not express joy or regard October 7 as some apocalyptic victory.

Israel is easy to hate—precisely because it is the Jewish state. History has shown that it takes almost no effort at all. But these are abnormal times. Nowadays, the hatred of Jews is a sign of virtue, not bigotry. In the perverse logic of identity politics, Jews are white oppressors. Hating them is looked upon favorably as making an antiracist statement. Antisemitism, which is never justified, suddenly has the virtue of a human rights crusade; Jew-hating *as* social justice.

But Palestinian antisemitism is not adopted because it is socially fashionable. While applauding the pro-Hamas protests, Gazans are not looking to make friends on campus. Their hatred of Jews is viral and endemic. Who knows whether it can ever be cured.

No wonder Liel Leibovitz, a columnist for *Tablet*, made his true feelings known when he discovered that the IDF's military prosecutor's office decided that civilians who actively participated in the October 7 melee could not be targeted—even if their identities are known. For instance, Shin Bet knows who kidnapped the Bibas brothers and their parents.

The reason is purely legalistic: unless civilians are attached to a Palestinian fighting force like Hamas and Islamic Jihad, they cannot be targeted for death.

The Netanyahu government had promised the Israeli people that everyone who pillaged, murdered, raped, and kidnapped Israelis on October 7 will pay the ultimate price. Apparently, that price has been severely discounted for crimes committed by "civilians."

"To argue that the Bibas' kidnappers deserve a pass because [they are] not considered a terror organization at war with Israel prior to Oct. 7 is a bit of maddening sophistry," Leibovitz wrote. "To allow such intellectual self-pleasuring to dictate military strategies when a five-year-old and a one-year-old are held captive is nothing short of national suicide."[60]

CHAPTER 4

The Singular Dilemma of Fighting a War in Gaza: The Relentless Gaze of the Globe

In America, being part of the "Greatest Generation" is still the gold standard of what it means to have fought in a just war. American soldiers landed on European beaches, parachuted behind enemy lines, manned submarines, and served on naval fleets in treacherous Pacific waters.

The wars Israel is obligated to wage in Gaza and Lebanon are never described in such heroic or glorious terms. It is a thankless task and a moral morass. When the world gazes at Israel's moral dilemma in Gaza, and when the media reports on Israel's necessary wartime conduct, it is never through sympathetic eyes.

The world never seems to honestly believe that Israeli self-defense is ever justified. All the wars it wages, especially in this century, are perceived as illegitimate, not worthy of global support, the actions of an aggressor.

Internally, Israelis have a far more favorable opinion of itself. Israel is one of the few nations around the world where the people genuinely take pride in the agility and morality of its armed services. Military service is, in fact, mandatory for both men and women—and there are few shirkers of that responsibility (other than the widely resented exemption for religious Jews). Outside of Israel, however, the military of this tiny nation has the reputation of neighborhood bully.

World War II was waged under political and military conditions that most people could understand. The aims of the Axis powers—Germany, Italy, and Japan—were unmistakable: world domination; the creation of a Thousand-Year Reich; wholesale conquests over Austria, Czechoslovakia, and Poland; the fall of France and then northern Europe; the bombings of London; the hopscotch capturing of Pacific Islands; and, of course, the attack on Pearl Harbor.

The Holocaust was not even a consideration in the moral calculus that guided the Allies. Germany had already crossed too many red geopolitical lines. A coalition of Western nations and the Soviet Union assembled to defeat the Nazis without regard to a genocide that was happening to European Jewry. In fact, the mass murdering of civilians wasn't alleged against the Allies, either. Wholly apart from the devastation brought to German cities by British and American bombers, Soviet soldiers raped hundreds—if not thousands—of German women. Hardly is that ever mentioned. All of it chalked up to the horrors of war.

The reasons to enter the war were plenty, and only with the arrival of V-E Day (victory in Europe) and V-J Day (victory over Japan) would World War II come to an end. There was no talk of ceasefires or civilian death tolls. Everyone seemed to understand that "total victory" meant that soldiers, and civilians, were going to die—unless Germany and Japan were prepared to surrender, which they most certainly were not. The bombings over Hiroshima, Nagasaki, and Dresden resulted in the death of tens of thousands of Japanese and Germans. These were excessive deaths, but also expected outcomes of a war fought on such a grand and grisly scale.

And it took many years for the people of Germany and Japan, even after each armistice was signed, to accept defeat. The "day after" is not a seamlessly cooperative, magnanimous day. Defeated nations don't instantly take responsibility for how the war got started. After World War II, for instance, the German and Japanese people needed to be deprogrammed from the nationalist propaganda that caused them to be so destructively led and misled. This was one of the reasons why measures as the Marshall Plan were so necessary. But such plans are not fully developed or even necessarily imagined while the wars are ongoing. A fictitious "world community" did not demand of the Allies that the war cannot continue unless they had a plan to rebuild their enemies once an armistice was declared.

Making such a demand would be ludicrous. But it is precisely what President Biden insisted of Israel.

Soon into the postwar era, the Nuremberg Trials were convened to punish the Germans for perpetrating a war of aggression and crimes against humanity. And the parallel Tokyo Trials similarly resulted in the prosecution of Japanese officials and top generals. No one suggested that the United States should also be prosecuted for dropping two nuclear bombs over Japan. There was no moral confusion over the reasons why so many civilians had perished around the world—the bad guys killed, and the good guys killed. There were reasons that accounted for those deaths. Crimes against humanity were not judged solely on the number of civilian dead.

Germany launched an aggressive war to conquer European nations and commit mass murder of Europe's Jews. The war was being fought over the former, and not the latter. The latter introduced a separate and new crime that would require a special remedy of its own. The Japanese provoked America's direct involvement in World War II with two words: "Pearl Harbor." Those words would forever become synonymous with being blindsided. But no one was blind to what happens in war. The United States and its Allies were fighting a large-scale war on many fronts. Given its scope and the destination of warzones, many soldiers, and some civilians, were going to get killed. But everyone understood that casualties of war are not the same thing as what was happening to European Jewry.

Public support for wars helps when there are clear and definable boundaries. With distinct armies who wear identifiable uniforms and face-off against one another, distinguishing between combatants and noncombatants is much clearer and easier to disentangle. Armies are trained to fight wars of attrition, waged under the laws of armed conflict and rules of engagement. The bombing of military targets has clear military objectives. They present few if any moral quandaries because, in theory, the targets are separately located from where civilian life happens to be.

Hitler's air-raid bombing of Britain, known as the Blitz; Britain's firebombing against Germany; and America's dropping of nuclear bombs on Japan ultimately turned what could have been the conventional warfare of World War II into urban battlefields with tens of thousands of civilian dead.

And, yet, the bombing campaigns over London, Rotterdam, Hamburg, Dresden, and Tokyo bear no relationship to the tunnels underneath and rooftops above—the hospitals, mosques, and schools that Hamas uses as its command centers and launching pads. The Allies bombed cities using, by comparison to today's high-tech munitions, imprecise weaponry—lots of payload but very little accuracy. Allied leaders knew that without precision, which didn't exist at the time, civilians would be killed. To some extent, that was why some leaders ordered the bombings in the first place. The goal was to demoralize the people and undermine their resolve.

In his book on just wars, Michael Walzer recalled, "Harry Truman's flat statement that he never lost a night's sleep over his decision to drop the atomic bomb on Hiroshima."[61] As for Winston Churchill and his terror bombing of Germany, Walzer wrote, "The purpose of the raids was explicitly declared to be the destruction of civilian morale... 'to create conditions intolerable to the mass of the German population.'"[62] Harry Truman offered similar justifications for why two atomic bombs were dropped on the civilians of Japan. He said: "We have used it in order to shorten the agony of war,[63] believing that, given Japanese aggression, the Americans could do *anything at all* to win."[64]

Anything at all? Didn't President Truman realize that such eliminationist rhetoric and finality of action would lead to nationwide student protests and demonstrators blocking bridges and the disruption of Christmas tree lighting ceremonies? He would be regaled as "Genocide Harry!"

No such thing happened. Surely the Democratic progressives who had preferred Roosevelt's prior vice-president, Henry Wallace, to Truman would erupt in outrage after learning that the president believed that saving the lives of American serviceman in the Pacific was more important than sparing innocent Japanese civilians. But they didn't. Obviously, there were no Squad members in Congress during World War II. Very few Americans said a peep. Everyone was thrilled that V-J Day had finally arrived.

Walzer recognized the military and emotional wisdom in that approach. Faced with implacable enemies waging a ruthless war, one that was taking its toll on Allied forces and the morale of British and American civilians back home, the wartime actions against Germany and Japan presented "a supreme emergency, where one might well be required to override the rights of innocent people and shatter the war convention."[65]

That means the following obvious point, unless you are an Islamist slumming at an Ivy League university or a screeching mentally impaired freshman with pink hair: Collateral damage in wartime is never unanticipated. Some civilian deaths are accidental, but the reality of war is that nations should expect to see large number of civilian dead—and that reality is no accident. Until Israel came along, followed by Hamas and Hezbollah, the world pretty much accepted these consequences of war without screaming "genocide" every time a civilian was inadvertently killed. Collateral damage is very much part of the calculus of warfare. It takes place whether nations at war want it or not. And it is especially predictable in asymmetric wars against nonstate actors with Islamist agendas.

The reason for that is ghastly, but otherwise really quite simple: Terrorists prefer fighting within cities because it offsets the significant advantages in weaponry that actual armies possess. States have advanced technological firepower, including fighter-jet air support. Nonstate terrorists may not have an air force, but suicide attacks and IEDs are effective weapons in urban areas. Cities also provide nonstate insurgents with significant defensive advantages.[66]

Cities, actually, can serve as a gauntlet, writ large, an endless array of funhouse mirrors, or haunted houses—all in one. Concrete cover that allows for evasion and concealment. Walls, corners, hallways, and staircases for an ambush and counterattack against invading armies that have no idea which direction to turn. Scientists have been working on x-ray technology that could neutralize this asymmetric advantage, but for now, it's basically walking in the dark. A terrorist's turf isn't really a turf at all—because it's mostly vertical terrain. There are tunnels, corridors, and rooftops. Buildings are all boobytrapped—welcoming infantry soldiers with a free tour.

Cities packed with civilians are the death knell of Western armies. Urban areas like Baghdad, Mogadishu, and Fallujah paralyze them. Bound by military guidelines and international law, soldiers are compelled to hesitate, misread body movements, second-guess every time they fire a weapon. Israel is forced to fight under a microscope. But even for nations that face no scrutiny at all, commanders often agonize over decisions to deploy certain weapons or undertake certain operations—precisely because of the civilian presence.

The agony of an enemy fearful of collateral damage can serve the same function as an Iron Dome for terrorists who could care less about the death of their own people.

And try as one might to avoid the unavoidable, the sight of dead civilians is only going to get worse. The days of conventional warfare are slowly coming to an end. Russia's invasion of Ukraine may be the last war not fought entirely in urban areas. And we have Hamas and Hezbollah largely to thank for that. Far more of the world's population now reside in cities. And world militaries are much smaller in size than they were during World War II. The combined armed forces in the United States decreased from 731,700 in 1991 to 481,750 in 2019. (Israel is one of the few nations that has more active military personnel than it did twenty years ago—with hundreds of thousands available for reservist duty.)

In 1960, the world's 3.5 billion population, only a mere five hundred million lived in cities. By 2020, the world's population grew to seven billion, with nearly half living in cities. By 2050, 70 percent of the world's population will live in urban areas.[67] That means that urban warfare will increasingly become more inevitable. So far, the world is only squeamish when it comes to Israel's wars in Gaza and Lebanon. But we must be prepared, psychologically and emotionally, to accept mounting civilian death tolls whenever nations and rogue states go to war.

Collateral damage has already become more ubiquitous in places like Gaza, Beirut, and Mosul, where American coalition forces killed as many as eleven thousand civilians in order to rid Iraq of twelve thousand ISIS terrorists. But large civilian death tolls were not invented by terrorists. Wartime always presented such inevitabilities. In fact, over 2,500 years ago, in 612 BCE, Mosul was the capital of the Assyrian Empire—the biblical area called Nineveh, beside the Tigris River. We know from archeological evidence that ancient Mosul was sacked by the Babylonians, with excavations uncovering the remains of children and babies killed by arrows.[68]

All the biblical and Greek battles were urban in nature. The Greek conquest over Troy required scaling its insurmountable wall—ultimately bypassing it altogether with the ingenuity of that Trojan Horse. Once on the other side, the Greeks discovered not just the Trojan army, but sleeping women and children. The Old Testament, which can be traced as far back as 5000 BCE, describes battles in such places as Ninevah, Jericho, and Elam, also with unscalable walls, and sieges that resulted in civilian death. The Romans invented the most effective weapons of its time to prevail in siege warfare: catapults and battering rams.[69] Armies did not always have the luxury of open battlefields marked off quite a distance from population centers.

But even in more recent battlefronts, such as the First and Second World Wars, modern armies squared off in capital cities such as Antwerp, Leningrad, Moscow, Stalingrad, Berlin, and Warsaw.[70]

Israel should be receiving global support for these campaigns against nonstate terrorists. As a democratic nation observing the laws of armed combat, Israel is the canary in the wartime coal mine. The world should take heed. The nature of asymmetric warfare, and what is being asked of conventional armies committed to military ethics, is maddening. So, too, are the moral quandaries young soldiers face. Israel is never credited with the risks its soldiers undertake in hostile environments where terrorists are indistinguishable from mild-mannered dentists. One scholar of military history put it this way: "Urban warfare demands a great deal more of fighting soldiers and officers; higher levels of mental agility and psychological resilience, and the experience of more physical and emotional stress."[71]

Clearly not enough deference is afforded soldiers who are placed in impossible situations. One IDF infantry commander reported his experience: "The weight of the decision, of the discretion. Sometimes one hit can make a lot of harm;… It could be that there are ten girls around him, so it's better not to shoot so that no girl will gets hit…[otherwise it will] be written in the newspaper that the IDF killed two terrorists and that as a result two girls were killed."[72] A tank commander said, "There is a fear throughout the IDF of shooting. Every time a shot is fired, you have all these commanders coming down to investigate you."[73] A paratrooper reported, "The guys were very frightened, very frightened. Before entering Nablus for the first time, the city was like the dark forest that you don't enter."[74] Similarly, a platoon commander said, "We were under a flood of stones. Molotov bottles and homemade explosives. The general instruction was not to open fire until we would be subject to a close and certain danger to our lives; but we had been ordered not to open fire at all, because there were civilians among the Palestinian terrorists. It was very hard for the soldiers to swallow this."[75]

Does this sound like the marching orders of a genocidal army—soldiers unloading weapons indiscriminately—or does it more resemble terrified young soldiers and older reservists deeply aware of the oversight and scrutiny that will be brought down on them if they make the wrong wartime decision? It is an environment of uncontrolled chaos and risk—to themselves and to civilians. They fear the military judgment of their superior offices and the moral judgment of the people of Israel. And they can't be inured to self-scrutiny. They know the consequences of carrying a weapon among so many civilians. And, yet they also know that some of those civilians are not civilians at all—they are Hamas operatives. How can they tell the difference?

Pampered Ivy League college students and their antisemitic professors know nothing about any of this, and they don't care. They just know that Gaza gives them license to hate Jews, and they will make good use of that opportunity.

Unlike terrorists, the IDF keeps track of when they fall short of their ethical obligations. The IDF holds itself accountable to a set of its own codified ideals and the ethos of Jewish morality. Israeli soldiers knew quite well why they were deployed: the inhumanity of the October 7 attack. Many knew victims or survivors. The crimes were too unspeakable to vindicate. Torching babies, gang raping girls. Who knows how one will handle him or herself when faced with such otherworldly pressures and emotions?

The *Washington Post* published photographs and videos created by IDF soldiers that depicted homes being burned to the ground, property destroyed, Hamas prisoners taunted, dead bodies mocked, graffiti left behind, and narrations invoking Israeli vengeance for what Hamas did on October 7. The news source undoubtedly wanted to discredit Israel, to expose the lack of professionalism of the IDF. Maybe it did. But it also showed soldiers operating under enormous stress levels while being placed in impossible moral and emotional situations.

"Keep watching us from above and we will avenge from below," Elishav Libman, an IDF soldier speaks into the camera. His brother was among the mass murdered at the Nova Music Festival. His video also captures the devastation of Gazan street life. There is graffiti scrawled on a wall: "We demand revenge." Yet, he denied that his amateur filmmaking was motivated by a vengeful impulse. "Ultimately, my target audience is the citizens of Israel. I know what gives our citizens strength."[76]

Elsewhere in the story, a lieutenant colonel is quoted as saying, "As far as we were concerned, everyone who was around there was an enemy. Whether he had a weapon on him or not, it doesn't matter."[77]

Clearly the IDF is not being captured in its most flattering light. These homemade newsreels from the front could be used as examples of soldiers and officers toying with the principles of military necessity. Might the International Court of Justice and the International Criminal Court regard such evidence as breached ethical military conduct and probative of indictable offenses?

The answer is possibly, yes. But Hamas took videos of atrocities committed by their own hands and posted them for all the world to see. The *Washington Post* wasn't all that interested in such *cinema verité*. But Israeli soldiers torching the homes of terrorists with no one in them? Enormously newsworthy. Hamas placed infants in ovens and forced Jewish families to watch their children burned to death. The IDF scrawled graffiti.

There were also reports of forty Israeli infants who were beheaded. Soldiers reported such sightings when they returned from southern Israel in the days following October 7. The Israeli government never confirmed those claims, however.

But journalists were invited to examine some of the remains of Hamas' victims on October 7. And they spoke with forensic pathologists. Dr. Chen Kugel, the head of Israel's National Center of Forensic Medicine, confirmed that that the ages of the victims ranged from three months to eighty or ninety years. He said that many bodies, including those of babies, were detached from heads.[78]

Remember that female student from the University of Toronto? Since torched babies is, apparently, of no consequence to the *Washington Post*, are they, too, saying, "No one has the right to question how Hamas chooses to resist"? A large segment of global public opinion is essentially saying: "If a nation occupies another, subjects it to apartheid policies, and ethnically cleanses its people, what did that nation expect would ultimately happen? We won't demonize freedom fighters by getting hung up on the semantics of terrorism."

These are the very same people who unflinchingly accept charges of Israel's land-theft, apartheid policies, and ethnic cleanings. They'll believe anything if it stigmatizes the Jewish state. They also reject that Israel should ever have the right to imprison Palestinians, demolish their homes, and withhold essential services. The national security threat Palestinians have presented to Israelis since the mid-1960s, which would justify these measures, are irrelevant to them.

But there is a vast difference between burning babies and torching unoccupied homes that double as terrorist dens. A news source with a motto, "Democracy Dies in Darkness," should be able to recognize darkness when confronted with it. What's more, it should be reporting on it, shining a light on Hamas rather than refracting the light toward Israel. A major mainstream newspaper chose to report on a few examples of unbecoming military behavior, while ignoring the barbarism of terrorists that ignited a full-scale war. Apparently, the *Washington Post* sees no reason to impugn Hamas' motives and methods.

The moral equivocation is appalling. And the lack of compassion for young soldiers who would much rather be elsewhere—who often can't know what they are shooting at—is journalistically irresponsible. As a day job, Israeli soldiers would prefer inventing the next miracle drug or engineering the next wave of microprocessors. Gazans of the same age would simply like to kill another Jew.

The pressure placed on Israeli soldiers is immense—for the younger ones, but for battle-tested reservists, too. The IDF's military code, moral scrutiny, and personal honor is never far from their minds. But there are ethical lapses and military mistakes, which the IDF never fails to address. By contrast, what's on the mind of a terrorist, and in what ways are they disciplined for falling short on the imperatives of terror?

With so many phantom targets, Israeli soldiers can either fire away randomly or be killed. What choice would you want your son or daughter to make? Terrorists enjoy the tactical freedom to disguise themselves as civilians engaged in ordinary acts. Edward Luttwak, an American military strategist, observed that "Hamas fighters can be perfect civilians walking alongside women and children right up until the moment they duck into the right doorway to take up prepared weapons and come out shooting."[79]

The horrific battlefield conditions of urban warfare cannot be underestimated. No amount of training can minimize the risk and steady a young soldier's nerves. Once boots hit the ground in Gaza, a soldier's life is imperiled. The rules governing *jus in bello*—whether warfare is being waged justly—seem ill-suited to the circumstances.

That's why there has been an ongoing debate within Israeli society, and especially within the Israeli defense establishment, as to whether the laws of armed conflict should even be applied strictly in Gaza. This is the essence of the Dahiya Doctrine—terrorists fight dirty, so when at war with them, the gloves come off, and some of the rules of armed conflict must, by necessity, be modified. It is a commonsense response to asymmetric, urban warfare. The Doctrine takes collateral damage entirely out of the military calculus. The death of civilians is a given. Better their civilians than ours.

Terrorists essentially have chosen their battlefield and weapons: urban settings surrounded by human shields. Israel must be permitted to choose a war strategy that offsets both the threat level and battlefield conditions of the enemy. Anything less compromises the chance of victory, and no one goes to war to lose. If an apartment building becomes a command center and launching pad, it is now a legitimate target. That decision was made by Hamas and Hezbollah. Israel must do what it must do.

It's an argument worth having, even though the various IDF chiefs of the general staff since Lebanon in 2006 have not adopted Dahiya—at least not formally or spoken much about it. Given the deadfall environment that is Gaza—with maximum enemy concealment of snipers and bombers, the presence of human shields, the absence of uniforms, the required split-second decision-making, and the hemmed in nature of the fighting—and with Israeli soldiers being asked to accomplish morally impossible tasks, Israel's *jus in bello* under such conditions must be given more leeway; it must be allowed to suit the circumstances.

Most of the soldiers are themselves only teenagers. Meanwhile, a good many of the Palestinians carrying weapons, planting explosives, or serving Hamas in some capacities are teenagers, too, and not children. It may be true that Israel has been forced to kill teenagers, but these teenagers were most certainly killed in action, and not while attending school. The Gaza Health Ministry's own records confirm that among the terrorists fighting under either the command of Hamas or Islamic Jihad, there are 225 seventeen-year-olds and 226 sixteen-year-olds.[80] If they are actually admitting the deployment of teenagers, then those numbers must be higher.

Under what moral principle must an Israeli mother sacrifice her son or daughter in order to save the child of a Palestinian mother, when the child is actually a teenager, and the mother willingly volunteers her child to assist Hamas in whatever sacrificial task suits the terrorists best? For many, it makes no difference whether the child is a teenager trained to kill Jews, whose mother is proud of her son's *jihadist* convictions. But the Israeli soldier is himself, or herself, only a year or two past being a kid, as well.

Professor Asa Kasher, who drafted the IDF's Code of Ethics, and Major General Amos Yadlin, the chief of Military Intelligence, published the book, *The Ethical Fight Against Terror*. When interviewed, Kasher said, "Sending a soldier there to fight terrorists is justified, but why should I force him to endanger himself much more than that so that the terrorist's neighbor is not killed?… If it's between the soldier and the terrorist's neighbor, the priority is the soldier. Any country would do the same."[81]

A United States Marine fighting in urban Iraq, where combatants and noncombatants were also, in greater numbers, essentially the same, described the heat of the moment and moral dilemma best in stating, "Large segments of the civilian population are expected to be armed with AK-47s, so that the armed and not hostile civilians will be mixed up with enemy fighters dressed in civilian clothes. Therefore, the usual battlefield rules—shoot guys wearing enemy uniforms, shoot guys with weapons—don't apply."[82]

The machinery of warfare has dramatically changed, as well. Drone warfare, for instance, allows for the delivery of precision-guided missiles operated by someone who need not wear a uniform because the aviator is on the ground, possibly not even on the same continent as his or her target. A mastery over video games doesn't hurt when it comes to this kind of killing. Basic training can be accomplished with an Xbox. Same with cyberwarfare, which in a digital theater of war, often dispenses with bloodshed altogether. Taking an enemy nation offline—disabling its digital infrastructure and communications centers—can, in many instances, inflict greater damage and make the nation more vulnerable than dead bodies. But Hamas hates that kind of warfare. Downed cable TV and weak internet access receives less attention from an antisemitic world. Cyberwarfare takes away Hamas' secret weapon: dead Gazans.

The entire formula for military ethics—the playbook and guidelines—get tossed anyway since terrorists aren't adhering to them. All Hamas wants is for Israel to be forced to join them in forsaking the rules. The mainstream media will then instantly sensationalize Israel's breach of *jus in bello*. This happened in December 2024 when the *New York Times* ran what appeared to be a blockbuster discovery of a deliberate ethical military failure. After the horror show that was October 7 and the discovery of the depth of those tunnels, military lawyers decided that the IDF could target even lower-valued Hamas commanders, using two-thousand-pound "dumb bombs" that would produce a larger number of civilian casualties than would be permissible under established rules.

Despite the prominence of this featured story and its bloated 4,413 word-count, the news was unsurprising given what had happened on October 7 and how high the stakes had been raised.[83] The *New York Times* has never featured Hamas' war strategy and military aims. The real story is always a non-story: Hamas' preferred form of warfare entirely ignores all conventional military models. Its military strategy depends entirely on shock value, moral revulsion, and an avoidance of rules altogether. And that's just fine because terrorists are justified in breaking all the rules and Israel deserves none of the benefits of those rules or allowances owing to Hamas' breach.

The media lap up and bury all departures from international law, and instantly zero in on any deviation committed by Israel. If the Dahiya Doctrine was ever actually invoked by Israel, the legacy media would have a field day on the propaganda battlefield.

This is the perversely grotesque innovation in modern warfare that Islamists have introduced to the world—a guerrilla warfare too uncivilized, even for guerillas. No battlefields. No uniforms. The enemy's civilians are deemed legitimate targets. The terrorists' own civilians are deployed as human shields. Civilian infrastructure—such as homes, schools, hospitals, and religious buildings—become indistinguishable from military infrastructure: they are used as command centers, for the warehousing of weapons, and as bases of operations. The rooftops of residential buildings serve as rocket launching pads with families one floor below. Hamas uses bedrooms, kitchens, backyards, and balconies—baby diapers are on the same shelf as mortar shells; a computer used by a middle-schooler doubles as an IP address for a terrorist. Neither the mainstream media, nor ostensibly "pro-Palestinian activists," seems to care one bit about how this monstrous war strategy immorally endangers civilian lives.[84]

This is the fight that Israel must wage, the position it continues to find itself in. The conventional rules of warfare are ill-suited to this terrain and against such a lawless foe. International humanitarian law is an oxymoron when one side instigates a war by mutilating teenagers and torching infants. Armed conflict had never before contemplated a war strategy depending so thoroughly upon civilian death—targeting the civilians of the enemy, then placing one's own civilians in harm's way, followed by counting the killing of terrorists as if they were civilians, too.

It would be difficult to explain, no less justify, such a *jus in bello*—the justice in how one side conducts itself in war—to students of warfare. And no doubt those attending military academies in the United States and in Western nations are watching Israel's dilemma with great interest. Some lessons were learned from their own experiences in Afghanistan and Iraq—where the fighting quarters were not nearly as narrow, but where insurgents could be nearly anyone.

Welcome to the world of today's warfare, where sacrificing one's own civilians is viewed as a win—so long as the world is paying attention, which they always seem to whenever the Jewish state is provoked to fight in self-defense.

Napoleon and George Washington would have been at a loss how to proceed. War is an inherently chaotic, a largely zero-sum affair. But Hamas has turned what was always understood to be a mess into something monstrous. In this new iteration of a warzone, residential buildings are potential military targets. Every mosque and hospital have a dual purpose—prayer and healing one day; terror and mass murder the next.

Israel's ground forces take command of a hospital, being fired upon by terrorists hiding behind the nurses' station. ICU machines blink and beep in the background. The basement under the hospital leads to tunnels where Israeli hostages are hidden or their remains are being stored. In the basement of another hospital, nearly the entire floor is committed to war-making. There's a missile launch control center that has more gadgets than anything in the facility's surgical rooms. Bandages are given less priority than drones. Such places are supposed to serve as sanctuaries where civilians are kept safe. But not when they also house operations that are not surgical but lethal in nature.

Israel has seen this all before and knows very well what a thankless task they have and how the world will react. In October 2002, Palestinian terrorists, this time in the West Bank, while exchanging gunfire with Israeli forces, dashed into the Church of the Nativity in Bethlehem—the town where Jesus was born. For nearly forty days, dozens of terrorists, among whom were several high-value targets who had planned a wave of suicide bombings, commandeered the Church, surrounded by the IDF. They were not alone, among them, forty-nine church clergy and forty-five unarmed Palestinians. Four Greek monks reported that the terrorists seized stockpiles of food and "ate like greedy monsters," while Christians, and Palestinians, received little.[85] They also slept in comfortable apartments reserved for priests, while civilians, and dislodged priests, were consigned to the floors of the main sanctuary.

What was learned years later, in a book about the siege, was that the entire affair was staged by the terrorists. The plan was to lure the IDF into heavy fighting in Manger Square and then flee inside the Church with bullets flying after them and taking civilians hostages. The mainstream media, naturally, couldn't get enough footage and photos.[86]

"The conspiracy was to make a siege and put all the fighters inside the church so Israel would make the siege. People from the Palestinian Authority collaborated with this conspiracy," said Elman Abu Eita, who was, at the time, an al-Aqsa Brigades chief.[87]

No army wishes to exchange fire in hospitals and mosques—and, in the worst possible of all settings—the Church that literally gave birth to Christianity! But can such ordinarily peaceful structures be immune from the presence of ground troops when they are being hijacked by killers hoping to bait the Israelis into a terrible press day? Israel is fighting a war of propaganda, moral confusion, and awful optics—the terrorists' most effective and disarming weapon in its arsenal.

The sight of the IDF razing houses and bombing apartment buildings appears vindictive, punitive, and unnecessarily cruel. It is therefore taken as a sign that what Israel really wants is to punish the Gazan population as a whole and ultimately drive them out as part of an unstated policy of ethnic cleansing. But in places like Gaza and the towns of the West Bank, each civilian home is a trap in which to kill or kidnap an Israeli soldier, or keep a civilian hostage. It's anyone's guess what's on the other side of the door to a child's bedroom: a terrorist activating a bomb; a teenager ready to hurl a Molotov cocktail; a small girl with her headphones on, listening to music.

Explosives are one thing, but what's far worse is the age of the Gazan attached to the weapon. Civilians are assisting terrorists in their dirty work with dirty bombs. When the press falsely reports the number of civilians caught in an Israeli counterstrike, they neglect to mention that far too many of them, including sixteen-year-old "children," are tantamount to terrorists themselves.

In 2021, United Nations Secretary-General António Guterres acknowledged this when he demanded that Hamas and Islamic Jihad stop inserting children into their terrorist war games: "I call upon the al-Qassam Brigades to cease the recruitment and use of children and to abide by their national and international legal obligations. I urge all Palestinian armed groups to protect children, including by preventing them from being exposed to the risk of violence or from being exploited for political purposes."[88]

This is not new information. It's just that when the world hears about the IDF killing Palestinian children, the association is immediately that of a woman cradling a dead baby in her arms. Of course, sometimes that is true, but some of those "children" are much older and have joined the fight voluntarily. Yes, minors are innocent, but these "minors" are trained to take the lives of Israeli soldiers, and they don't hesitate in doing so. They are not exactly the same as the kids on your block who attend the local junior high school. Their inherent innocence may be identical, but in Gaza, they are not mere bystanders.

Hamas has deployed children under the age of fifteen for decades. They operate military summer camps for children, where they receive training from foot soldiers with the al-Qassam Brigades. Daniel Pérez-García—who is affiliated with the radicalization, prevention, and security area of the research and projects department of the Euro-Arab Foundation for Higher Studies—has provided more details about the involvement of these children: "In addition to training in the handling of weapons such as the well-known AK-47, they are trained in…asymmetric and irregular warfare,…[where] their youngest members [are taught how] to kidnap IDF soldiers."[89]

When that's the enemy a soldier is facing, a just war—the justified reasons for entering the fight (*jus ad bellum*)—can easily seem irreconcilable with the justness of the fighting itself, the way in which the war is being conducted (*jus in bello*).

And this is only the havoc that awaits the IDF above ground. What about the vast network of tunnels—totaling over 310 miles all throughout Gaza—with numerous exits serving as death traps and hidden dangers for Jews in southern Israel? This is something that surprised the IDF soon after invading Gaza: the sheer depth and size of the tunnels. Some were laid with tracks to enable the swift movement of men and munitions underground; others were dug 250 feet deep, which is the equivalent of a twenty-five-story building turned upside-down. The sophistication and scale of the tunnels truly caught the IDF off guard. They didn't quite know what was being engineered on the other side of the security fence. The magnitude of this intelligence failure will not soon be forgiven or forgotten among Israelis.

Of course, Israel knew about the tunnels since the last major conflict with Hamas back in 2014. But at the time these underground structures had a more limited purpose: cleverly concealed to penetrate into Israel to kidnap soldiers and civilians, dragging them underground and into Gaza. These were single file in width, crudely constructed, and not in any way habitable, lacking the lavish amenities and structural improvements they possessed on October 7.

Back in 2014, the Jewish state agreed to a ceasefire after fifty days of fighting—knowing full well that Hamas still had three thousand rockets in its arsenal, and ten tunnels left undestroyed. Many Israelis implored the IDF to press on until Hamas and its weapons were no more. On October 8, 2023, they could not refrain from saying, "We told you so!" They were none too happy to be proven correct. To placate global public opinion, and primarily to appease President Barack Obama, the IDF failed to finish the job.

A decade later, the tunnels had the width to allow trucks to disappear underground. Command and communications centers were deep enough to survive Israeli airstrikes. And they probably also offer Netflix and Pornhub a keystroke away.

Without this labyrinthine expanse of passageways and hideouts, this most recent war in Gaza would have been over much sooner. Instead, Israel soon came to learn that most of the hostages were being held in the tunnels, chained to beds, alone in the dark, visited by terrorists who repeatedly tormented and (in the case of women) sexually assaulted them. Israeli civilians were now serving as human shields for Hamas, too. Every Hamas commander needed an Israeli civilian to hide behind. Yahya Sinwar reportedly had half a dozen.

"I cannot overstate [how] [t]he tunnels impact the pace of the operations," said Daphné Richemond-Barak, who specializes in tunnel warfare at Israel's Reichman University. "You can't advance. You can't secure the terrain.... You're dealing with two wars.... One on the surface and one on the subsurface."[90]

Hamas terrorists venture out of the dark for three reasons alone: to kill Jews, to steal food and humanitarian aid, and to photograph dead Gazans. Those civilians would be alive today had Hamas shared those tunnels with their people. But a ground covered in corpses, and the wreckage of buildings with bodies buried underneath, was far more valuable. And Hamas knew that the media would label it evidence of genocide.

As reported in the *New York Times*, Israel recovered a manual in one of its raids, written in 2019, that anticipated what the next war would look like, including how Hamas could wage it and the new obstacles Israel would face. It essentially contemplated the war that the October 7 massacre unleashed. The goal was to create an underground strategic complex that Israel would not know how to penetrate, or navigate. It even instructed terrorists on how to move through the various maze-like entry points—including how long it should take to move from one area to the next—and fire weapons from awkward angles.[91]

The tunnel network not only slowed the pace of Israel's military operations, it created yet another dangerous terrain for Israeli soldiers to traverse. Gaza's home-turf was not only underground; it was also sheathed in darkness. A trip-wired world onto itself, constructed with impressive engineering ingenuity.

How could such an elaborate underworld of terror have been created with Israel not knowing about it? Its critics have complained about Israel's blockade of Gaza for over fifteen years. Former British Prime Minister David Cameron said that "Gaza cannot and must not be allowed to remain a prison camp. People in Gaza are living under constant attacks and pressure in an open-air prison." No friend of Israel, hard-left linguistic professor, Noam Chomsky, wrote that "it hardly takes more than a day in Gaza to appreciate what it must be like to try to survive in the world's largest open-air prison."

Is there any wonder why Israel continues its air and naval blockade of Gaza? It's because materials in which to make bombs and build tunnels is all Gazans seem interested in. They could have built swanky hotels with casinos along the Mediterranean, modern hospitals, first-class internet infrastructure, cantilever bridges, glistening buildings on university campuses. Nothing stopped them from doing so. Instead, they built 310 miles of tunnels to help facilitate their genocidal aspirations.

By now the degree to which UNRWA has collaborated with Hamas is well known. No better proof exists than the discovery of a Nokia telecommunications system right underneath UNRWA's offices.[92] The tunnels have entranceways and escape portals below schools and hospitals operated by UNRWA. Some arteries connect command centers with underground weapons factories. Above ground, weapons are warehoused in the homes of civilians. Below, weapons systems are manufactured. IDF soldiers are often in the dark, with landmines everywhere.[93]

The date, and the contents, of the discovered manual indicated that Hamas spent at least five years preparing for the October 7 surprise attack. During that entire time, Israel's Shin Bet and IDF special forces had no idea just how sophisticated and widespread these underground battlefields would become.

Daphné Richemond-Barak wrote in *Foreign Policy*, "Never in the history of tunnel warfare has a defender been able to spend months in such confined spaces. The digging itself, the innovative way Hamas had made use of the tunnels, and the group's survival underground for this long have been unprecedented."[94] The tunnels give new meaning to the asymmetries that accompany Islamic terror. The entire theater of war has been compressed. Dimensions are more vertical than horizontal, without any true open terrain. It's impossible to avoid the resulting collateral damage.

One effective strategy in navigating these tunnels has been to first send in dogs to sniff out bombs before soldiers specializing in these operations begin searching for hostages and collapsing the tunnels. The dogs have been trained for any number of assignments. Sometimes their efforts accidentally set off a bomb. One wonders when PETA will join protest groups like Queers for Palestine, Feminists for Palestine, and Black Lives Matter, all of whom are great admirers of Hamas.

Israel's need to detonate the tunnels is more bad news for ordinary Gazans. Given their strategic significance, it became a military priority to destroy this entire subterranean infrastructure.

The problem is that the tunnels run beneath densely populated areas. And given the depth of the targets with the greatest military significance—including the operational headquarters and living quarters of Hamas commanders—the IDF was forced to choose appropriate weapons to accomplish the task. The resulting destruction invariably killed more Palestinian civilians. It took an enormous payload and kill radius to demolish those tunnels—more than sixteen tons of explosives per kilometer.

As Amos Oz once asked his German audience: What is Israel to do? The civilian death toll from the October 7 Gaza War is larger than the two earlier campaigns. The reasons are many.

All three had the same origins and military objectives. Whether it was tens of thousands of rockets in 2014, or a savage ambush in 2023, in each instance, Israel was provoked into a just war that presented complexities that would raise questions about the manner in which it waged these wars. The same story, time and again: defeating Hamas required being lured into a trap of the terrorists' own design, one intentionally rigged to produce a disproportionate number of civilian dead.

But the circumstances surrounding the October 7 War was much worse. For one thing, it took much longer to reach its conclusion. Gaza had grown larger in population density; the number of human shields had multiplied; and the willingness of the citizenry to serve in that capacity had reached new levels of commitment. Terrorism in Gaza got more sophisticated. Hamas and Islamic Jihad improved their training and fighting capabilities.

There were now 250 hostages to consider. It weighed on the hearts of Israelis and complicated the national consensus to rid the enclave of terror outfits once and for all. The tunnelling of Gaza made leveling it that much more difficult. To collapse the tunnels required larger bombs that also spelled greater civilians loss above ground. And many of the hostages were being held inside those tunnels. Surgical strikes became more important, yet difficult to achieve.

The United States, Israel's most important ally, led by a Democratic administration where bipartisan support for the Jewish state was fraying, delivered mixed messages about how far Israel could go in setting the bar for what winning the war would look like. President Joe Biden, and then presidential candidate Kamala Harris, felt obligated to listen to the hectoring progressives within their party and on college campuses, and the rising Islamic influence within the United States.

The enormity of the attack on southern Israel resulted in sharpening Israel's national resolve. Yes, the hostages who were still alive, and the remains of those who had been killed, needed to be returned to Israel, but not at the expense of a premature ceasefire that would leave Hamas and Islamic Jihad still intact and capable of reconstituting.

The more the war dragged on—fifteen months, the longest in Israel's history—the greater the price for both Israel and Gaza. In addition to the 1,200 slaughtered on October 7 (a number that would translate into roughly fifty thousand Americans on 9/11), Israel lost nine hundred soldiers and police officers. And, yes, the Gaza Health Ministry reports that forty-eight thousand Gazans have lost their lives.

Israel's tragic fate is that from the world's perspective, it is only the last number that matters, and not the events that necessitated the war, or the circumstances that contributed to the casualty count, which was largely out of Israel's control.

CHAPTER 5

Do the Laws of Armed Conflict Apply to Terrorists Who Surround Themselves with Civilians?

There is a scene in the feature film, *The Patriot* (2000), starring Mel Gibson, that might help better understand how the laws of war occasionally need to be modified to suit the landscape of the battleground. One side has chosen the off-ramp on permissible warfare. Its adversary can continue to play by the rules or adjust its own war strategy, accordingly.

The film takes place during the American Revolutionary War. Gibson plays Benjamin Martin, a Colonel in the South Carolina militia tasked with holding back the advance of the mighty Red Coats in the South led by Lieutenant General Charles Cornwallis, played by Tom Wilkinson.

The story takes a dramatic turn, which may not be historically accurate, when a renegade British colonel decides to intentionally kill American civilians in order to hasten victory, and to obtain information on the whereabouts of Martin and his men.

Colonel Martin's young son was one of those civilians who was murdered by such an illegal military action that violated the principles of *jus in bello*.

The killing of colonial civilians was clearly a war crime. They were mostly farmers with families who were not involved in the war. They were precisely what the Geneva Conventions had in mind when codifying laws to protect innocent civilians nearly two hundred years later. Moreover, unlike Hamas, the militia fighting the British were not holed up among these civilians, hiding behind women and children, using them as human shields.

In one crucial scene, Colonel Martin meets with Lieutenant General Cornwallis to discuss a prisoner exchange. Cornwallis begins by invoking a military term, "aggrieved status," which essentially means that he has a problem with the colonial militia's *jus in bello*—the way in which Martin is leading his men in war.

Apparently, Martin is targeting both ordinary soldiers *and* British officers. Cornwallis objects to the tactic, suggesting that it is unbecoming of "gentlemen" to kill high-ranking officers. Colonel Martin points out that the British are "targeting civilians. Women, children and such." The General replies, "That's a separate issue," to which the Colonel responds, "No, no. I consider them linked. And as long as your soldiers attack civilians, I will order the shooting of officers at every engagement. And my men are excellent marksmen."

The Patriot leaves the audience thinking: When an army strays from the laws of armed conflict, it then perhaps forfeits any right to complain about an objectionable tactic deployed by the opposing army. Target our civilians, and don't be surprised when we start shooting at your officers.

Israel has repeatedly been placed in the same situation. It adheres to the laws of war against terrorists who don't believe such rules apply to them. They are nonstate actors, after all. Perhaps they are right: outlaws operate outside the boundaries of the law. They make their own rules and take full advantage of all deviations from the norm. Why then must Israel treat Hamas as if it is at war with a professional army, identified by its uniform and the ethical obligations that come with wearing stripes and medals, and hold fast to the norms and customs of waging warfare—the ground rules that all armies accept as a matter of course? The terrorists' code of conduct, by contrast, is always à la carte—catch-as-catch-can, whatever goes, nice knowing you. Why shouldn't Israel, to some degree, be expected to order off the *prix fixe* war menu, as well?

All but Islamists grant that Israel's war in Gaza is a just war, but many question whether Israel has been fighting justly—the treacherousness of the terrain and Hamas' lawlessness, notwithstanding. This is really the primary question because much of the world begrudgingly concedes that Israel has met its *jus ad bellum* burden—its war aims are just. Its methods in fighting this war in Gaza, however, the *jus in bello*, is where many critics find fault.

Despite the very public denunciations, Israel has been fighting justly. But perhaps it should be allowed some leeway, militarily, to address the significant disadvantages it faces given the way Hamas wages war?

When the enemy deliberately surrounds itself with civilians, and there is no way to distinguish between them, a moral quagmire is presented wholly unlike other more conventional war. But international humanitarian law was written to establish ground rules for conventional warfare—to carve out some humanity within warfare itself. Terrorists have but one organizing principle, however: to strike fear in humanity. The laws of war simply do not apply easily when the objectives are so irreconcilable.

One commentator wrote, "A just war demands one fight with one hand bound, but not both. For that is to make wars of self-defence impossible, and to grant complete immunity to an adversary, in this case of Hamas, that is sufficiently skilled and unscrupulous enough to use civilians as human shields. To demand that solicitude for civilian casualties go so far as to preclude military operations altogether is to concede the right of self-defence in the abstract, but deny it in the particular."[95]

Immediately after October 7, leaders of many nations acknowledged that Israel had the right, under Article 51 of the United Nations Charter, to defend itself—the same right that would apply to any other member state.

That right is meaningless, however, if the same statesmen, which at times even included President Joe Biden, denounce Israel for the Palestinian civilians killed while the IDF hunted down Hamas. And yet a rightful retaliation is bound to result in collateral damage. There is no avoiding it, unless both of Israel's hand are tied, in which case, self-defense is nothing but a sham, a misnomer. By going too far in its own self-defense, the argument goes, Israel is engaging in collective punishment against the Palestinian people who have no way to escape the hostilities between the Jewish state and the terrorist state Gaza has long become.

Perhaps what we have are irreconcilable applications of law. When a nation is attacked, it has a right and duty to retaliate in self-defense, to eliminate the threat, and to establish deterrence against any future act of aggression. Its actions are sanctioned under the laws of armed conflict. And under such laws, civilian deaths are deemed casualties of war, provided that a nation's *jus in bello* is proportionate.

But collateral damage is not the right term of art to describe Israel's actions in Gaza, so say Israel's many critics. The disproportionate number of Palestinian dead provides all the tangible evidence to prove that Israel's self-defense is a sham, a pretext to eliminate the Palestinians of Gaza from the entire Strip. Its war against Hamas and Islamic Jihad is not being waged judiciously. In the end, Israel could care less who it kills. It claims to be targeting terrorists, but the means by which it has been doing so far more resembles collective punishment.

How would one actually know when collective punishment is even taking place in the context of a war? When the Allies bombed Hiroshima, Nagasaki, Dresden, and other cities within the constellation of Axis Powers during World War II, the targets were not exclusively military in nature. In fact, in many cases, they were deliberately selected to get the attention of civilians who cheered on the Nazis and kamikazes. The United States, England, and the Soviet Union were holding the people of Germany and Japan responsible for allowing these fascist governments to seize power with their blessing. Hitler and Hirohito were embraced as glorious heroes, not tyrants.

Was that not collective punishment masquerading as a military war strategy? Perhaps it can be both. Perhaps civilians are, at times, enablers of the wicked nations they become. In the case of Gaza, unlike Germany and Japan, the terrorist entities that represent Gazans are deliberately targeting, and have succeeding in killing, Israeli civilians. (The Japanese bombed Pearl Harbor, not Brooklyn.) What should Gazan civilians expect in return? What did they think was going to happen when they elected a terrorist organization to govern the enclave immediately after Israel withdrew in 2005?

Israel *is* and always *has* conducted itself in self-defense in Gaza. But are Gazans who celebrated the savagery against Israeli civilians on October 7—who jeered and spit on hostages as they were paraded, broken and traumatized on the streets of Gaza—really in a position to complain about collective punishment?

Israel is being accused of far more than simply excessive self-defense. The far more damning accusation, the one that has piqued the world's attention and won't let go, is one of genocide, a crime that defies any pretense of proportionality, and thoroughly dispenses with any claim to self-defense

Can one nation's war strategy be defined by an enraged world as a cynical genocidal campaign?

War and genocide can occur at the same time, and it happens that wars can mask genocides—which is largely what happened in the civil wars that took place in Bosnia, Congo, and Sudan. Nazi Germany was charged under the Nuremberg Trials with launching a war of aggression—the absence of *jus ad bellum*—and crimes against humanity. The latter had nothing to do with *jus in bello*—when it comes to genocide, there can be no justification. And those crimes were unrelated to Germany's war against the Allied Powers. Crimes against humanity was a newly created legal category and referred to the genocide of Jews, gypsies, the mentally handicapped, and homosexuals.

Those who accuse Israel of genocide in Gaza are conflating two very different legal principles that apply to completely separate classifications of noncombatants: civilians caught in the very nucleus of a war; and civilians who are systematically marked for death. A genocide in Gaza would require a showing that the Palestinian *people* were the very targets of Israel's war strategy—the premeditated intention to eliminate the people and not just the terrorists who govern them.

As long as Israel has been conducting its war pursuant to the rules of engagement, the first category is not implicated. The second category has nothing to do with war, unless it's merely a pretext to "destroying, in whole or in part, a national, ethnical, racial or religious group," pursuant to the Convention on the Prevention and Punishment of the Crime of Genocide. The

Convention, which is essentially a contract enforceable against signatories, sets forth the legal definition of genocide that was established not long after the Nuremberg Trials concluded.

If it was true that Israel was fighting Hamas in a just war, but fighting it unjustly, the legal charge would be waging a war of aggression. No matter how Israel was conducting this war, so long as its intent was focused on vanquishing Hamas, no number of civilian deaths would constitute genocide.

Israel was attacked on October 7. It did not initiate the fighting. Hamas chooses to fight among its own civilians, deploying them as human shields. Civilian death in this circumstance does not meet the legal standard for genocide, although there are war crimes galore in Hamas targeting Israeli civilians and exposing its own civilians to certain death. And there may be legitimate claims against Israel for war crimes, too, such as for the use of imprecise, maliciously destructive weaponry—if that's what an impartial finder-of-fact might conclude.

It is legally incorrect to definitively conclude that large numbers of civilian casualties equate to genocide, as a matter of law. Shrieking college students, pro-Hamas activists and the charlatans of international law who administer the International Criminal Court, can't prove a crime simply by shouting its name. Unless the United Nations introduces an amendment to its Genocide Convention that changes the legal definition, Israel's critics are stuck with an unmet standard. A new definition would require a provision that now clarifies that genocide is not only the "intent to destroy a people"; genocide can also take place in a war in which "one side kills an inordinate number of civilians."

In the case of the mass murder of ethnic Muslims in the former Yugoslavia, which occurred from 1992–1995, international tribunals were reluctant to rule that anything more than war crimes had taken place—apart from the massacre in Srebrenica in 1995, when eight thousand men and boys were intentionally killed unrelated to any Serbian wartime objective.

In 2007, the International Court of Justice identified crimes that occurred in Bosnia and Herzegovina, a list that included widespread and deliberate killings, the siege of towns, mass rapes, torture, and deportation to camps and detention centers. But none involved the legal elements for a genocide. The president of the ICJ, Rosalyn Higgins, ruled that what took place were largely war crimes and, in some cases, crimes against humanity, but "Serbia has not committed genocide" nor "conspired to" or "incited the commission of genocide."[96]

If international tribunals had difficulty finding the necessary facts that would justify convicting Serbia with the crime of genocide in Bosnia, they have nothing to see in Gaza that approaches mass rapes, torture, and the specific intent to kill civilians. What you have in Gaza is a specific intent to kill *terrorists* who insist on standing right beside civilians.

Far too many self-appointed humanitarians who are avowedly antisemitic refuse to accept that Jews have a right to self-determination in their ancestral homeland. It is for this reason that to them, *any* aggression committed by Jewish interlopers against a Palestinian violates international law because Jews are alien to the land. Trespassers have no claim of right to self-defense. Those who hold such views reject the geographical details of the Old Testament, the existence of the Western Wall of the Second Temple, and the treasure trove of archeological evidence uncovered over centuries that conclusively prove that Jews are indigenous to the land of Israel and its disputed territories, especially the towns that comprise the West Bank.

That doesn't mean that Arabs were not living on the land, too, over many centuries. But Islam didn't come into existence until roughly seven hundred years after the death of Jesus Christ and the birth of Christianity. While the Jewish people are over four thousand years old, their first nation, the Kingdom of Judah, existed six hundred years *before* Christ and three hundred years *before* the Ancient Greeks.

This is the central absurdity of the slanderous libel that Jews have stolen Palestinian land. Throughout all recorded history, there never once was an Arab nation called Palestine. Not for ten minutes. No currency; no founding fathers; no national flag; no national capital; no governmental buildings; no consulates, ambassadors, or official diplomatic appointments.

The only time the land Palestinians claim as their own was officially a nation was during the biblical period of King David and King Solomon, and after Israel declared statehood in 1948. At all other times in between, the land was occupied by foreign invaders—Greeks, Babylonians, Romans, Persians, Assyrians, Ottomans, and the British. By the time the Jews established the modern state of Israel, the land had finally returned to its rightful owners. The Jews aren't colonizers of Israel, they are the dispossessed owners of a nation who finally, two millennia later, reclaimed their property and sovereignty.

So, what does fighting a just war, one that adheres to laws of armed conflict, look like?

First, let's examine the relevant laws surrounding warfare.

The first and most important question is whether the laws of armed conflict even apply when a state actor is at war with a terrorist entity. Should the laws of war govern a state's military conduct to protect terrorists who exercise no restraints at all in how they fight?

States have political goals in mind when waging war; they have no interest in destruction for its own sake. Liberation movements and organized terrorism are not necessarily the same. Terrorists favor terror and destruction; liberation movements seek self-determination.

There is no evidence at all that Hamas and Islamic Jihad are liberation movements. The same observation applies to the PLO and Fatah in the West Bank. There is plenty of evidence, however, that they are largely in the business of blowing things up, slitting Jewish throats, and stealing international aid.

The laws of war were designed to address the symmetries and reciprocities in warfare between actual states. The original Geneva Conventions don't even mention the word "terrorist," although terrorism is covered in the Updated Protocols to the Conventions in 1977.

The laws of armed conflict start with the presumption that states are rational actors with political goals and will respond to incentives that would curtail the amount of suffering that takes place in war. But this is less true when it comes to terrorism in general and has no application to Hamas at all. As law professor Eric Posner has written in discussing when the laws of war should apply to a state's war against a terrorist entity, "Although each side has an interest in defeating the other side, each side also has an interest in minimizing its own losses prior to victory or defeat, as the case may be."[97]

But such life-affirming rationales are not true of Hamas, Islamic Jihad, and Hezbollah. Just read their Charters and hear their public statements. They speak entirely in eliminationist language, target their adversary's civilians indiscriminately, and treat their own civilians as human shields, their lives entirely disposable. None of that behavior appears to have a political motive. In no way does it resemble the rationale of an actual nation-state. And there are no Fail-safe precautions because the desired endgame requires an actual end of days.

Moreover, the Palestinians have rejected five offers of statehood since 1947. Obviously, politics and nation-building are not objective goals. Dead Jews, however, are most definitely an organizational priority. Because those who represent the Palestinian people are "not amenable to reason and are unable to exercise self-discipline," the rational actor thesis is not available to justify strict compliance with the laws of armed combat.[98]

It just might be the case that many of the elements embodied in the laws of armed conflict have no application in Gaza whatsoever—Hamas is not a state actor and has never behaved even like a quasi-state actor. The broader laws of war might still apply, and international humanitarian law might apply, as well.

But let's start with the basics of Just War Theory.

A nation-state must have the proper justification to wage war and pursue its war aims justly, all pursuant to the general laws of war, international humanitarian law, and the Geneva Conventions. Several long-established elements must be met:

1. The wartime actions must prompted by a *military necessity*;
2. The targets chosen must make clear *distinctions* between enemy combatants and noncombatant civilians—when it's possible to do so;
3. The actions are *proportionate* to achieving the defined military aims;
4. The weapons being used are *appropriate* for the military task and deployed with *precision*;
5. Operational decisions are undertaken pursuant to *verifiable intelligence*;
6. *Humanitarian assistance* is offered to civilians.[99]

Military necessity means that the action an army is taking is justified and necessary to achieve a legitimate military goal. Firing upon enemy troops is perfectly legal under international law. The intention behind the military actions that are being taken matters most. There must be a reasonable rationale for doing so. Aiming at targets for the express purpose of killing civilians, however, is absolutely not permissible under international law because it is not a military necessity and achieves no wartime purpose.

To establish military necessity, an army can target storage facilities that warehouse weapons, transportation systems, or launching sites. Given the way in which Hamas uses all of Gaza—below and above ground—as an obstacle course for the IDF to guess what to shoot at, whether they be mosques, hospitals, bridges, schools, or apartment buildings, all can present a military necessity and contribute to a military objective.

Therein lies the essential problem.

The principle of *distinction* is important because it places the burden on an army to ensure that all of its military operations are directed at military targets to achieve a military end. It is required to distinguish between combatants and noncombatants. The laws of armed conflict, including the Geneva Conventions, absolutely prohibit direct attacks against civilians.

The problem here is the disparate treatment and deference shown to terrorists when it comes to the principle of distinction. And make no mistake, in the case of Hamas, Islamic Jihad, and Hezbollah, departments of state, foreign ministries, and intelligence services from countries around the world, have all designated these groups to be practitioners of terrorism.

Yet, the global community of international law "experts" do not seem to mind that Hamas and Hezbollah, for nearly two decades, have aimed rockets and missiles directly at Israeli civilian population centers. They have shown far less interest in attacking IDF facilities and its soldiers. This special targeting of Israeli civilians clearly violates the rule of distinction—a rule that Islamists seeking the death of Jews, no matter where they live, avowedly reject. And this makes them clearly in violation of international law.

We learned with the world's reaction to October 7—despite the gruesomeness of an attack against civilians that served no military purpose—that Palestinians are given a pass. Observing the laws of war don't, apparently, apply to them. They are presumptively permitted to engage in any act of violence against Jews without exposing themselves to violations of international law. Israel's retaliation to October 7, and whatever harm may have come to Palestinians—whether they be terrorists or civilians—is a different matter altogether, however. When it came to who was getting killed, there was great moral equivocation and immoral equivalencies. The loss of life among Palestinians in the context of a just war, no matter who they might be, was deemed more important than the 1,200 Israeli civilians who had already been murdered.

Now to the matter of the choice of weaponry. The general laws of war, and respect for military symmetries, require that the weapon be appropriate, precise and commensurate with the military necessity of the operation. Anyone who watched the critically–acclaimed, award–winning film, *Oppenheimer* (2023), is aware that being in possession of a secret offensive weapon raises all kinds of ethical dilemmas—even when nations are at war. Knowing what it could do—its unambiguous lethality; the scope of its destruction—should two atomic bombs have been dropped on Japan in order to bring an end to the war and pay Japan back for Pearl Harbor?

The chattering crowd of Israel detractors have long argued that more precise weapons should be chosen in Gaza to reduce the kill radius, given the densely urbanized conditions of the warzone. They have insisted that Israel's choice of artillery guaranteed needless civilian deaths. The purpose behind Israel's airstrikes is destructive by design, rather than the achievement of military goals.

Yet, a number of high-ranking military officers in the Pentagon and the British Armed Forces have meticulously examined the IDF's conduct in Gaza—during the 2014, and now in its October 7 campaign. Based on what they have observed, Israel should actually be praised for undertaking appropriate humanitarian precautions and strictly adhering to the rules of engagement. And while not without mistakes, all of its military actions occurred under extremely volatile, unpredictable conditions. Israel should be commended, not vilified, for exercising proper levels of military force that each military situation demanded.[100]

International humanitarian law does not have two sets of rules: one for nation states and another for nonstate actors practicing terrorism. The wars may be asymmetric in nature, but the rules of ethical warfare are supposed to be strictly adhered to, nonetheless. That means Hamas can't seek protection from the Geneva Conventions and international humanitarian law when it routinely flaunts the laws of war, generally. They don't get to cry "Uncle!" if they refuse to observe the laws of war that apply to the family of nations.

And, yet that's precisely what the community of international lawyers and legacy media apparently believed was appropriate in this particular war. We heard outrageous claims with disastrously lawless implications that beheadings and rape are "acceptable forms of resistance," and that Hamas was permitted to achieve its genocidal goals "by any means necessary"—a carte blanche exemption that sanctions savagery.

Targeting civilians with indiscriminate rocket fire. Having terrorists dress indistinguishably from ordinary civilians. Counting terrorists among the total civilian dead so as to exaggerate the casualty numbers and blame Israel for committing war crimes. Using civilians as shields and civilian infrastructure as staging grounds for military purposes. Defining and utilizing rape as a weapon.

All of these are clear violations of the principle of distinction, not to mention the laws of war, generally. Hamas makes no distinction between Israeli soldiers and civilians, and it makes no distinction between its own civilians and home-grown terrorists. How should an army observing the rules of engagement fight such a shape-shifting enemy? The only uniformity is that all Gazans are not wearing military uniforms. No one is saluting or marching or carrying on any of the duties of a standing army that would be instantly recognizable as combatants.

Street clothes allow for no distinctions to be made at all. Wearing a keffiyeh in Gaza is like wearing Levi's in San Francisco. Terrorists walk in and out of apartment buildings followed by children who appear to belong to them. Terrorists drive around in ambulances with the sirens on—while carrying weapons as cargo. Terrorists could walk the Gazan streets holding shopping bags with baguettes (maybe in Beirut, but not Gaza, where pita is more likely) sticking out from the top and mortar shells concealed at the bottom. Doctors in white coats have Hamas affiliations. All civilians are standby shields.

Israel is being dared to fire away at a rotating, never-ending shooting gallery. Simply madness.

Even Walzer, who normally holds nations strictly accountable to the laws of war, has recognized that sometimes military necessity forces a conflict between the collective survival of army personnel, and humanitarian considerations owed to civilians who have become sacrificial to a relentless cause. Given these grim stakes, a nation such as Israel might have to choose its own national survival over the human rights owed to civilians placed in harm's way.[101]

The military standards are obligatory no matter how much purported "experts" in international law—confined mostly to lawyers working within nongovernmental human rights organizations like Human Rights Watch, Amnesty International, and the United Nations Independent International Commission of Inquiry on the Occupied Palestinian Territory—impose a double standard that cynically strips Israel of its sovereign rights to defend itself. Western nations faced with Islamist internal threats of their own will gladly demonize Israel if it means the avoidance of rioting on their once civilized streets. Remember, Osama bin Laden was a Saudi; so, too, were many of his 9/11 henchmen. The Gulf nations and their royal families, and many European capitals inundated with Islamic terror, are quietly rooting for Israel—very quietly. But that does nothing for Israel if these states continually slam the Jewish one, publicly and loudly, in order to buy themselves another day of peace.

Setting aside all the antisemitic noise for a moment, if Israel has rights under international law to defend itself, and it satisfies the "military necessity" and "distinction" elements of the laws of armed combat, then its specific intent is what becomes most relevant. Are they aiming at Hamas and Islamic Jihad? That's all that matter. The collateral damage that predictably arises from the exercise of self-defense is neither surprising nor unlawful.

What is Israel seeking to accomplish in Gaza? What intention is plainly in evidence? It most certainly is *not* a joy ride to kill civilians.

Walzer recalls the emergency circumstances the Allied Powers faced during World War II: "[T]he more certain a German victory appeared to be in the absence of a bomber offensive, the more justifiable was the decision to launch the offensive.... Here was a supreme emergency, where one might well be required to override the rights of innocent people and shatter the war convention."[102] Walzer wasn't merely speaking in generalities by invoking the Nazis as the ultimate boogeymen, suggesting that deviation from the laws of war in that special instance was an aberration. The Nazi onslaught was singular, but so, too, was the orgy of inhumanity that Hamas and its civilian collaborators left behind in blood-soaked southern Israel. Walzer instantly understood the situation that Israel was placed in, and what response it was politically, legally and morally obligated to deliver to the people of Gaza.

Hamas deserved an earth-shattering retaliation, and that's the reason why the landscape of Gaza now resembles Mars. Walzer was not surprised by the damage Israel would inflict. Shortly after Hamas attacked Israel on October 7, he presciently wrote, "I had better make this terrifying argument more specific: the defeat of Hamas is a moral necessity, and it requires the kind of moral toughness that isn't always admirable."[103]

That statement came from the godfather of Just War Theory!

Two leading Middle East experts, based at the Washington Institute for Near East Policy, one with official negotiator status—at both Camp David and the Oslo Accords—both committed to diplomatic solutions, put the endgame of this war in the starkest terms possible: "Any talk of a postwar political process is meaningless without Israel battlefield success: There can be no serious discussion of a two-state solution or any other political objective with Hamas either still governing Gaza or commanding a coherent military force."[104]

What Walzer and other military theorists have been forced to concede and conclude is that Israel is continually placed in a morally untenable situation. In this most recent campaign, they were engaged in wars on seven fronts, fighting either terrorists or a meddlesome, fanatical Iran that actively finances all terrorism in the region. And let's not forget to include the rage-filled wars taking place on college campuses, on the Arab streets of Western capitals, and the mainstream media. These are all theaters of war like no other historical battlefields—all taking place simultaneously.

After fighting numerous wars in wide-open deserts and skies, against Egyptian, Syrian, Jordanian, Lebanese, and Iraqi militaries, nations that observed the basic principles of international humanitarian law, Israel had to adopt, and adapt to, a very different kind of aggression that has none of the nobility of a national army. Nation-states have the self-disciple to accept defeat and hand over their swords as a sign of surrender. Hamas commanders would prefer to simply blow themselves up while standing beside a child.

On July 31, 2024, Hamas' political leader, Ismail Haniyeh, was assassinated by an Israeli explosive while in a safehouse in Tehran. For the entire war until his death, Haniyeh was safely holed up in a luxury hotel in Qatar. He was largely sheltered, but his family was not. Months earlier, on April 11, 2024, three of his sons were killed in an Israeli airstrike in Gaza. The Gaza Health Ministry alleged that four of Haniyeh's grandchildren were killed in the blast, too.

According to the IDF and the Israel Security Agency (ISA), all three sons were senior commanders and military operatives in Hamas. How does a terrorist kingpin grieve the losses of his children and grandchildren? Haniyeh immediately issued a statement that these killings would not impact any ceasefire discussions or result in the return of the Israeli hostages. He stated emphatically that Hamas would "not surrender, and… not compromise…no matter how great our sacrifices are."[105]

The war in Vietnam forced the United States to learn how to fight against an insurgency embedded in a jungle. Israel was being forced to engage in an even more maddening minefield, where terrorists were embedded among *people*—not Israeli hostages, but their *own* people. True, many a North Vietnamese village was napalmed with full knowledge that women and children were scampering for breathable air. But the Viet Cong were not trying to get their own people killed. They weren't playing a PR game. They saw no advantage in displaying their own dead civilians in order to get the American bombing campaigns to stop. (Such efforts were underway on college campuses, however.) Globally, it wouldn't have worked. The world cared far less for North Vietnamese villages than it does for Gazans with terrorist ties. The United States concluded, as does Israel in Gaza, that the military value and operational necessity of these targets offset the certainty of civilian death.

Only an antisemite, or someone seriously misinformed, can fail to understand the simple logic of this. Civilians are going to perish in places like Gaza and Beirut, and the blame for those deaths must fall on Hamas and Hezbollah, and not on the country that was attacked and is responding in self-defense. The asymmetries are exploited by terrorists to produce disproportionate death tolls. The answer is to punish the terrorists who resort to such barbaric tactics, and not the nation that is operating in accordance with its own code of ethical military conduct, and in a manner that is also consistent with the principles of international humanitarian law.

Two military historians wrote a treatise arguing that asymmetric warfare may require a fresh look at the laws of war. One major modification that needs to be considered is the more prevalent use of human shields whenever Islamists go to war. Civilians being used as shields foretells more collateral damages. Generations of military ethicists never contemplated using civilians as a war tactic—as both offensive and defensive weapons. These two historians concluded, "When human shields are being used to shield an important military target,... the direct military necessity of the attack soars, and the proportionality analysis allows for more civilian casualties."[106]

That means: Expect more casualties of war and adjust your proportionality assessments accordingly. Hamas is creating targets Israel cannot ignore. But whether they are in the form of high-value terrorists or weapons warehouses, Hamas is flooding the warzone with civilians. The more important the terrorist, the more civilians should be expected in his immediate vicinity. He can never die alone. Another dead terrorist means nothing. His wife, children and relatives—well, that begins to look like a war crime. The same is true with weapons and launch sites. Store them in a civilian home. If an apartment building has an unusually large number of toddlers, then terrorists must be nearby. The more kids in the house, the better.

What is Israel to do? Surrender to these tactics? The Jewish state has chosen to fight on.

You can pretty much rest assured that if you find an empty lot in Gaza with no civilians in sight, there is nothing to bomb. This madness would leave the drafters of the Geneva Conventions with their heads spinning.

Want to know the relationship between human shields and disproportionate loss? In America's War on Terror in Iraq in 2003, the United States military command ordered that no more than thirty Iraqi civilians could be killed as collateral damage in the targeting of Saddam Hussein, the highest valued target imaginable. More than thirty, and they'd have to catch him at another location on some other day. In Gaza, in 2024, Israel targeted and killed Hamas commanders—just the commanders and not the two leaders of the military wing—and such operations resulted in as many as one hundred civilian casualties of war! Doesn't that meet the standard of "excessive" for the purposes of proportionality?

Perhaps Saddam Hussein didn't surround himself with human shields. Had he done so, far more than thirty Iraqis would have been fated to die with him. But then, theoretically, the United States would never have been able to assassinate him from the air. Remember, in the end, they found him hiding in a hole.

No other conflict around the world demands the same kind of numerical attention. In no other battlefield are combatants and noncombatants treated the same and counted the same—the killing of an armed terrorist gets added to the death toll as a "civilian" death. Nowhere else are civilians such a ubiquitous part of the military landscape. Moreover, nowhere else are civilians aiding and abetting terrorists at their own volition.

Both those with civilian status and armed combatants are legally and morally blurred. The Gaza Health Ministry manifestly obscures the identity of each casualty, and neither the press nor the United Nations is troubled by the statistical anomalies and lack of correlation. Perhaps most egregious of all: in no other war is collateral damage so casually relabeled as genocide.

In all other contexts, the distinction is clear. Nations go to war to defeat an opposing adversary's military. The grievances are political in nature and will result in some territorial compromise. Genocide takes place when a nation is attempting to eradicate an entire people, and there can be no resolution other than erasing all evidence of a population that once existed. The United Nations enacted the Genocide Convention on December 9, 1948, which criminalized genocide under international law "only if and when committed with the *specific intent to destroy a protected group*."[107]

Civilian death in war is always accidental if the nation is fighting justly. With genocide, a nation acts with the intention to kill everyone, or a significant part of the population. It is not accidental or unanticipated; it is the entire point.

Therein lies the irony of accusing Israel of perpetrating genocide against the Gazan people. Where is the evidence in all of Israel's brief history of an intent to destroy all remnants of the Palestinian population? Is it in Israel's founding documents and Declaration of Independence? Quite the opposite: Arabs were granted identical civil rights and privileges of citizenship. By contrast, the intention of Palestinian terrorists has always been unambiguous: the Charters of both the PLO and Hamas specifically speak of slaughtering all Jews.

The side that takes affirmative steps to preserve civilian life is accused of genocide. The other side expressly pronounces its genocidal intentions—demonstrated quite convincingly in beheading and gang raping civilians and indiscriminately firing rockets—and that other side is purportedly only engaged in "resistance."

If Israel was, indeed, a genocidal army, guilty as charged based on the death toll in Gaza alone, then the Jewish state would be the least effective genocidal nation in history. The IDF agonizes over every offensive strike precisely because it wants to preserve civilian life. Most airstrikes and bombings are determined by committee: the War Cabinet, Israel's Attorney General, the Chief Military Advocate General, the Deputy for International Affairs. Military legal advisors—40 full-time lawyers and over 100 reservists—work around the clock to make sure that commanders and soldiers are in compliance with international law. They are present at both command centers and division-level headquarters, which are closer to the actual target sites, in real time. They examine the operational "target bank" and make sure that the IDF's "high-level targeting" is based on "military necessity." They then consult on whether the correct weapon is being used to destroy the target without causing needless and avoidable civilian harm. These military overseers have the authority to override senior IDF commanders on decisions whether to launch drone and missile strikes.[108]

An IDF investigation into the 2023 Christmas Eve bombing of the Maghazi refugee camp concluded that the wrong weapon was chosen for the task, which resulted in the killing of seventy civilians.[109] This was an internal investigation, the kind of public acknowledgment rarely seen by other armies. All those responsible were held accountable and received some meaningful punishment or reprimand.

Under what oversight authority and fidelity to international law and humanitarian considerations does Hamas operate? What committee of military ethicists are standing behind Hamas commanders, counseling against firing rockets directly at Tel Aviv beaches?

The Palestinian population has tripled since the "Occupation." That's a pretty disqualifying statistic. Because when it comes right down to it: Genocide is a matter of math. Nations that have experienced genocide end up having fewer people in their overall population. There is a pronounced and not insubstantial subtraction from the last census. If your people have multiplied over a given period of time, you are not, by any legal definition, victims of genocide. And using the words "ethnic cleansing" might confuse already brainwashed college kids, but it doesn't change the status of war casualties.

The purpose of war is to eliminate an enemy; the purpose of genocide is to eliminate an entire people. In war, civilians die; in genocide, they are murdered. And far more are murdered in a genocide than those that die in battle. Political scientist Daniel Jonah Goldhagen coined the phrase describing genocide as, "Worse Than War."[110] Collateral damage is tragic; genocide is an atrocity.

There were two million Armenians in 1914, and four hundred thousand in 1917. There were sixteen million Jews in

1930, and ten million worldwide in 1945. Rwanda had seven hundred thousand Tutsi in April 1994, and fewer than 150,000 in July 1994. The Congolese have lost six million of its people since 1998. Between 1975 and 1979, two million Cambodians were annihilated. Tens of thousands of Mayans were mass murdered in Guatemala from 1981 to 1983. Since 2005, four hundred thousand Darfurians, comprising three separate ethnic groups, have been murdered, tortured, and raped in Sudan. And most recently, three hundred thousand Tigray civilians have been killed in Ethiopia.

These are the documented, legally recognized genocides of our recent history. The absolute death toll in each is greater than all the wars Israel has been dragged into—not just against Palestinian terrorists, but also other neighboring Arab and Muslim countries. Yet, global outrage for all the truly mass murdered is muted. Charges of genocide are rarely invoked against any of these other nations, and press coverage is always obscured if not altogether ignored.

Turkey makes it a crime to even mention the Armenian genocide and Turkey in the same sentence. Seriously, one is sent to prison for merely associating Turkey with the decimated Armenian population. No one is shy about leveling such charges against Israel, however, and unlike the Armenians, the Palestinian population has grown exponentially.

The number of Palestinians in the West Bank and Gaza in 1967 was 1.6 million; the number living in those territories today is 5.5 million.[111] For all this talk of genocide, the population growth among Palestinians is booming. Tripling in number is the very opposite of ethnic cleansing. It is repulsive to equate actual victims of genocide with the explosive population growth Palestinians have enjoyed. Armenians, Cambodians, and Rwandans—most especially global Jewry—should be morally outraged.

If Israel was trying to rid Gaza of Palestinians, it wouldn't need to risk the lives of IDF soldiers to do so. It has a vast arsenal of lethal projectiles. Gaza has no missile defense system to speak of. Israel's bombers and fighter-jet superiority would flatten Gaza in a matter of hours. By placing its soldiers on the ground in Gaza—moving house-to-house, building-to-building and in and out of tunnels—they risked Israeli lives: Nearly nine hundred IDF soldiers have been killed in a nation of only eight million people. Those deaths could have been avoided if Israel simply sought to eliminate all Palestinians, which could have been accomplished with much greater efficiency and finality from the air.

Instead, well into the second year of a war they could have won instantly, Israel successfully eliminated scores of Hamas and Islamic Jihad battalions, killed all of its main leaders, and degraded a good deal of its military capabilities, but it still was not finished. The war continued and spread into Beirut to eliminate the terrorists that have plagued Israel from the north at the same time as it was still occupied, militarily, to its south. Clearly, the war was about terrorists all along and never about civilians.

Here's an anecdote worth contemplating: Israeli doctors cured Yahya Sinwar of brain cancer back in 2008 while he was imprisoned in Israel. It gave him a second chance to emerge fifteen years later as the mastermind of the October 7 massacre. If Israel didn't kill a first-tier terrorist who had many murders and mutilations to his name—by simply allowing him to succumb to cancer—why would they want to kill Palestinian children? Israeli doctors saved his life. They had taken the Hippocratic Oath; they did not pledge themselves to murder. It's not natural for Jews to kill (or even to let die), but among far too many Palestinians, it's positively second nature.

For all the talk among Western leaders, Muslim marchers, and college nuisance-makers about withholding arms shipments to Israel, what isn't being discussed is how much restraint the Israelis have actually shown. Most other nations that had its infants butchered and girls gang raped would show no mercy at all to anyone in Gaza with a kind word to say about Hamas. Israel had the firepower, but not the will.

One can point to the death toll in Gaza in horror, but if you discount the number of terrorists and family members who were killed, the civilian casualty count would most certainly have been much higher—especially on a land mass that congested and totally decimated. Clearly, Israel had undertaken humanitarian precautions to spare lives.

The Jewish state defended itself pursuant to the laws of war on a battlefield designed for death. Asa Kasher, an Israeli philosopher, drafted the IDF ethical code. He and Major General Amos Yadlin, a former chief of Israel's Military Intelligence, published "Military Ethics of Fighting Terror." It justified the targeted killing of terrorists, even at the risk of harming civilians.

"The Geneva Conventions are based on hundreds of years of tradition of the fair rules of combat," Kasher said. "They were appropriate for classic warfare, where one army fought another. But in our time the whole business of rules of fair combat has been pushed aside. There are international efforts underway to revise the rules to accommodate the war against terrorism."[112]

Kasher took a bold step further. Why must Israeli soldiers be placed in the center of such ungodly chaos, knowing they are surrounded by terrorists dressed like civilians—never knowing who are the killers, and being unable to decipher who they must not kill? "War is hell," said the merciless tactician of Sherman's March. War in Gaza is also maddening. Under international law, commanders are required to direct their troops to fire upon combatants only. Everyone, including Walzer's textbook on the subject, is clear about that.

But, in Gaza, how can anyone know for sure the direction of the incoming fire, and which identically dressed Arab—male, female, or teenager—is pulling the trigger? Hesitate, and take a bullet from a terrorist dressed in a burka. It is a hostile environment not just because it is deadly, but because it creates so much doubt. Soldiers are very often choosing the lives of civilians over their own. They shouldn't have to.

Avishai Margalit and Michael Walzer wrote, however, that soldiers are owed no assurances that they will survive in battle. It is the risk that comes with wearing a military uniform and swearing an oath. But a duty is imposed upon them to protect civilian life even at the risk of their own peril.[113] At least that partially explains why Israeli commandos invaded Gaza and placed their boots on the ground rather than conducting the campaign entirely from the air: so they could get a better look at just who they are killing—identifying terrorists, trying to separate them from their human shields, an exercise that is even more daunting from the sky.

Yet, Kasher and Yadlin do not agree that this is legally required. They are of the view that the entire concept of distinction needs to be modified—because it is becoming increasingly difficult to distinguish enemy combatants from noncombatants. The core reality of asymmetric warfare is that it is next to impossible to disentangle faithful human shields from civilians that want no part of Hamas.

In such urban settings, Kasher and Yadlin propose that the lives of Israeli soldiers should be prioritized *over* Palestinian civilians. To do otherwise only incentivizes Hamas' dead-civilian war strategy. It becomes a grotesque self-fulfilling prophesy and a corruption of international law: the more terrorists hide within the civilian population, the more legal protection they receive; and the more condemnation is heaped upon the nation-state goaded into a war with terrorists. The nation-state will be blamed no matter what humanitarian precautions it takes. Hamas banked on the belief that if human shields were their first line of defense, Israel would be forced into using less lethal weaponry to inflict less damage.[114]

For Kasher, applying the law of distinction any other way is simply suicidal. Hamas is not distinguishing between Israeli combatants and civilians. Israel is building bunkers to protect its civilians. Why should Israel place its soldiers at risk simply because Hamas could care less whether Gazans live or die? This is a war, after all. Is *jus in bello* without any common sense?

"There is no army in the world that will endanger its soldiers in order to avoid hitting the neighbors of an enemy or terrorist," Kasher said. "The media don't [sic] understand the nature of international law."[115]

In late December 2024, the *New York Times* published what it trumpeted as a blockbuster expose showing that Israel had relaxed its protocols in determining what targets it could bomb, and just who could order the bombing. Under its earlier guidelines, targets that included high-value terrorists warranted the use of advanced weaponry, but no more than ten civilians could be at risk. After October 7, apparently, Israel's rules of engagement changed: now mid-level IDF officers could order airstrikes against less valuable targets, and as many as twenty civilians could become collateral damage.

After October 7, the IDF made allowances for more civilian casualties with each strike. The kill radius had essentially expanded. An IDF commander of mid-level rank could now bomb a less significant target and not worry if the death toll ends up being higher.

The *Times* accused the IDF and its legal advisors of ordering airstrikes without sufficient intelligence to assess the potential for civilian loss—especially during the first few months of the war, when the highest number of Palestinian casualties were reported.

What was the *Times*' big revelation? "Suddenly, officers could decide to drop one-ton bombs on a vast array of military infrastructure—including small ammunition stockpiles and rocket factories—as well as on all Hamas and Islamic Jihad fighters. The definition of a military target included lookouts and money changers suspected of handling Hamas' funds, as well as the entrances to the group's underground tunnel network, which were often hidden in homes."[116]

So what? I should certainly hope that these targets would not have been spared. They sound strategically important. The *Times* isn't even referring to schools, hospitals, and mosques. The paper of record seems to be saying that those who assist Hamas in financing its terrorist activities are solid citizens who can't be touched. Should enablers of mass murder have a reasonable expectation that Israel won't kill them in their homes?

Responding to the *Times*' findings, the IDF acknowledged that its rules of engagement changed after October 7, but for obvious reasons: No such attack against Israel had ever been mounted before. At no other time in Israel's history had so many of its citizens been slaughtered. Never before had so many of its children—babies, in fact—been murdered, its girls gang raped, its families burned alive, and its elderly Holocaust survivors taken hostage. Until October 7, Israel had no knowledge of the sophistication and vastness of Gaza's underground tunnel network.

Apparently, the *New York Times* expected Israel to retaliate by dropping off bundt cakes to their barbarous neighbors, rather than actual bombs. The IDF spelled out why its military response was different from earlier campaigns: The scale of Hamas' October 7 attack, the degree of its hiding among civilians, and the depth of the tunnels was "unprecedented and hardly comparable to other theaters of hostilities worldwide.... Such key factors...bear implications on the...choice of military objectives and the operational constraints that dictate the conduct of hostilities, including the ability to take feasible precautions in strikes."[117]

Columnist Jonathan Tobin put it succinctly, "To claim that Israel's loosened rules are unjustified requires one to accept the idea that terrorists waging an active war with blood on their hands ought to have the impunity to commit as many crimes as they like so long as they keep their family and friends around them."[118]

What duties are owed to civilian populations that have not forfeited their status as noncombatants by having joined the fight? If they are not aiding and abetting the war effort, the burden is always to mitigate the risk to civilians. The destruction an army leaves behind in its wake should not be wanton and gratuitous. Sherman's March from Georgia through the Carolinas, for instance, was a quintessential scorched earth affair. It spared nothing and no one—military installations, private industry, civic infrastructure, and civilian property were on equal footing as legitimate targets all throughout the march. Starving the Confederate Army by destroying the South's agricultural base was deemed a military necessity.

Even more deliberately, the Allied Powers during World War II were very much aware that Dresden was a jewel of a German city, among Hitler's favorite in all of Europe. That's why British Prime Minister Churchill was especially pleased with the devastation his bombers inflicted. A great deal of the firebombing had no meaningful military significance. A magnificent city of Baroque architecture soon disappeared. The bombing was meant as collective punishment to the German people, whether they wore jackboots during the war, or not. "This is what we think of your beautiful city and the people who live there." It was an act of plain vindictiveness, which suited Churchill just fine. Yet he is considered by many, myself included, to be the ultimate wartime prime minister.

Dresden was much closer to being a war crime than anything Israel has visited upon Gaza, and in all its wars with the Arabs combined. Gaza is no architectural wonder. Its lone purpose is as a terrorist's paradise. It is a place that only an Islamist would love. But given that the entire Strip has been devoted to one pursuit—killing Jews—what is the moral argument for denying Israel the right to do to Gaza what Sherman did to Georgia? Dresden was not a Nazi stronghold. There were some factories that manufactured weapons. But for the most part, the city was known as the Jewel Box; Florence on the Elbe. A place recognized primarily for its high culture and museums. The same cannot be said of Gaza.

With each war that Israel got dragged into against Hamas, Gaza became progressively less habitable. The October 7 War has left it in even more ruin than before. Over two million Gazans have been displaced—nearly the entire population. It will need to be completely rebuilt. Whose job that will be is yet to be decided.

There is global precedent for rebuilding an enemy nation. The Marshall Plan was instituted specifically to bring life back to Germany in hopes of staving off a third World War. The rationale was grounded in precedent. World War I led to World War II because the burden of financial reparations imposed upon Germany proved to be too severe. The Allied Powers came to realize that German national suffering after the Great War—compounded by the global Depression of 1929—led to the rise of Adolf Hitler.

Should Israel consider the same rationale? Not if history is any guide. When Israel withdrew from the Gaza Strip in 2005, taking with them even the dead from their cemeteries, they left behind complete businesses—including greenhouses—that could have served as standing infrastructure and seed capital for a burgeoning Gazan economy. That's not how the Palestinians of Gaza saw it, however. Their first act was to destroy any and all structures soiled by Israeli hands—not just the synagogues, but industrial facilities that could have been used for their immediate economic benefit.

If you ask some who have followed the conflict over the decades, they might say that Israel owes Gaza everything it needs to rebuild and prosper. Palestinian-American academic Rashid Khalidi is among those who continue to invoke the lie that Gaza is "occupied" by Israel, even though not a single Jew has lived there since 2005. He has written that "Israel has subjected [Gaza] to periodic savage attacks as well as a blockade since 2007… Israel is…in flagrant violation of the Fourth Geneva Convention, which enjoins the occupying power to protect the population under its control…. [T]he people of Gaza are being punished collectively by the occupier that is supposed to protect them."[119]

First, simply because a country is protecting its homeland by preventing weapons from being shipped or flown into a neighboring territory committed to its destruction doesn't render such border protection an "occupation." Hamas controls every single aspect of what happens in Gaza. No one makes a move without Hamas granting permission. No Israeli is actually *in* Gaza! It's laughable when one compares Gaza to German-occupied

France or French-occupied Algeria. Palestinians are so used to exploiting the word "occupation," they invoke it as often as *pass the tahini*.[120]

Second, the reason for the blockade itself—both air and sea—is imperative. Gaza is an enclave of very minimalist taste. If the product can't be used to make a bomb or build a tunnel, what other purpose do imports have? Materials and machinery for the making of rockets, or concrete and steel used to construct tunnels, are prized over civilian infrastructure and other civic works. Egypt imposes the very same blockade on its border with Hamas, for the very same reason. Hamas are members of the Muslim Brotherhood. Many followers of the Brotherhood live in Egypt. Egypt's government reasonably fears the terrorism that materializes wherever the Muslim Brotherhood congregates. It doesn't want Gazans mingling with and possibly radicalizing Egyptians. (It bears mentioning that Egypt didn't properly secure the border at the Philadelphi Corridor when it came to Hamas' planning of the October 7 massacre. Those paraglides and advanced rocketry—that was far more lethal than had ever been available to Hamas before—came from somewhere. It didn't slip by Israel's border security.)

Notwithstanding Egypt's more recent failings in border control, no one seems to be complaining about its blockade over Gaza. No one complained when Egypt occupied Gaza from 1948 to 1967, either.

Israel owes Gaza no special protection or any kind of reparations. The enclave has shown only murderous contempt for the Jewish state. And Judaism imposes no religious obligation to love one's enemy. The Hamas Charter, and the curriculum that UNRWA has created for Palestinian children, are both a blueprint and preparatory school for the genocide of Jews.

CHAPTER 6

The Proportionality Trap: Why Death Tolls in War Need Not Add Up Equally

"Military necessity" and "distinction" are bedrock principles in international humanitarian law. But when it comes to the three wars Israel has fought with Hamas since 2008, another legal concept is invoked, often appearing in the mainstream press, and receiving greater attention in the academic and human rights communities: "proportionality." It is the third essential element in the rules governing armed conflict. In fact, it seems to demand greater public attention than any of the other laws of war.

How does this principle apply to Israel's war in Gaza? It goes like this: Israel has the right to defend itself. It must and may respond to the October 7 attack in a war that Hamas clearly instigated. But the manner in which Israel battles Hamas is having a disproportionate impact. Israel, as the more powerful of the combatants, is, therefore, required to exercise more restraint against Hamas—even if Hamas started the war, won't surrender, and continues to hold Israeli and American hostages.

Israel's counterstrikes are questioned and instantly condemned on the grounds of proportionality: that they go too far and result in disproportionate harm. Of course, like most things when Israel is involved, emotions run high and the flagrantly ignorant are suddenly experts. The same people who scream "genocide" also shriek "proportionality." They have no idea what either means. Israel's conduct in Gaza doesn't come close to meeting the legal standards for either.

Even United States senators get it wrong—especially Jewish ones. After Israel's war against Hamas in 2014, Senator Bernie Sanders sat for an interview with *CNN* and completely bungled the legal concept of proportionality. "Was Israel's response disproportionate? I think it was," he concluded. "Israel has a 100%...right to live in freedom, independently and in security without having to be subjected to terrorist attacks.... But I think that we will not succeed to ever bring peace into that region unless we also treat the Palestinians with dignity and respect, and that is my view."[121]

Sanders then recklessly went on to misstate that Israel killed ten thousand innocent civilians (the total dead at the time was actually 2,100, with the majority being terrorists). Israel's enemies very much appreciated the assist. He gave that interview two years *after* the war came to end, when the death toll information was more accurate. (The number ten thousand was never cited as the death toll before. The Jewish senator simply felt like tacking on.) He defaulted to the typical anti-Israel position: the IDF somehow only manages to kill women and children. Sanders casually blurted out a large number of dead Gazans and deemed them all innocent civilians.

While inflating the number of Palestinians killed that summer of 2014, Sanders somehow forgot to mention that the war didn't begin until Israel got tired of the ten thousand rockets Hamas and Islamic Jihad had launched at Israeli civilians. (Maybe that's where he came up with the number ten thousand!)

It was only then that Israel began its counteroffensive—which like October 7, made it a just war.

Would the killing of ten thousand Palestinian civilians, provided it achieved the military objectives of a just war, be a proportionate response to the launching of ten thousand rockets at Israelis, which ultimately killed very few?

Those rockets gave credence to a just war and served as the military necessity behind Israel's response. Sanders, however, could care less. He dispensed quickly with Israel's right to live in "freedom" and "security," and defaulted to the "dignity and respect" owed to Palestinians. He was fixated on dead Gazans, all presumptively innocent, their deaths all caused by Israel's violation of international law. The Vermont Senator did not provide the number of Israeli dead, by comparison. It was seventy-three, a low number largely due to the effectiveness of Israel's Iron Dome air-defense system. To Sanders, the extreme unbalanced body count reinforced the first impression that Israel had violated the tenets of proportionality.

Having a terribly misinformed United States senator—and a Jewish one, no less—appear on a global cable news service and, based on an inflated death toll, accuse Israel of war crimes, is not something the Jewish state can easily erase from the minds of *CNN* viewers—not that *CNN* felt compelled to correct the record. The damage was already done.

A proportionality argument is appealing even to those without senatorial credentials. It speaks to basic fairness when the strong are confronted by the confrontationally weak. Yes, Hamas provokes these fights, but it can't win these wars. So why not allow them to have their fun? A close friend of mine once compared Hamas to the little boy in the schoolyard swinging away at a larger boy who holds him at bay by stiff-arming his forehead. I remember replying: "Yes, but did the little boy just fire ten thousand rockets at the home of the larger boy?"

Restraint is not necessarily a virtue. No quarter is owed to a weaker enemy with genocidal aims.

As far as we know, at the time of this writing, forty-eight thousand Palestinians have been reputedly killed in Gaza. We won't know the final tally until long after the war is over. Based on past experience with the Gaza Health Ministry, the statistical data in Gaza is a moving target. Hamas disallows any other entity from handling or computing the death toll ledgers. Accuracy in the count is always in doubt. Israel reports that nearly half of the dead are terrorists, regardless of their ages. The veracity of those numbers aside, clearly far more Gazans were killed in 2023 to 2024 than back in 2014. Of course, that earlier war lasted only fifty days.

But for argument's sake, let's say that Sanders was correct in his estimation of ten thousand civilians, as against seventy-three Israelis. Would that have made Israel's claims to *jus in bello* false because it violated the rules regarding proportionality?

To some degree, Sanders' confusion is somewhat understandable, although perhaps not for a man who twice ran for President. Seemingly, many are confused about the meaning of a proportionate response—in part, because the winning side in a war sometimes gains victory so decisively, the outcome doesn't sit well. And proportionality has been the preferred way for global antisemites to side with Hamas over Israel. Finally, sometimes the ferociousness of an attack requires more than a mere tit-for-tat. The retaliation should not depend on whether there is a handy abacus lying around that can sort out what constitutes suitable payback.

The confusion surrounding the military concept of "proportionality" has even found its way into two iconic works of

American culture: a feature film, *Munich* (2005), directed by Steven Spielberg, and the award-winning television drama, *The West Wing* (1999), written by Aaron Sorkin (a third, too, when you consider that he included a similar scene in the screenplay for the movie, *The American President* (1995)).

Munich begins by telling the story of the murder of eleven Israeli athletes by Palestinian terrorists at the 1972 Olympic Games in Munich. But the film is really about what happened next. What did Israel choose to do in response?

The film depicts Israel's Prime Minister at the time, Golda Meir, assembling her senior officers in the IDF at what appears to be her kitchen table, along with certain cabinet ministers and key advisors. The Prime Minister wishes to know what Israel has done so far in retaliation, and what should be the next step. The meeting would result in recruiting a team of special Mossad operatives who would hunt down eleven high-value Palestinian terrorists responsible for planning and carrying out the attack. The agents would comprise a hit squad operating exclusively, and illegally, in Europe where these terrorists are based.

> ***Prime Minister Meir:*** *[Addressing her Attorney General] There's legitimacy for this—am I correct? Ambushed and slaughtered again. While the rest of the world is playing games, Olympic torches, and brass bands, and dead Jews in Germany—and the world couldn't care less.*
>
> ***Minister 1:*** *We've responded. We sent 70 fighter jets.*
>
> ***Minister 2:*** *A response no one heard.*
>
> ***Minister 1:*** *Airstrikes on guerrilla training centers—that's a response.*

> …
>
> ***Minister 1:*** *Sixty Arabs dead at least. Who knows how many wounded?*
>
> ***General Nadav:*** *This is about fixing the world's attention.*
>
> ***General Zamir:*** *Well, it's not just a publicity stunt. Let me remind you: Ali Hassan Salameh, he invented Black September. He is the architect of the Munich murders.*
>
> ***Prime Minister Meir:*** *These people. They're sworn to destroy us. Forget peace for now. We have to show them we're strong. We have laws. We represent civilization. Some people say we can't afford to be civilized. I've always resisted such people, but I don't know who these maniacs are and where they come from.… You tell me what law protects people like these.… Every civilization finds it necessary to negotiate compromises with its own values. I've made a decision. The responsibility is entirely mine.*

One of her generals tells the Prime Minister that bombing a PLO base and killing sixty terrorists is a reasonable and proportionate response to the murder of eleven Israeli athletes. The Prime Minister is unpersuaded that such a response constitutes a proportionate attack. She believes Israel is entitled to more justice than that. She isn't worried about what "experts" would deem to be proportionate. She wants to see *disproportionate* action. An assassination squad is what the Prime Minister orders even at the risk of possibly violating international law.

On one episode during the first season of *The West Wing*, a Syrian terrorist group successfully blows up an American military jet, killing everyone on board, including the President's personal physician. The fictional President Bartlet takes this attack on America personally. He assembles his global crisis team in the Situation Room and wants to hear advice on how the United States should best respond. An admiral within the Joint Chiefs of Staff lays out four possible targets.

> ***Admiral Fitzwallace:*** *All three scenarios are comprehensive, meet the obligations of proportional response and pose minimal threat to U.S. personnel and assets.*
>
> ***President Bartlet:*** *What is the virtue of a proportional response?… Why's it good? [beat] They hit an airplane, so we hit a transmitter, right? That's a proportional response.… They hit a barracks, so we hit two transmitters.*
>
> ***Admiral Fitzwallace:*** *That's roughly it, sir.*
>
> …
>
> ***President Bartlet:*** *Well, if it's what we do, if it's what we've always done, don't they know we're going to do it?*
>
> …
>
> ***Admiral Fitzwallace:*** *Those are four high rated military targets, sir.*
>
> ***President Bartlet:*** *They did that, so we did this, it's the cost of doing business, it's been factored in, right?… Am I right or am I missing something here?*

> ***Admiral Fitzwallace:*** *No sir, you're right sir.*
>
> ***President Bartlet:*** *Then I ask again, what is the virtue of a proportional response?*
>
> ***Admiral Fitzwallace:*** *It isn't virtuous Mr. President. It's all there is sir.*
>
> ***President Bartlet:*** *It is not all there is.*
>
> ***Admiral Fitzwallace:*** *...[B]ut pardon me, Mr. President, just what else is there?*
>
> ***President Bartlet:*** *A disproportional response! Let the word ring forth from this time and this place, you kill an American, any American, we don't come back with a proportional response, we come back [bangs fist on table] with total disaster!*

In both depictions of proportionality, the respective leaders of their nations are demanding not the customary "proportionate" response, which the experts on such matters—usually cautious men in military uniforms—reassure them is proper and appropriate, but something that goes *beyond* proportionality. The measure-for-measure, eye-for-an-eye logic of the *lex talionis*—a Biblical concept intended to limit the cycle of violence that in the pre-state era of feuding clans and tribes could consume an entire population—is unsatisfying at the level of modern societies because it does not send the aggressor a declarative message that *punishment* is what is being called for, and not mere proportionality. Getting even is what you deserve, but what you will receive instead is teeth-rattling payback.[122]

The problem is: when it comes right down to it, there is no precise measurement in determining whether a counteroffensive is proportionate or disproportionate. What we do know is that it's not simply a numbers game. After October 7, Israel wasn't looking for 1,200 Palestinians to murder, Gazan babies to burn alive, dozens of teenage girls to gang rape and mutilate, grandmothers to kidnap—measure for measure. Disproportion does not mean what Bernie Sanders thinks it does: whomever racks up the larger death toll can claim that its wartime enemy was fighting unfairly based solely on a head count, especially if a large percentage of those heads are women and children.[123]

Many get it wrong—especially the people and entities that uninformed people listen to, regrettably. Israel's many critics conclude that the disproportionate death toll—far more dead Palestinians than Israelis—must mean that Israel is violating the principle of *jus in bello*: fighting justly in just a war. But proportionality is measured by military objectives and outcomes, and not by lopsided death tallies.

The rule of proportionality takes full account that military operations will result in the loss of civilian life. Death tolls are wholly anticipated and de rigueur. Body counts do not lead to automatic presumptions about *jus in bello*. Gruesome though it may be to contemplate, the laws of armed conflict require only that the military value of the target justify the number of likely civilian deaths. If the target is legitimate and militarily necessary, civilians can be killed as collateral damage so long as the actions taken include efforts to minimize the damage. The more valuable the target, the more civilian deaths are permissibly tolerated without committing war crimes.

Proportionality, in the end, has nothing at all to do with unequal death tolls. Body counts are neither material, nor must death tolls be equally matched It is not a race to the bottom of humanity. If it was, all victorious armies would presumptively be judged guilty of war crimes.

But that's precisely what the International Court of Justice, and the International Criminal Court, have been trying to do with Israel. In their ongoing investigations and contemplated proceedings, they are pinning their allegations solely on the bad optics of civilian suffering. The legitimacy of the war itself, the *casus belli*—the events that prompted the war—and the separate war crimes committed by Hamas have largely escaped the attention of these tribunals.

All that proportionality requires is that the military necessity be sufficiently important to justify the loss of civilian life and destruction of property. And that all reasonable efforts are made to mitigate that loss of life, if possible. The military advantage must be proportionate to the civilian harm. If the anticipated civilian harm exceeds the foreseeable military advantage, then such an attack cannot be justified because it presents too grave an outcome for the surrounding civilians without a substantial enough corresponding wartime benefit.

Referring to the *Law of War Manual*, David B. Rivkin Jr. and Lee A. Casey, in an opinion piece in the *Wall Street Journal*, describe the proportionality test: "Proportionality requires that the expected harms to civilians and civilian property...can't be 'excessive' when compared with 'the concrete and direct military advantage expected to be gained.' The comparison isn't to the number of soldiers killed or to the number of casualties on each side of the conflict. Nor is there any upper limit on the number of civilian deaths that will trigger 'war crimes' if exceeded."[124]

"No upper limit on civilian deaths" is the strongest legal argument that Israel is neither committing war crimes nor genocide in Gaza. Emotionally, large numbers of civilian dead might be sickening. Legally, they are accepted in military doctrine as the costs of war. It is trivializing to reduce mass death to clinical, data-based terminology. But Israel is being accused of "war crimes" and "genocide." Mounting a legal defense requires a showing that the proportionality principle has not be violated.

The catalogue of war crimes lodged against Israel is extensive: ranging from crimes against humanity, which refers to indiscriminate killings, to deprivations—such as water, electricity, and food—along with the denial of access to, and destruction of, medical personnel and facilities. Essentially, Israel is being charged with inflicting a siege on Gaza.[125]

All of these charges are variations on the same theme, however: Gazans paying the price for Hamas' actions; collective punishment against an innocent people; and the moral eyesore of disproportionate death.

These accusations have not just been prejudged by ignorant students at prestigious universities. The allegations have been taken up by the International Criminal Court and the International Court of Justice in The Hague. These tribunals plan to hear evidence that will prove these claims against Israel. The presumption of innocence is not strictly applied in cases against the Jewish state. In fact, quite the opposite is true: What's the point of prosecuting a pariah state unless it comes with a guilty verdict.

Prosecutors will have to interrogate the intent and motive of the Jewish state in waging this latest war in Gaza. They will seek to provide an evidentiary basis for what led to all those civilian deaths. The legal standard on what constitutes proportionality will become vitally important to understand.

The most relevant legal question will be: What was Israel aiming at, and what was the military significance of the target? Was Israel indiscriminately firing upon Palestinian civilians in vengeance for October 7? One trier of fact's collateral damage is another's collective punishment. With plenty of bad faith and moral confusion against Israel to go around, Palestinians in

Gaza are generally spoken of as if they have been "murdered," killed in action in a war that has nothing to do with them.

But they weren't targeted for death. And it is not at all clear how many were killed in action by Israel. First, far too often Gazans are killed by Hamas' own errant rockets—which constitute the most unfriendliest fire of all. Second, the majority of Gazans have officially joined the fight, placing their civilian status in question.

Israel is *always* targeting terrorists, and not civilians who choose to ignore Israel's warnings to evacuate their homes, mosques, and schools—civilian locations that Hamas utilizes as command centers, weapons warehouses, and launching pads. All of Gaza is a gray zone of appearances that truly are deceiving. Structures that anywhere else would have no wartime utility, in Gaza could very well unveil a military mother lode that could bring a war to an end. So the question must always be asked: Were the civilian deaths in excess of the military benefit?

It is a cruel calculation, but it is the only analysis that matters under international law.

No serious person questions whether the Nazis needed to be defeated at all costs. Many people came to believe late into World War II that Japan would simply never surrender, the war in the Pacific would drag on, and American soldiers would be killed every day it continued. The two atomic bombs ended the war in the Pacific, and many American mothers with sons deployed overseas were thrilled by the decision to drop them. The civilians of Japan were not their concern, just like those same civilians cared little for the loss of life at Pearl Harbor.

Applying proportionality analysis to the atomic bombings in Hiroshima and Nagasaki balanced an inordinate number of civilian dead against bringing finality to the war itself. It did not matter that American servicemen did not die in those bombing missions, and that the death toll—among Japanese civilians—was substantial.

With Nazi Germany, given the threat that Hitler presented as a mass murderer and ruthless conqueror of nations, Michael Walzer formulated the proportionality calculation this way: "If the end is defeating the Nazis, then, suddenly, 1,000 lives, or even 10,000, do not seem disproportionate."[126] In Walzer's seminal work, *Just and Unjust Wars*, he made the Nazi analogy even more starkly and definitively, not pulling any punches on either military necessity or proportionality: "[T]he more certain a German victory appeared to be in the absence of a bomber offensive, the more justifiable was the decision to launch the offensive"[127] Walzer also questions the war in Vietnam: "Who is responsible for this war? Surely all those men and women who voted for it and who cooperated in planning, initiating, and waging it."[128]

That sounds a lot like the situation in Gaza. The people are *not* passive bystanders. They voted for Hamas, and many cooperated in the planning phases and execution of terrorism. Others played lesser but not unessential roles, whether it be lending their homes as communication centers, storing weapons, or taking custody of hostages. They had joined the fight for purposes of the Geneva Conventions.

Until Israel's wars with Hamas, there was always moral clarity that Dresden and the Holocaust existed on radically different moral plains. Bombing Dresden brought the Allies closer to ending the war in Europe; the Holocaust nearly brought an end to all European Jewry.

There is great danger in all this irresponsible, inflammatory rhetoric that equates a war in Gaza with a genocide of the Palestinian people. The various indictments of Israel trivialize the meaning of war crimes—conflating genocide with legitimate war aims. The word genocide should never be used when referring to Gaza. War crimes, however, do raise legitimate questions, and if Israel can't successfully rebut them, they should be made to answer for them.

But in judging Israel, these truths must always be kept at eye level: Hamas scored a massive victory on October 7, 2023. Palestinians continue to assert that the staging of the attack was justified resistance. They have promised repeat performances—"again and again." Israelis were placed on notice to prepare for similar dark days until Jewish life in the Middle East is finally extinguished. The murderous language in the Hamas and PLO Charters has remained unchanged. No Hamas leader ever conceded that after twenty years of launching tens of thousands of rockets at Israeli civilian population centers, this practice will finally come to an end. Each war with terrorist groups were instigated by Hamas, Islamic Jihad, and Hezbollah. Terrorists were showing no hint of an early retirement—and they were training another generation to be just as brutal and barbaric.

Under any fair interpretation of international law, Israel's government had every right, after October 7, to order the IDF to utterly destroy Hamas—once and for all. To leave no further trace of terrorists, tunnels, and their weapons. That's what became the official Israeli war aim, which it had every right to pursue.

And with the war soon followed casualties of that war—the vast majority of them, Palestinian. Given Israel's superior air-defense systems—Iron Dome, David's Sling, and Arrow—its civilians were far less likely to fall from Hamas' incoming rocket attacks and Hezbollah's missiles. Some argue that these air-defense systems negate the threat from Palestinian rockets. Of course it does! That's the whole point. A good defense only magnifies its military advantage because there is no actual threat to Israeli civilians. But sparing the lives of its own citizens does not render Israel's actions illegal or disproportionate.

Yes, the Iron Dome is a technological marvel. But it doesn't eliminate the threat to Israelis. Rockets and missiles are still headed its way—and more recently they are being launched by yet another terror group, this one from Yemen, the Houthis. Hezbollah's arsenal is supplied by Iran. They are precision-guided missiles, far more technologically advanced than the rocketry that Hamas deploys. Most of that stockpile has been destroyed by Israeli counteroffensives when the Gaza War turned from Gaza to the suburbs of Beirut. But it is important to remember that these projectiles are all capable of penetrating Israeli air space. Iron Dome is not fool proof; it doesn't detonate every single one headed toward Israel. The system can be overwhelmed by the number being launched at any given time. Rockets and missiles always have the potential to land and cause death.

More importantly, merely possessing an arsenal of defensive weapons does not undermine the intentions and motivations of Israel's enemies. No nation should be required to have its people continuously run for cover—forced to duck into fallout shelters or huddle inside safe rooms—while a neighboring enemy unleashes all of its airborne weaponry until its entire arsenal is discharged. Israel's military has an obligation to eliminate the existential threat that Hamas' and Hezbollah's firepower poses. Thus far its civilians have been spared mass casualties. The best way to protect them is to destroy the airpower before they reach air. (This is the strategy Israel employed in the 1967 Six-Day War when, in a preemptive strike, it bombed the Egyptian Air Force before any of those planes left the tarmac, rendering them permanently grounded.) Failing that, prevent them from landing.

Despite the nonsense that pours out of the mouths of anti-Zionist pundits, Israel's capacity to knock incoming rockets out of the sky does not violate the principle of proportionality. Israel is under no legal or moral obligation to fail to protect its citizens so that the death tolls on each side are more equal.

For its part, Israel clearly announced its intention to completely eradicate terrorism in Gaza. Ending Hamas' reign in Gaza would take longer to achieve—partly because Israel was taking humanitarian precautions to spare Palestinian lives, and because the United States was applying pressure on Israel to "de-escalate" its operations to placate Jew-hating progressives and American Muslims.

The overall objective was ambitious, and perhaps not entirely achievable. Israel did not have the same objective in its earlier wars with Hamas in 2008 and 2014. Everything about this campaign was different.

Israelis wanted October 7 to be the last time it would ever face this enemy again. Yes, it is true: given Palestinian and Islamist fanaticism, and the failure of Palestinian society and Islamic extremism to reform itself, another Hamas could reemerge with a new face. All Israel could do for now was ensure that it would never again be *this* Hamas. That required a much larger troop deployment and a more lethal weapons package—the depth and width of the tunnels necessitating the use of more two-thousand-pound bombs.

Of course, the mainstream media, along with terrorism-fanboys on campus and the Biden State Department, always focus on the tonnage of the bombs as a way to indict Israel for not deploying the most precise weaponry. According to its critics, Israel deliberately chose bombs with an especially large blast radius to indiscriminately kill more Palestinian civilians. What they repeatedly failed to mention is that these two-thousand-pound bombs are designed to detonate underground, to collapse Hamas' vast labyrinthine tunnel network. The effect of underground explosions ultimately mitigated the blast radius above ground.[129]

As the war progressed from airstrikes to the invasion of ground troops, the Gazan death toll climbed. The reflexive blaming of Israel commenced—all without regard to the devastated crime scene on October 7, Israel's lawful right to rid itself of the Hamas menace forevermore, and Hamas' own war crimes in using its citizens as shields.

And so global media reported the story as Israel murdering civilians instead of waging a just war against Hamas. Collateral damage and destroyed property and infrastructure mounted. The common language used to delegitimize Israel—to call its very existence into question—was proportionality.

A rabbi and ethicist on war, Shlomo Brody, wrote: "A body count doesn't indicate whether an army acted excessively or immorally. The question is always the relationship between the damage to the military gain...."[130] Israeli philosopher Asa Kasher explained how proportionality figures into the calculation of disparate civilian losses: "There is no logic in comparing the number of civilians and armed fighters killed on the Palestinian side, or comparing the number of Israelis killed by Qassam rockets to the number of Palestinians killed in Gaza."[131]

Bernie Sanders, and most of the world, deliberately distort the legal concept of proportionality. Loss is always a given in a just war. How much depends on the military objective that justifies the war itself, and the precautions taken to minimize the harm.

Is the Palestinian death toll in an asymmetric campaign where its home court is baited for greater casualties disproportionate under the laws of war? Is Israel's *jus in bello* ultimately just?

If an enemy launches a war of aggression, which Hamas did, and Israel is allowed to defend itself by targeting those responsible for the attack, which it has been doing, it is under no legal obligation to compromise whatever military advantage it possesses simply because of the presence of civilians. If the military target is vital and verifiable—where the terrorists are located, weapons stashed, rockets launched, and communication and command centers based—then military necessity governs the legality of the strike. It would take an insurmountably high bar of disproportionate loss to negate the lawfulness of that strike. Daniel Reisner, a former head of the IDF's international law division, believes that a proportionality analysis may have as much to do with politics as it does with law. He said, "The numbers of dead on both sides are tragic, if you limited the discussion to legality, the numbers are not the thing to measure. It's *why* they died and in what circumstances they died, *not how many* of them died."[132]

To do or think otherwise would be unfeasible given the realities of war. Wars could not be conducted if armies were squeamish about killing civilians. Military necessity guides the proportionality analysis. And intention is ultimately what matters most.

Israel's obvious intent makes charges of genocide outrageous. Destroying Hamas is the aim; civilian deaths are the undesirable consequence—it is collateral to the objective, not the objective itself. Israel haters have it backwards: Proportionality is not the first level of analysis. And it does not receive the highest priority because there's "no explicit agreement as to how to apply the proportionality equation practically in real-life situations. No numerical weight is provided anywhere for each of the different variables."[133]

And to subject an army to the strictest proportionality protocols is a gift to those who resort to terrorist tactics—most especially, the use of civilians as human shields. That's why proportionality is a singular preoccupation in Gaza: human shields pad the disproportion; they are essential to Hamas' civilian death strategy.

But at what cost to Israeli civilian life? Giving into ceasefire demands in order to save Palestinian lives is a noble humanitarian impulse, but it presents an immediate national security risk to Israeli civilians. The ceasefire that was negotiated in mid-January 2025 contemplated the eventual release of over one thousand Palestinians from Israeli prisons. Many of them either murdered Israeli citizens or assisted in the manufacturing of weapons for that purpose. They are likely to return to their usual line of work. A permanent ceasefire would result in sparing the lives of the remaining terrorists still in Gaza who will escape punishment. This presents both a grave national security risk and a terribly unjust outcome.[134]

Civilians are at risk in both hot spots—Gaza and Israel. In the market economy of human life, the world is clearly valuing the lives of Palestinians over Israelis. Israeli civilians are fair game for an atrocity-filled future. Palestinian lives, however, are precious and must be spared at all costs.

Palestinian children present an even more unique case. As Bob Simon said back in 2014, the killing of children operates on a completely different moral plane. We must not allow for it. But he was speaking about all children (I hope), not just Palestinian. Surely Palestinian children are not more untouchable and valuable than other children caught in war-torn regions. Yet, we never hear about those other children. Where are the campus protests on their behalf, the insistent "by any means necessary" militancy directed at saving them? Children in

Sudan, Syria, Congo, Myanmar, Yemen, Iraq, China, or more locally, the children of Latin America and Mexico who are subject to human trafficking and exploitation by cartels, or the children of Chicago, who are often tragically killed in gun- and gang-related violence? These are all tragic losses, but Palestinian children are casualties of war—where very often parental choices are made to sacrifice them for a maniacally religious cause.[135] That is not true of the many other instances around the world where children are horrifically lost to violence. The parents in such places are not accomplices in their deaths.

Speaking of children that world governments, global media, the United Nations, and nongovernmental human rights entities couldn't care less about, why is there no discussion about the allegations of beheadings, which may have included Israeli infants, on October 7? IDF soldiers and forensic pathologists returned from the crime scene in southern Israel sickened. Where was the global outrage? One side shamelessly decapitated bodies; the other side conducts a just war in self-defense where children are inadvertently killed, while grossly negligent parents primp themselves up for screen time on the *BBC*.

There is absolutely no moral equivalence.

Once it became known that beheadings were part of the carnage, nothing further needed to have been said. No additional information was necessary about Hamas, and what Israel must do as both a moral imperative and duty to its citizenry. Everything one needed to know was right there, in its sheer barbarism. Sympathy for Israel should have been immediate and irrevocable.

Instead, all the emotional energy was devoted to an apparent obligation to spare all Palestinian life, while the lives of Jews, as has been true throughout history, were wholly dispensable.

One commentator pointedly observed that, "In a just war, victory is not merely a right, it is an obligation, and even premature peace has its casualties. Were Israel to accept a ceasefire in Gaza where Hamas retained its military infrastructure, it would spare many civilian lives. But it would also ensure further Hamas atrocities, and for the lives lost in those it would be as culpable as for the unintended casualties had it fought on to victory."[136]

The disconnect for most people comes down to pure moral confusion: blocking out that the targets are terrorists who started a war, and that Palestinian civilians, by and large, don't seem all that interested in getting out of the way.

But there are those who would say: Even if Israel has the legal right to inflict massive damage while in pursuit of terrorists, the moral universe must prevent them from doing so. The mounting civilian death toll cries out for the law's protection. After all, the carnage is unbearable, even if it is Hamas that has been orchestrating this grand plan of leveraging the lives of Palestinians to blanket terrorists from harm.

Bad optics, however, is a PR problem, not a violation of international humanitarian law. The question posed throughout this book—is Israel fighting a just war and is it fighting it justly?—is viewed under a different lens than a cable news TV screen. Proportionality analysis cuts right through the numerical dead—the only thing the media cares about.

Intent matters, but of the several warring parties here, Israel is the only one that wishes to avoid civilian deaths. The intent to kill civilians is a terrorist's gambit, not democratic governments. Hamas knows how easy it is to get the *BBC* and *MSNBC* to turn its cameras on Israel, inverting the pyramid, placing self-defense on the bottom, punishing the IDF for doing its job while getting suckered into a moral morass of Hamas' creation.

But it's precisely Hamas' twisted *jus in bello* that justifies, and makes a foregone conclusion, the civilian death ratios that the world decries. The terrorists' manner of fighting becomes a self-fulfilling prophesy. As two military historians recently observed, "When human shields are being used to shield an important military target,...the direct military necessity of the attack soars, and the proportionality analysis allows for more civilian casualties."[137]

Which means that when Israel uses verifiable intelligence to pinpoint a valuable military target, the fact that it is being shielded by civilians does not diminish the military necessity, nor does it obligate Israel to show restraint.

Nonetheless, Israel largely stands alone on these legal issues. They have few defenders. Someday this most recent war in Gaza might receive a hearing before the International Court of Justice, which has nominal jurisdiction over Israel. The International Criminal Court has no jurisdiction over the Jewish state (or the United States, for that matter), and even less enforcement powers, but charges have already been filed against Israeli officials.[138]

It is unlikely to end well for Israel, even if the results have no material consequences. The Jewish state will have to make do with the cadre of intellectually honest and morally upright legal and military experts—a dwindling group if there ever was one—who know that these are sham proceedings motivated by antisemitism and not the rule of law.

Because the law, itself, is otherwise clear. Distorted notions of human rights, and garden variety antisemitism, has become the convenient excuse not to apply the law in Israel's favor. It is far too easy to simply blame Israel for collapsed buildings on top of dead Palestinians. The media, the human rights community, Western nations, all refuse to hold Hamas accountable for sacrificing its own civilians. And in doing so, they all fail to draw the correct moral and legal conclusions about why disproportionate deaths are magnified in Gaza. Such blatant bias must be seen for what it is: urban warfare agitprop.

An opinion piece in the *Wall Street Journal*, written by two esteemed military analysts, cut to the core of this ruse in stating that:

> "each party to a conflict is primarily responsible for protecting its own civilian population by moving them away from military targets and taking other measures to shield them. Hamas not only fails to meet these obligations; it uses civilians as human shields and invites casualties for propaganda purposes.... [T]he [Department of Defense *Law of War*] manual makes clear that additional civilian injuries resulting from this illegal tactic are 'a factor that may be considered in determining whether such harm is excessive.'"[139]

More specifically, the language of the *Law of War Manual* makes plain that the party that places civilians near the fighting "assumes responsibility for their injury."[140] The killing of human shields is the fault of those who place them in harm's way—and not the nation targeting, justifiably, those responsible for concocting such monstrous war strategies.

The word "proportionality" became a cudgel to be used against Israel without anyone really knowing what it meant in the context of the laws of armed conflict. Those that did know manipulated the public into believing that Bernie Sanders was correct: All you need to show is disproportionate death. Military necessity and justification, distinction and intention, are irrelevant—even though these are essential elements in establishing a war crime.

Here is an example of a pro forma statement from the head of the United Nations Human Rights Office, stating matter-of-factly that civilian casualties in Gaza are "a direct consequence of the failure to comply with fundamental principles of international humanitarian law—namely the principles of distinction, proportionality and precautions in attack."[141]

It's as if Israel is fighting a war without cause, and against no one in particular.

It is preposterous to say that the very existence of casualties of war is *prima facia* proof that the country responsible for civilian deaths must be violating international humanitarian law. But that's precisely what cynics say and the gullible believe.

CHAPTER 7

When Global Politics and An Ancient Prejudice Hijack International Law

A favorite pastime of the international law and human rights communities is to gang up on Israel. And a selective application of the rules is the best way to demonstrate this singular form of moral bullying.

The Geneva Conventions provide a useful example. Each of them are generally used as legal authority against Israel, even when the various treaties must be contorted in order to apply even vaguely to Israel's actions. For instance, Article 49 of the Fourth Geneva Convention concerns the obligation of an "Occupying Power" to protect civilians under its control. But Israel does not occupy Gaza and hasn't since 2005. If Israel had occupied Gaza, October 7 would never have happened. During the war, it wasn't occupying Gaza, either. It was heavily engaged in hunting down and dodging crossfire from Hamas terrorists. No matter, you will hear international law "experts" invoke Article 49 all the time in various situations that are wholly inapposite to Israel's reasons for being in the enclave now.

Among these very same arbiters of international law, it is strictly forbidden to interpret any of the laws of war favorably in defense of the Jewish state. The rules outlining the outlawing of human shields, the full rights to self-defense, and what is permissible for an army embroiled in asymmetric warfare, are positively taboo.

The protected status of noncombatants caught in a warzone, among other matters concerning defenseless parties, is why 196 nations came together in 1949 to ratify the first of these treaties. Those critical of Israel are applying the Geneva Conventions strictly to protect Gazan civilians; Israeli civilians, however, are to receive no such reciprocal protection. They are essentially being directed to find some other law that deals with their existential dilemma. There is no such other law. Israelis are precisely the type of civilians the drafters of the Geneva Conventions, and subsequent Protocols, had in mind. But the Conventions are, seemingly, off-limits to Jews.

The madness of fighting wars with terrorists in closely quartered, densely populated urban areas was beyond the imagination of the original drafters of the Geneva Conventions. These laws were eventually modified and codified so that they could pertain to unique asymmetric situations. In 1977, international lawyers, nearly thirty years after the first treaty, drafted the First Additional Protocols of the Geneva Conventions. It serves many valuable purposes, chief among them, formally establishing the principle of proportionality.

Article 51(5)(b): prohibits "an attack which may be expected to cause incidental loss of civilian life, injury to civilians, damage to civilian objects,...which would be *excessive in relation to the concrete and direct military advantage*."[142]

This section specifically cautions armies that large numbers of civilian casualties can only be excused if it follows a military action that was absolutely necessary—the killing of civilians cannot be done for its own sake.

The Protocols also anticipate the possibility that one party would intentionally place civilian life at risk.

Article 51(7): "The Parties to the conflict shall not direct the movement of the civilian population or individual civilians in order to attempt to *shield military objectives from attacks or to shield military operations.*"[143]

Given the language of this provision, and what it seeks to protect—prohibiting civilians from being used to "*shield* military operations"—why has it never been applied to charge Hamas and Islamic Jihad with war crimes? The Protocols were drafted years before anyone had ever heard the term "human shields." What Hamas has done in Gaza, repeatedly over three wars and countless skirmishes, is a direct violation of the Geneva Conventions. When was the last time you heard that bit of information?

Similarly, the Protocols not only prohibit using civilians as human shields, but they also prohibit deliberately choosing to fight exactly where civilians happen to be.

Article 58: "avoid locating military objectives within or near densely populated areas."[144]

That means that asymmetric warfare itself, as a military strategy, is categorically illegal under the Geneva Conventions.

Even before the Geneva Conventions codified the principles of proportionality in its 1977 Protocols, the International Committee of the Red Cross, in 1956, created Draft Rules for the Limitation of the Dangers incurred by the Civilian Population in Time of War. This, too, adopts proportionality as a legal standard that incorporates military necessity, the use of precise weapons, and the mitigation of losses to the civilian population, but does *not* outlaw armies that leave collateral damage behind.

Article 8: "He is required to refrain from the attack if, after due consideration, it is apparent that the loss and destruction would be *disproportionate to the military advantage* anticipated."[145]

Article 9: "All possible precautions shall be taken, both in the *choice of the weapons* and methods to be used...to ensure that no losses or damage are caused to the civilian population...or that such *losses or damages are at least reduced to a minimum.*"[146]

The Geneva Conventions may have been initially drafted to establish rules for the treatment of captured soldiers and the rights of civilians surviving through conventional wars. But it was updated to account for urban, Fourth Generation Warfare, precisely what we are seeing in Gaza.

Why aren't we hearing more about that? The Protocols to the Geneva Conventions specifically address the situation we find with terrorist organizations, like Hamas, that endanger its own civilians. The Protocols address the responsibility of nations, like Israel, that find themselves stuck in a quagmire of asymmetric warfare. Fighting justly requires that excessive, disproportionate force not be used unless the military target is of significant value.

These codified rules are, apparently, only being applied against Israel without regard to how terrorists wage war. Taking children and the elderly hostage without so much as allowing a visit from the Red Cross is the epitome of looking the other way. How is it possible that Israeli and American hostages were denied the basic humanitarian courtesy of receiving a visit from the Red Cross to check on their condition and treatment?

Bloody and broken warzones do not portend war crimes; they only show the ravages of war. War crimes require more than that to be actionable. John Spencer, a leading authority on urban warfare and West Point professor, has taken a special interest in Israel's wars in Gaza. He wrote, "There is no escaping that pursuing a terrorist organization touches off a nightmarish landscape of war.... [D]estruction and suffering, as awful as they are, don't automatically constitute war crimes—otherwise, nearly any military action in a populated area would violate the laws of armed conflict,... [W]ar crimes must be assessed on evidence and the standards of armed conflict, not a quick glimpse at the harrowing aftermath of an attack."[147]

Unlike British common law, which America has adopted, and European Roman Law, which has been in existence for centuries, international law is a post-World War II phenomenon, largely coinciding with the birth of the human rights movement and the creation of the United Nations.

But anyone who has been paying any attention at all knows that the United Nations is a morally corrupt body. Iran has held a seat on the Human Rights Council. Need anything more be said?

On November 14, 2024, the UN Special Committee to Investigate Israeli Practices issued a report accusing Israel of genocide in Gaza. It provided a list of the usual libels against the Jewish state: "breaches of international humanitarian and human rights laws" and "the possibility of genocide in Gaza and an apartheid system in the West Bank." At the same time, it declined to renew the contract of Alice Wairimu Nderitu, the Kenyan who served as a Special Advisor on the Prevention of Genocide. Why? Because she refused to endorse the report, stating definitively that Israel is at war and is not committing genocide. More importantly, she objected to misusing the word "genocide" itself, trivializing its meaning and misapplying it to losses of life that do not meet the legal standard or recognized definition.[148]

It's no surprise, given its history of double standards and doublespeak, that the United Nations would purge supporters of Israel, and anyone calling attention to the international body's hypocrisy. If you're not bashing Israel, there is no room for you at the international table where laws are selective and provisional, especially if Israel is under consideration.

The good news is that the United Nations, and its International Court of Justice, have no real jurisdictional or enforcement powers over its individual member states. Like everything about the United Nations, its work is purely symbolic, and its hypocrisies are offset by insufferable ficklessness.

Israel is a member state of the United Nations. So is South Africa, which charged Israel with genocide before the ICJ in connection with this recent war in Gaza. (Ireland formally joined South Africa as a complaining party.) It's possible that Israel will have to defend its military conduct given the Special Committee's Report. Should some proceeding be held, expect no acquittal for the Jewish state. But no punishment will follow, either. The purpose of a guilty verdict is largely to shame Israel, without any further action.

The International Criminal Court, by contrast, prosecutes individuals and has already issued arrest warrants for Israel's Prime Minister Benjamin Netanyahu and its former Defense Minister, Yoav Gallant. This is the first time in the court's twenty-five-year history that leaders of democratic nations were indicted on criminal charges.

Israel is not a signatory to the Rome Statute, which created the ICC (neither is the United States), meaning that both men have no obligation to surrender themselves to the jurisdiction of the ICC for prosecution. And don't expect either of them to make a voluntary appearance. In yet another sign of the West's capitulation to Islamist demands, and its fomenting of antisemitism globally, nations such as Italy, the Netherlands, Norway, Sweden, Ireland, and Canada have pledged to arrest Netanyahu or Gallant should either visit their nations while the warrants remain in effect.[149] Even if arrested, it might make for interesting TV, but the ICC still has no jurisdiction over Israeli leaders. It would be an unimaginable spectacle to see either of them in the dock.

An arrest warrant for the Sudanese head of state, Omar al-Bashir, accused of genocide, crimes against humanity, and war crimes in Darfur, was issued in 2009. It was only after a new Sudanese government deposed him in 2020 that he was transferred to the ICC, where he was sentenced to a mere two years in prison.

Amnesty International released a Report on December 5, 2024, determining that Israel has committed genocide against the Palestinian people due to the "scale and severity of the casualties and destruction" arising out of its post-October 7 War in Gaza. [150] The key word here is "casualties," which is a term that is used to describe war, and not genocide. One is a "victim" of genocide, and not a "casualty."

The Report neglected to mention that its researchers never consulted with colleagues in Amnesty International's own branch in Israel. The Israeli members completely distanced themselves from the Report's conclusions on the genocide charge.[151]After all, they were closer to the scene. You would think they would have been consulted. Two board members, and the board chair, resigned in protest over the Report.

Worse still, in order to have arrived at such a conclusion, Amnesty International unilaterally redefined the meaning of genocide. It would have had to. The Convention on the Prevention and Punishment of the Crime of Genocide clearly states that the guilty nation must have exhibited the specific "intent to destroy in whole or in part, a national, ethnic, racial or religious group."[152] When a nation is at war, it has other priorities—aside from more apparent intentions—than committing genocide.

Here the Report would have to circumvent several inconvenient truths: Israel was at war with Hamas; it made unprecedented efforts to spare civilian lives; and it allowed caravans of food and medicine to enter the enclave for humanitarian purposes. These are not the actions of a genocidal nation. A finding of genocidal intent is wholly lacking here, and without that intent, there can be no genocide.

Why let the law get in the way?, Amnesty International apparently concluded. It simply skirted the legal technicality, acknowledging that the actual legal definition of genocide is an "overly cramped interpretation of international jurisprudence and one that would effectively preclude a finding of genocide in the context of an armed conflict."[153]

Yes, exactly. It does, under the law, preclude a finding of genocide. The signatories to the Convention knew what they were signing: in the context of an armed conflict, unless you are operating an Auschwitz on the side, you're probably not engaging in genocide. That's how the Genocide Convention reads, and that's how it has always been applied. Amnesty International went to the trouble of inventing a new crime, which looks a lot like the old one—because it is! And guess what? By complete coincidence, they decided to name it "genocide," too. How original. All except for the fact that Amnesty International has no legal authority to alter the customary definition of a crime, and, in doing so, contort its application.

All three actions—from the ICJ, ICC, and Amnesty International—are legally without merit and factually groundless.[154] They were brought solely for the purpose of isolating Israel even further from the community of nations—if such a thing is possible. That's how threatening the Abraham Accords proved to be to Iran and its proxies, and scores of other nations that hate the West, and those who are jealous of Israel's economy and technological superiority.

Fine, collect your Nobel Prizes in the sciences and go ahead and invent life-altering devices and life-saving drugs. But in our eyes, you are a mass murdering, white supremacist nation that has no right to exist. We'd rather do without cell phones that depend on your patented technology than reconcile ourselves to the reality of a thriving Jewish state.

Universities, or groups like Human Rights Watch and Amnesty International, are not lacking in law professors and lawyers who well know that Israel has not, and is not, violating international humanitarian law. Each of them simply allows pernicious antisemitic groupthink to get in the way. None of these bodies and very few individuals will stand beside the Jewish state and exonerate it from these baseless accusations. President Biden did call the arrest warrants from the ICC "outrageous." Perhaps he was defending an ally, or, more likely, he knows that if this can happen to one democratic nation, then the United States can one day expect similar treatment from the anti-Western "have nots" of the world.

It's a good thing the ICC wasn't around after World War II. One commentator crisply explained why: "[T]he ICC would have issued arrest warrants for Churchill and Eisenhower. While invading Italy in 1943, the Allies caused old men, women, and children to be torn apart by bombs and shells, exposed to the wintry elements by the destruction of their homes, and starved of food and water. They did this 'knowingly,' aware of the effects of their unavoidably imprecise bombing and shelling."[155]

So much for justice, or respect for the rule of law, under international law. Cases brought against Israel are the very definition of kangaroo courts, although they would be better named camel courts—given the region in which Israel resides and the blinding desert conditions. A leading British columnist deriding his government's tilt against Israel and the absurdity of South Africa, of all nations, charging Israel with genocide, wrote, "The fact that the International Criminal Court and the International Court of Justice have the trappings of a legitimate legal setting does not mean they necessarily embody justice. The fact that their rulings are deemed legitimate by Left-wing elites doesn't automatically make them such. The fact that today's blood libels take on the language of 'human rights' doesn't make them less monstrous."[156]

Don't be fooled by the black robes, powdered wigs, and turgid legalese. International law is not settled law. It is evolving law, and largely unenforceable. And it is law that, due to its unequal application and shape-shifting shenanigans, has little public legitimacy. No nation has paid any price for standing before the ICJ. As historian Jack Cunningham observed about the slipperiness of the International Court of Justice, and its comparison to the ICC, "Under the Rome Statute, the ICC can invent international law on the fly and signatories can vote to change what constitutes a crime and how it may be tried, while rogue prosecutors have a free hand."[157]

Even members of the Bar, in countries the world over, have no idea how international law works, whether it enjoys any international consensus or whether it is ever binding on anyone or any nation. International law is not a required course in any of the accredited American law schools. As a practice area of the law, it doesn't even appear on bar exams! Attorneys can't make a living as international lawyers. It may be widely cited on cable news channels, largely to condemn Israel, but it's a lot of smoke and mirrors—sounds serious, but not taken seriously, at all.

And there is a reason for it: all that hypocrisy is a disqualifier. It is very easy to confuse and manipulate a layperson with reckless talk that Israel has "violated international law." People, politicians, and members of the press, do it all the time. No one questions it because even lawyers themselves are unfamiliar with the legal standards, the relevant statutes, treaties and resolutions.

International law is being leveraged to libel Israel by a cabal of global lawyers with a lot of free time on their hands. George Clooney's wife, Amal, a Lebanese lawyer of some renown in the human rights community, is one such person.[158] On numerous instances, she has weighed in against Israel. After Israel's last major war against Hamas in 2014, she was appointed as one of only three committee members to serve on the United Nations Fact Finding Mission on the 2014 Israel–Gaza Conflict. She ultimately turned down the offer. One suspects that her future husband's publicist had something to do with it. They were not yet married, and it was too provocative a topic for an A-list actor. Since their marriage, however, she has regained her voice and public hatred of Israel in connection with the October 7 War, serving as one of the consultants to the ICC's decision to indict Israeli Prime Minister Netanyahu.[159]

After each of the wars Israel has fought with Hamas, the United Nations assigned a fact-finding commission to investigate Israel's wartime conduct. (Amal Clooney has joined this effort, too.) The reasons that provoked the war and compelled Israel to retaliate are usually left out of the investigation. So, too, are the words "terrorist" or "terrorism" never used, lending credence to the falsehood and deception that Hamas are nothing more than combatants in a liberationist movement for Palestinian self-determination. Hamas' genocidal aims, fueled by its fanatical religious beliefs, go unmentioned and unaddressed.

So, too, do the mandate, and the ultimate fact-findings, fail to devote any attention to the tens of thousands of rockets fired toward Israeli population centers, and the deployment of Palestinian human shields. Both are indisputable war crimes, yet somehow, they fall outside of the parameters of the Commission's purview. Not only are these crimes unindicted, but it is as if they never took place.

Like clockwork, the results of these UN commissions invariably conclude, once the fighting was over and the relative numbers of civilian dead were counted, that the Palestinian death toll was disproportionate. Hardly an unexpected outcome *after* the war concludes and the cleanup creates moral discomfort. But "[p]roportionality is a question of judgment in the moment, not in hindsight. Is the potential risk to civilians excessive in relation to its military advantage? That favors military advantage, since civilian risk is a given and must only not be 'excessive.'"[160]

Moreover, the condition of the battlefield—with the presence of human shields guarding terrorists, weapons caches, and launching sites both below and above civilian structures—should inhere to Israel's favor under any proportionality analysis. No such luck. A fair reading of international humanitarian law—and international human rights law—should always start with the premise that in war, civilian casualties cannot be avoided. And surely not on such a boobytrapped battlefield. As two military ethicists wrote, "There is more flexibility in the application of the rule when the non-state party intentionally manipulates the battlefield in order to involve civilians in the armed conflict."[161] Yoram Dinstein, a law professor who specializes in the laws of war, wrote, "[T]he appraisal whether civilian casualties are excessive in relation to the military advantage anticipated must make allowances for the fact that—if an attempt is made to shield military objectives with civilians—civilian casualties will be higher…."[162]

But none of that ever factors into the mandate of United Nations commissions empaneled for the ostensible purpose of calling the one Jewish state's existence into question. With all that one-sided bias and ballast behind it, Israel will be ultimately accused of war crimes and possible crimes against humanity.

And there are lesser charges that Israel will no doubt be expected to answer for, more common and less fanciful war crimes such as indiscriminate killings; the withholding of water, electricity, and humanitarian aid; mass starvation; and the denial of access to, and destruction of, medical personnel and facilities. This list encompasses what essentially amounts to a siege on Gaza.[163]

No one can deny Palestinian suffering. What can be disputed is who is to blame for the misery. Israel may not be a perfect society, but under the laws of war, it bears no responsibility for what has happened to the people of Gaza. That doesn't mean there will be no tribunals passing judgment on Israel. Manifold investigative reports issued by international bodies wearing blinders to all manner of human suffering except for what has happened in Gaza will mount. Israel will most assuredly be held blameworthy. Israelis all know to expect it. But we should all know that these accusers are not impartial, honest brokers.

In each of the many past investigations, those judging Israel created a moral equivalence between a nation defending itself against terrorists and terrorists who indiscriminately attack Israeli civilians and position their own civilians as human shields.

Following these news-grabbing, sensationalized provocations against the Jewish state, regardless of any uncovered facts that might exonerate Israel, the damage is already done. The blood libel has infected public opinion. Long prejudiced minds receive their confirmation bias. Facts no longer matter when Israel is judged, as it always is, to be guilty.

After the 2008–2009 Gaza war, the UN appointed Judge Richard Goldstone as the head of that fact-finding mission. Goldstone had been a High Court jurist in South Africa, and the first chief prosecutor assigned by the UN International Criminal Tribunal in the cases brought against those believed to be responsible for crimes in the former Yugoslavia and Rwanda. What made Goldstone even more qualified to condemn Israel was that he, himself, was a Jew.

The mission ultimately published its findings near the end of 2009. It was titled: The Goldstone Report. Naturally, Israel was found guilty, relying mostly on evidence supplied by Hamas. The Goldstone Report concluded that Israel's wartime conduct was not guided by military necessity. Moreover, the damage it inflicted was disproportionate. And, most damningly, it stated that Israel targeted innocent civilians.

The verdict could not have been worse.

The Goldstone Report acknowledged that the mission "wasn't a judicial investigation," and that the war crimes conclusion "was always intended as conditional." Moreover, the findings were not subject to "the criminal standard of proof beyond a reasonable doubt."[164] The evidence the Report had relied upon and obtained would not be admissible in an actual court of law.[165] But it was surely good enough for the predictable prejudgments of the United Nations.

Two years later, however, after Israel produced its own detailed report on the 2008 Gaza War, Goldstone recanted the most damning and slanderous claim of his Report: that Israel had intentionally targeted civilians.[166] He specifically disavowed that non-Hamas civilians were "intentionally targeted as a matter of policy." And equally important, he finally concluded that Hamas' rockets "were purposefully and indiscriminately aimed at civilian targets." He went on to confess: "If I had known then what I know now, the 'Goldstone Report' would have been a different document."[167]

Thanks for nothing. Two years after the fact, when the wartime dust had settled, denunciations against Israel had already poisoned the world, and the media's demonization of Israel lessened to a quieter roar, the man behind the Report's biased and irrevocable conclusion decided to disown its worst findings. His ax-grinding antisemitic colleagues, however, publicly distanced themselves from the former judge's change of heart. Israel-bashers ran with the Report, anyway, acting as if it was composed and brought down from Mount Sinai.

Meanwhile, the 2024 genocide charge lodged against Israel by the government of South Africa in The Hague, where the International Court of Justice is based, is, yet again, heavy on prejudice and light on law. And its preliminary ruling was deceitfully vague. The former president of the court, Joan Donoghue, speaking to the *BBC*, clarified the court's January 2024 ruling because it was being misread to indict Israel for having violated the Genocide Convention. She stated, "[Our ruling] did not decide, and this is something where *I'm correcting something that's often said in the media. It did not decide that the claim of genocide was plausible.*"[168]

And that's how international law works.

CHAPTER 8

Civilians Voluntarily Serving As Human Shields Lose Their Innocence

No one appreciates living life under a microscope, especially if everyone wearing a lab coat wishes for your demise. In the annals of nationhood, this pretty much sums up Israel's dilemma with its coexistence among the family of nations. Israel was never even given its own white coat.

When it comes to Hamas and Hezbollah and the existential threats they present, and the genocidal fears they evoke, would Israel's PR problem be any different if these terrorist groups fought Israel on some open battlefield, away from civilian life and infrastructure? Obviously, Hamas and Islamic Jihad would never agree to it. They have had too much success exploiting their own people as defensive weapons, an antidote for all that asymmetry they face and create, making it a more fair fight. Palestinians sleeping serenely in their beds is a nightmare for them.

It is no longer true that Hamas and Islamic Jihad are a bunch of ragtag terrorists, light on training and weaponry, sky high on religious rapture. On October 7, 2023, and for the year that followed, Hamas demonstrated that they possessed more punch than Israel saw from them in the past. Yes, still martyrdom—their own, and the people of Gaza—but militarily, they raised their game. The October 7 campaign was, for Israel, more like a full-scale war—one they could surely win, but not without challenges.

Hamas showed a surprising amount of conventional army capability. They mounted a combat-ready ground force of over forty thousand insurgents. They possessed artillery, infantry, armored attack vehicles, drone-strike aviation, and, most importantly, more precision-guided rockets that traveled farther into Israel than any projectile they were able to launch in prior wars. Hamas and Islamic Jihad presented a much more formidable threat, without forsaking the dark arts of terrorism.

But here's a thought experiment: If Palestinian civilians were not involved at all, if they were completely removed from the heaviest artillery shelling and cross-firing, would the world have less of a problem with an Israeli victory? IDF versus terrorists—mano-to-monsters, with no civilian middlemen? Or are civilians merely a pretext, a humanitarian fabrication, an excuse to call for the end of the Jewish state because Israel commits war crimes against Palestinians?

It is one thing for civilian death to be incidental to legitimate wartime aims. That's the true meaning of "collateral" damage. It is quite another when civilian death is all but certain. The German firebombing of England, the British bombing of Dresden, the two atomic bombs America dropped on Hiroshima and Nagasaki, the napalm in Vietnam, and the "shock and awe" over Baghdad, presented similar assurances of civilian death. Israel's airstrikes on Gaza are just such a place, too.

But the difference is that assurances of civilian death in Gaza are never evaluated as tragic examples of collateral damage. If deaths are caused by Israel, there is automatic global prejudgment of war crimes. Hamas initiating these wars, firing upon Israeli civilians, and then hiding among Palestinian civilians, are minor details. "Oh, that," can be heard with shrugged shoulders the world over. The Middle East backstory becomes irrelevant; the premise of a just war is completely inverted. Terrorists sleep with the just; Israel's self-defense is an abomination. Whatever means Israel chooses to defend itself can never be rationalized or excused.

Gaza, for one special reason, is a different theater of war. Each confirmed Israeli kill is treated like opening night. Counting the civilian Palestinian dead is a global obsession. Israel's failure to live up to the world's condescending expectations is smugly recited. Actual war crimes and genocides being committed in other hot spots around the world are deliberately unseen—involving victims and casualty rates that are multiples of what is reported in Gaza. Without Jews, there is simply no crime worth mentioning.

The United States and Allied Coalition Forces faced similar moral quandaries with civilian casualties in Afghanistan and Iraq. The main difference was the absence of bad press. Those wars generated none of the same public outcry. No fact-finding missions ordered by the United Nations. International tribunals were never convened. No passing of judgment on the moral morass of fighting in combat zones swarming with civilians. The numbers of civilians killed in those warzones were not insignificant: fifty thousand in Afghanistan; two hundred thousand in Iraq. And, yes, naturally, women and children were among the dead.

But in those cases, the bombings in densely populated areas were legally permissible under the laws of war—because they don't necessarily violate those laws. More likely, no one paid enough attention to even contemplate whether crimes had been committed. Most assuredly, allegations of genocide were not even remotely entertained.

What we know about Israel's military campaigns in Gaza—in 2008 to 2009, 2014, and 2023 to 2025—is that fighting in self-defense can be judged more harshly than the original act of aggression itself. Israel knows all too well that global public opinion sidesteps the justness of the war and fixates on its *jus in bello* alone—unjust solely on account of lopsided death tolls. But as discussed earlier, those numbers have nothing to do with proportionality, nor do they sully the IDF's manner of fighting.

When warfare is asymmetric, references to body counts are prejudiced against the side forced to wage war under such inhuman conditions. Humanitarian concerns are just smoke screens. If body counts were that important, college campus unrest would be convulsing on behalf of the dead civilians from Syria, Darfur, Ethiopia, and Ukraine.

Now that Syrian strongman Bashar al-Assad has been deposed and evidence of his use of chemicals weapons is once again in the news, like it was when Barack Obama drew his "red line" in 2012, why aren't college students walking out of classrooms in protest, where are the activists shutting down major thoroughfares?

In a very important way, not all civilians are the same, especially the ones from Gaza. One need not be a card-carrying member of a terrorist organization to be treated like a wartime militant. Under the laws of armed combat, a civilian up to no good can forfeit his or her civilian status. In Gaza, very much unlike in neighboring Syria, civilians largely act like an auxiliary military force without portfolio.

Claims like this one are often spoken and are wholly preposterous: "The vast majority of civilians in Gaza are neither terrorists nor terrorist supporters. They are normal human beings who would like to live normal lives, but are caught between the IDF, who will not let them leave Gaza, and Hamas militants, who use them as shields."[169] This statement is demonstrably false: Israel isn't stopping anyone from leaving Gaza, civilians choose to remain in their homes and not flee to a humanitarian corridor even after being warned of an impending airstrike, and polling shows that Hamas remains immensely popular.

The question I raised back in 2014 with my *Wall Street Journal* op-ed should be asked again: Are Gazans complicit in their own deaths? Civilians, yes, they may be, but not necessarily innocent ones.

Children, of course, are innocent, although far too many Hamas fighters are underage. If they are carrying weapons, Israel can't very well be held responsible—although the Gaza Health Ministry will list them among the civilian dead as "children." The life and death choices Gaza's parents make for their children also can't be blamed on Israel. If parents are warned to leave their apartment buildings and choose to stay with their children right beside them, those deaths become unavoidable. Gazans might as well place their children on rooftops and instruct them to bare their teeth and dare Israel to fire away. Over the past three wars, impossible as it may be to believe, there have been reports of that very thing taking place.

Only two outcomes are possible under such surreal circumstances: children serve the wishes of their parents and terrorist overseers and are martyred as human shields; or Israeli fighter pilots flinch and fly away, giving Hamas free rein to rain rockets down on Israeli children.

Let's remember how we got here. Hamas was popularly elected in 2006 by the Gazan people, who voted in favor of a terrorist organization that ran on a single policy plank—eliminate Israel and all Jews that live there (and everywhere, time permitting); reclaim Israeli cities and designate *all* the land under Islamist control. It wasn't as if the Palestinians of Gaza were unaware of Israel's history of responding to wars brought by its Arab neighbors and handing them resounding defeats. Casting your vote for Hamas was tantamount to a death sentence. And, yet, that's what the Gazans, apparently, wanted for their families and their future. If they didn't, why has there not been a single uprising against Hamas' control over the Strip? Why is terrorism still the governance of choice in Gaza?

A shocking moment that flipped the script did take place over a year after the October 7 massacre, something that, of course, received little attention. Professor Salman al-Dayah, the former dean of the faculty of Sharia and Law at the Islamic University of Gaza, issued a *fatwa*—a legal ruling—against Hamas for "violating Islamic principles governing *jihad*."[170] Yes, you heard that right—the leading Palestinian legal and religious scholar on the Koran condemned Hamas, under Islamic law! And he based his ruling on the significant civilian casualties, and the destruction of Gazan infrastructure, arising out of Hamas' actions on October 7. The consequences of the attack, he argued, which Hamas brought upon the Palestinian people, violated the teachings of Islam.

Which Koran is he reading? If you listen to lunatic ayatollahs from Iran or the equally unhinged clerics in Lebanon, or frankly every other religious figure in the West Bank and Gaza, you will believe that the Koran demands the killing of all infidels, especially Jews, and that it is the will of Allah that Muslims sacrifice themselves in the demented cause of destroying the enemies of Islam. In case you're curious, here's one of my favorite passages in the Koran, 3:151-52: "strike *terror* into the hearts of the unbelievers."[171]

It actually invokes the word "terror"! The Muslim Brotherhood, perhaps not surprisingly, goes by the book.

What passage of sacred text is al-Dayah relying upon? Has there been a Koranic reformation that the world is unaware of? And where has he been all this time? Al-Dayah's *fatwa* literally decrees that Hamas had a sacred duty to *not* allow Palestinians to be used as human shields. He wrote that Hamas should be "keeping fighters away from the homes of defenceless [Palestinian] civilians." And even more astoundingly, al-Dayah reads the Koran as demanding that jihad avoid taking actions that will provoke an adversary to retaliate with an excessive and disproportionate response.[172]

That means, if you can believe this: October 7 somehow escaped the judgment of the Geneva Conventions but directly violated the teachings of the Koran! Professor Salman al-Dayah is stating the obvious: what Hamas did to innocent Israeli civilians would naturally result in disproportionate harm to Muslims.

I have two thoughts: Will someone please take the professor immediately to a safe house because he will surely be assassinated by Hamas operatives; and how will Gaza's general public respond to this *fatwa*, given that they overwhelmingly support the barbaric methods of Hamas, are generally happy to die or sacrifice their children as martyrs, and are absolutely thrilled with the results of October 7?

Given the popular appeal of Hamas, and the IDF's retaliatory track record, one must dumbfoundingly ask: What did Gazans actually expect to happen in the days, weeks, and months after October 7? They cheered as half-naked Israeli teenagers were dragged through their streets, as terrorists and fellow citizens carried severed Jewish heads and lifted them in the air in triumph. They celebrated a victory even as they had to know that tens of thousands of them would soon be dead.

Ask yourself: As bloodthirsty terrorists and their civilian henchmen basked in the glory of all this orgiastic barbarism, if you were a parent, wouldn't you pack a few bags and drive, run, or walk, as far away as possible from anyone associated with Hamas? When Israel repeatedly gave warnings of looming attacks and provided notice of areas set aside for shelter—dropping leaflets, handing out pamphlets, providing safe passage and havens making seventy thousand telephone calls, thirteen million text messages, and fifteen million voicemails to vacate, dropping giant speakers from parachutes to broadcast warnings, alerting its enemy with online military maps where operations will be taking place, taking four-hour daily pauses to leave combat areas—would you not be racing for the nearest humanitarian corridor?[173]

If you didn't, and instead chose to stay, would that be Israel's fault?

In the Protocols to the Geneva Conventions, Article 57(2)(c) provides that "effective advanced warning shall be given of attacks which may affect the civilian population, unless circumstances do not permit."

That's what Israel has always done and what the Palestinians, and the world, largely ignore. Legal experts continue to insist that Israel is violating international law when Israel happens to be the only entity scrupulously trying to operate within its framework.

I think it is high time for Israel to stop apologizing for fighting a war in self-defense. It has to stop listening to people who have never been to war, like Joe Biden, Antony Blinken, and Barack Obama, and have no understanding about the Middle East where Jews have always faced murderous enemies. These enemies will never become converts to Western universalist ideals. They don't comport themselves according to the foolish wisdom of the faculty lounge.

The fog of war in the Middle East is even more murky. Armchair quarterbacking is especially galling in such terrain. Israel should long be sick and tired of receiving political and moral advice from ignorant American leaders, and even more disgusted by progressive Jews standing in judgment of fellow tribesmen whose children serve in the IDF while the children of American Jews are shopping for summer homes in the Hamptons.[174]

What message do Palestinians time and again convey to the world about their aspirations for their people? Self-determination and nation-building, apparently, interest them very little. Nothing stopped Gazans from building their state once Israel withdrew from the Strip in 2005. Hamas took control in 2006, and rather than learn how to fire rockets and train their children to become martyrs, they could have dedicated their efforts to developing the Gaza Strip into a glistening jewel on the Mediterranean.

There was no air or naval blockade at the time. There was no "open air prison." Had Gazans demonstrated a desire to live in peace and establish the foundations toward a Palestinian future, Israelis—especially those in the south, the ones that Hamas slaughtered—would have been the first to cross the border with hammers and nails and said, "How can we help?"

The Palestinian Authority in the West Bank sets aside over $300 million each year for its "pay-for-slay" martyr program, where Palestinians are incentivized to kill or harm Israelis with monthly salaries, stipends, tuition benefits, and life insurance for family members, including prized civil service positions after being released from Israeli prisons.[175] Is this how a people inspire a generation of future statesmen? The bounty system and human shields are indicative of a morally bankrupt society interested only in violence and contemptuous of the necessary work required to become a nation.

Surely there are longstanding wartime distinctions between combatants and noncombatants. But the demarcation does not end there. There are also differences between civilians who aid and abet terrorism, and those who want no part in the fight. The latter are truly innocent. Each night they pray for the war to end, for their families to survive unharmed, their homes to be spared, the lingering smoke from nearby shelling to keep its distance, and the deafening sound of explosions to quiet. If given a chance to get out of harm's way, they would do anything and everything to protect their families from the near certainty of becoming casualties of war.

Michael Walzer, the foremost moral philosopher on what constitutes a just war, had this to say about when disproportionate civilian death does not raise concerns over war crimes. He wrote, "When we judge the unintended killing of civilians, we need to know how those civilians came to be in a battle zone in the first place.... [W]ho put them at risk and what positive efforts were made to save them?"[176]

Walzer makes a clarifying, yet patently obvious presumption about civilians who find themselves trapped inside a smothering warzone. Why wouldn't someone who isn't a terrorist and knows that he or she, and their family, are smack in the middle of the worst kind of danger, seek cover elsewhere—if humanitarian options are made available? Even Gazans who despise Israel and adore Hamas would surely not wish to remain in an apartment building that serves as a command center for terrorists. The IDF has issued clear warnings that a home will soon be reduced to rubble with terrorists, and noncombatants, buried underneath. Why would anyone wish to have those ruins as one's final resting place?

Two explanations come to mind: Hamas coerces the people to serve as human shields against their will; or civilians accede to Allah's will and await the splendor of becoming a *shahid*. The former is belied by the popular support that Hamas have enjoyed for decades, even after Israel pummels the enclave into the Stone Age. All three wars and several skirmishes between Israel and Hamas since 2007 produced the same outcomes. How can then Hamas remain so beloved? When civilian death becomes both a war strategy and a vile inevitability, how can the world luridly watch and not blame Hamas? Are there no Gazans who think it is a good idea to live beside Israel as a peaceable neighbor instead of a murderous rogue nonstate?

The question of Palestinian complicity in their own suffering must be taken seriously. There is nothing racist or Islamophobic about it. It is simply an observation about group conduct and personal responsibility at wartime. Complicity means active assistance—material aiding and abetting—and the consequences of doing so. The participation of civilians in the conduct of war may result in the forfeiture of "innocent" civilian status.

Walzer offers a conclusion that clearly applies to Gazans. In situations when a nonstate actor is "fighting among the people, it is best to assume that they have some serious political support among the people. The people, or some of them, are complicitous in guerrilla war, and the war would be impossible without their complicity."[177] Scholars on military history and ethics have long maintained that "[C]ivilians do not enjoy protection at all times and under all circumstances. When civilians take a direct part in the hostilities,...they lose their civilian protection and can be lawfully targeted."[178]

Do you need to read that again? I suggest you do because you won't see that stark conclusion and moral judgment elsewhere, either in print or on cable news. It is far too inconvenient and obvious a truth. Such a fate can't possibly be true about innocent civilians.

Don't be seduced by the white privilege of self-sacrifice: Israel has no legal or ethical obligation to compromise its military advantage because of the death wish of Palestinians. It has the right to defend itself with the full knowledge that its bombings, counterstrikes, and ground troop operations will result in civilian loss. Walzer writes that there is a "moral difference between…aiming at particular people because of things they have done or are doing, and aiming at whole groups of people, indiscriminately, because of who they are."[179]

Again, the moral philosopher who many believe must be unalterably opposed to Israel's war efforts and aims in Gaza has, actually, written a great deal that places the IDF's reasons to go to war, and the way it has been executing that war, on solid footing. Israel is aiming at Gaza not "indiscriminately" but under circumstances of extreme discrimination and precaution—seeking to kill all those responsible for October 7, whether they be terrorists or accomplices, for, as Walzer justifies, "the things they have *done*."[180] It is also on account of acts of terrorism that were done to Israeli civilians for decades—with October 7 reaching an apex where Israel simply could no longer afford to allow Hamas to remain as the governing power to its south. Ceasefires only prolonged the suffering of Israelis. Hamas and Islamic Jihad needed to be no more.

Every other country in the world would have done the same.

Here's a good example of military ethics from a rabbi who has struggled with the morality of war. He recalls a military operation on July 22, 2002, during the Second Intifada, in which one thousand Israelis lost their lives to suicide bombings on buses, in pizza shops, and even a Passover Seder held at a hotel. Trying to finally put a halt to all this violence, Israel bombed a small apartment building in Gaza City. The IDF was aiming at Salah Shehade, who at the time commanded the al-Qassam Brigades, the military wing of Hamas. More importantly, he was regarded as the "Godfather of suicide bombers," recruiting Palestinian children for the task, and other gruesome, sickening tradecraft. Over that year alone, he was responsible for killing 474 Israelis and wounding 2,649. He wasn't finished, yet. Other handiwork was being set in motion, which never materialized owing to a successful Israeli airstrike.

Shehade was in that building, but so were his chief deputy, his wife, his teenage daughter, and thirteen civilians. All were killed and over one hundred were wounded.

When the media reported the story, the focus was entirely on the collateral damage—the wife, daughter, and thirteen civilians. It made for good anti-Israel copy—"Israel Kills Wife and Daughter of Freedom Fighter." But those civilian deaths did not render the airstrike illegitimate—nor do we know whether some of the one hundred "civilian" dead had any tangible connections to terrorist activity. Why would anyone knowingly live in the same apartment building with the "godfather of suicide bombing"?

Rabbi Shlomo Brody wrote, "They don't ask whether the strike was excessive in proportion to the military advantage of killing, in the midst of an extended war on terror, the lead terrorist commander responsible for thousands of Israeli casualties."[181] Over the years Israel has neglected to avail themselves of the chance to eliminate terrorists because of persistent backlash and international condemnation over collateral damage. "Fears of 'disproportionate' accusations, led Israel to shirk its primary moral responsibility, which is to protect its own citizens from being murdered by terrorists."[182]

International humanitarian law is ultimately lawless when the distinction between combatants and civilians is an impossible judgment call. In Gaza, civilians are serving as quasi-combatants; the entire analysis on distinction begs for some reasonable modification to reflect how these wars are fought.

How does a military commander make such a call when his judgment might result in a war crime? Recent revisions to the United States Department of Defense *Law of War Manual* now prescribe: "The law of war does not require that commanders and other decision-makers apply a fixed standard of evidence or proof.... [T]he law of war requires commanders and other decision-makers to exercise professional judgment in making any assessment that a person or object is a military objective, and what is reasonable in making that assessment depends on the circumstances."[183]

As it should. No one would wish to be placed in a situation that is always a step away from a court martial. Asymmetric urban warfare demands split-second decision-making rendered in good faith, with full recognition that nearly everyone will appear to be a possible moving target. The proportionality analysis can't be made in hindsight. It happens in real time, under brutal wartime conditions.

Of course, any military decision will likely have consequences to civilians—but none more harrowing than what's presented in Gaza. Wholly incredulous in the annals of civilian behavior, Gazans are not committed to fleeing warzones. They are unique from other Arabs in the region, including the Palestinians in the West Bank, whose Islamist convictions are, seemingly, much less fanatical when it comes to matters of life and death.

But assessing the strategic military benefits is the first order of business when a nation is at war.

Similarly, as the October 7 Gaza War subsided, Israel's tit-for-tat encounters with Hezbollah in Lebanon and the Houthis in Yemen widened. Israel stepped up its offensives in the region. After killing Yahya Sinwar, Hamas' military commander, Israel's attention shifted to eliminating Hezbollah's military command in Beirut, including its longtime leader, Hassan Nasrallah.

But here's an interesting sidenote. After extensive aerial bombings and a ground invasion into Lebanon, the collateral damage in Beirut was surprisingly low. Lebanese civilians did the responsible thing: after being warned by the IDF that apartment buildings that housed Hezbollah were scheduled to be bombed, they instinctively fled.[184]

In the end, there is a consequence to complicity, and that ought to be so. You are either an innocent civilian who wants no part in the fighting and the assurance of death from Israel's bullseye retaliations, or you are a terrorist enabler and willful martyr. You can't be both.

Hamas, however, and the global antisemites that endorse its methods, want it both ways: "We start wars with our patented barbarism, and then demand immediate ceasefires the moment you kill the civilians we fiendishly place in your sightlines." There is a preciousness granted to the lives of Palestinian civilians that only antisemitism can explain. Deliberately positioned in harm's way, yet demanding that such civilians be immune from collateral damage.

It is especially galling for Israel to hear that its efforts to rescue the hostages taken by Hamas are criticized because some Palestinians, including the civilian keepers of those hostages, lost their lives during the operation.

Two of the leading scholars on military ethics, soon after one of those daring and successful Israeli Special Forces rescue operations occurred, wrote in *Newsweek*, "Let's get something straight from the outset: When you take hostages, you risk death. The moral and legal responsibility for any casualties resulting from the operation to free the hostages rests fully with Hamas and those holding hostages captive."[185]

The laws of war are not really all that complicated. Certain things require common sense, not a law degree: When warned of an impending airstrike, get the hell out of the building and take your children with you. If you are warehousing weapons in your apartment, or making your home available as a command center, or holding hostages captive in one of your rooms, then you *are* Hamas—you have joined forces with the dark arts of terrorism, and you are an accomplice to everything that arises from their terrorist acts, and directly culpable for the crimes you commit on your own accord. You have joined a criminal conspiracy, and you have no one but yourself to blame if your life comes to an end in a war with the Jewish state.

You elected Hamas, you enabled them, you assisted them, you cheered them on. You broke what could have been your promising country and sealed its decrepit fate. In a just universe where the rule of law also makes common sense, your participation in the crimes of Hamas makes you not an innocent civilian, but a war criminal.

As Arsen Ostrovsky and John Spencer concluded, "[O]ne should not need to be a legal scholar to understand that if you are a journalist or physician holding hostages, you are no longer a 'civilian.' In fact, the Geneva Convention makes it unequivocally clear that civilians lose that protection when they take direct part in the hostilities. In other words, when you hold hostages captive, you become a legitimate military target and should not be surprised when the Israel Defense Forces come knocking on your door."[186]

CHAPTER 9

When Body Counts and Death Tolls Can't Be Trusted

It is nothing new that Israel is being held to a different standard than other nations at war. Hypocrisy is another word for diplomacy when it comes to the world's treatment of the Jewish state—the only state, and the only democracy, deemed illegitimate, its very existence routinely questioned.

Israel is the only nation where history and geography are entirely inverted. The indigenous people of Israel and territories legally in dispute are called colonizing invaders. They are accused of stealing land from another nation that never, in fact, was a nation. Accused of maintaining Gaza as an "open air prison" when the enclave is governed by terrorists who make an air and naval blockade essential. As for the West Bank, it is governed by an entity called the Palestinian Authority, not the Jewish Authority. The nation is accused of being settled by white supremacists when more than half its citizens are people of color. Denounced as an apartheid state when every citizen possesses the same civil rights, where there is no forcible separation between the citizens, and where Arabs, Druze, Bedouins, and Africans are elected to the legislature and serve on the Supreme Court.

All the usual terms of art are deliberately upended to manufacture propaganda and feed a false narrative. A massacre perpetrated by Hamas is an act of resistance against an "occupation" when not a single Jew or Israeli has set foot in Gaza since 2005—aside from a very brief incursion at the tail end of 2014 to end the war. Israel's right to self-defense is re-characterized as war of aggression that demands a ceasefire—even *before* the IDF fired a single shot or set boots on the Gazan ground. Decapitated Israelis and gang raped teenage girls go unaddressed, legally, but every Palestinian child that may or may not have been killed constitutes an indisputable war crime.

Israel purportedly has the right of self-defense under Article 51 of the United Nations Charter, but apparently not if that means killing the people who attacked them because doing so would leave behind collateral damage. Ironically, like Shakespeare's Shylock in *The Merchant of Venice*, Israel is permitted its pound of flesh, but not if it accompanies the spilling of blood.

The laws of armed conflict, in the case of a law-abiding nation, are being used against Israel and in favor of terrorists who abide by absolutely no laws. And most surreal of all, the murderous conduct of keffiyeh-cladded terrorists, and their public statements, are not taken at face value—wholly trivialized, as if it is the work and words of children.

For instance, the Gaza Health Ministry provides the numbers and attests to the accuracy of Palestinian casualties of this war. Dead Palestinians are the reasons for the genocidal charge against the Jewish state. So, the accuracy of the total number of dead—and who are among the dead—is a pretty important assignment to hand over exclusively to the people who are decisive winners in the PR war against Israel. Those statistics are universally relied upon even though the United Nations Human Rights Office, the European Union, nongovernmental "human rights" organizations, and major media outlets all know that the Gaza Health Ministry is in the fuzzy math business.

In October 2023, not even a month into the war, President Joe Biden acknowledged that he had no confidence in the veracity of the Gaza death toll. Biden had been around the block. He was Vice-President during the last Israel–Gaza war. He knows Hamas to be notorious for lying, and its casualty figures are not to be trusted. That realization escaped his memory throughout the war, however. He occasionally berated Israel for killing Palestinians—who may or may not have actually been killed.

Yet, the Gaza Health Ministry's statistics are the only numbers *CNN* and competing media outlets, and the UN's Office for the Coordination of Humanitarian Affairs, relies upon in its own reporting. Independent journalists don't report from Gaza. They simply restate whatever the Health Ministry makes available to the public. In fact, Hamas refuses journalists access to observe anything related to the use of human shields; the hiding and launching of weapons from civilian homes, hospitals, and mosques; or the vastness and sophistication of those terror tunnels.[187]

The Gaza Health Ministry are agents of stealth, not health; propagandists, not statisticians. Proportionality in the Middle East is itself nothing but propaganda. The Health Ministry is a misnomer. It's in the death promotion business, doing the bidding of Hamas by cooking the books.

The world, however, is more than happy doing without the kind of ordinarily essential, independent verification required of truth-seekers and fact-checkers. Hamas, a blue-chip terrorist organization that set a new standard for depravity on October 7, 2023, seems to be placed on an honor system. Why would they lie? They have nothing to hide.

Assessing collateral damage in Gaza is a fool's errand where everyone is willing play the fool. If death tolls can be used to demonize the Jewish state, why quarrel over decimals?

When the smoke clears, Palestinian casualties always seem to include statistically suspicious and disproportionate numbers of dead women and children. All throughout the war, the media and the United Nations, based entirely on the good faith and math skills of Hamas, took it on faith that Israeli airstrikes have disproportionately killed Palestinian women and children—and each attack, coincidentally, always arrives at the same figure: 70 percent.[188] The genocide charge is directly traceable to the exclusion of men from the death rolls. If the death toll in Gaza is dominated by women and children, Israel must be targeting them and bypassing terrorists altogether.

However, as anyone who has ever attended grade school surely knows: if you don't show your work, and the answer is always the same, your math is way off.

Cynical though it may be, there's a brilliance to the endgame. Hamas knows that in a woke Western world where math itself is politically incorrect, where calculus is deemed a racist subject, no one will question the numbers of dark-skinned people. One would instantly be called a racist.

A report that completely debunked the Health Ministry's ledgers and spreadsheets, prepared by the Washington Institute for Near East Policy, concluded, "[B]y failing to distinguish between civilians and combatants, it [the Health Ministry] seeks to obscure its military losses and magnify civilian deaths. The use of human shields thus presents an advantage on the battlefield and in the fight for public opinion."[189]

Based on Hamas' official fatality count, the Israeli Defense Forces hardly ever kills Palestinian men, and most certainly not any terrorists. Indeed, no actual Hamas fighters are ever listed among the dead in reports filed by the Gaza Health Ministry. If everyone in Gaza is a civilian, then no one in Gaza is a civilian—since the whole enclave is run by Hamas. The Gaza Health Ministry seems to be making the case for human shields: You're either a Hamas terrorist or civilian cannon fodder—in either case, you are more valuable as a statistic to be used in the PR war against Israel than you are in carrying an assault rifle. The whole point of deploying civilians as shields is to assure higher death tolls, and to shield terrorists to allow them to fight another day.

What other conclusion can one reach? Israel's aim can't possibly be that bad. If one accepts the numbers provided by the Health Ministry, Israel is abysmal at conducting an actual war. The IDF is, apparently, in the sole business of killing women and children—not even civilian men, or the elderly, for that matter. So goes the pride of investigative journalism in the Middle East. The mass media would print or broadcast any damning, but ultimately improbable statistic that maligns the Jewish state.

The logic of warfare becomes wholly corrupted in such a setting. This being the third time Israel has gone to war against Hamas since 2008, the Health Ministry knows that the world will not keep track of who started the war, and under what un-neighborly conditions Israelis were living before they decided to put an end to it. It's all a sucker's game of false numbers, the global gas-lighting of disproportionate death.

Anne Bayefsky, director of Human Rights and the Holocaust Center at Touro University, said, the UN has

> systematically blasted false numbers of Palestinian casualties across the globe since Oct. 8. Their source has always been Hamas knowing full well that Hamas has a vested interest in

> lying about the numbers.... They run civilian and combatant figures together knowing full well that it is legal to kill Hamas combatants and the lawfulness of civilian casualties depends entirely on different standards.... This isn't math. It's antisemitism.[190]

During this October 7 War, unlike past wars, experts in statistical analysis examined the Health Ministry's numbers—the kind of due diligence any self-respecting journalist would do—and determined that the design pattern of the deaths could not be accounted for. When President Biden started to turn against Israel, capitulating to the global drumbeat against mounting civilian deaths, which was damaging his re-election campaign, he accused Israel's pursuit of terrorists as "over the top."

Abraham Wyner, a professor of data science at the University of Pennsylvania's Wharton School, concluded that it was impossible for Israeli airstrikes to cause such consistent collateral damage, where 70 percent of the casualties were categorized as women and children. "[T]hese numbers aren't right...instead of, being 70% women and children, it's probably closer to 30% to 35% women and children."[191]

How can Wyner be so sure that the Health Ministry is intentionally lying? Simply put, "there just aren't enough [of their] civilian men dying.... [T]he number of people dying every day is almost the same.... In war, there should be variability. Variability coming from war plans, from lulls, from intense increases in activity. And none of that was observable in the data. There was what we call too little dispersion."[192]

The Health Ministry are not just liars. They are bad liars. They report the same casualty counts each day, without any variation—even on days when there is little to no fighting or bombing. Wyner continued: "The basic idea is that on days where there isn't very much bombing, you should see just a few children and women dying.... You should see more women and children dying on days where there's lots of civilian casualties as opposed to fighters."[193]

Without variation, the only conclusion a reasonable person can draw is that no correlation exists between what's actually happening in Gaza and what is being reported by the only entity charged with supplying the data. Michael Spagat is a professor at the University of London who is affiliated with a British NGO that tracks civilian casualties of war around the world. He's also admittedly no fan of Israel. Yet, he reviewed the Health Ministry's data and discovered 3,407 obvious errors—15.7 percent of the total! They included: duplicate names appearing on the list, no ID numbers or ID numbers with too few digits, and other numerical and statistical reasons to question the validity of the report. "The oft-cited claim that 70 percent of the Gazans killed in the conflict are women and children seems increasingly untenable," Spagat said.[194]

The motive is obvious: keep the focus on Israeli weapons and not on Hamas' tactics. Two experts in military ethics put it this way: "Its statistical sleight-of-hand is meant to draw attention away from Hamas' criminal conduct of the war, built around the exploitation of hospitals, schools, mosques, and UN buildings as military assets."[195]

Even Israel's most left-wing newspaper, *Haaretz*, in a 2011 report detailing some of the discoveries made about Hamas' chicanery in its war reporting in 2008 to 2009, wrote, "Hamas admitted that the numbers that it had been telling the public about the size of their fighter losses (terrorists), which they had reported to be 49, was actually over 700, which was exactly what Israel had said it was in the very beginning."[196]

Hamas' inflated numbers has become more shameless over time. And the entities who should be demanding more accuracy in the Palestinian death tolls have been become even less curious and committed to truth. It's hard to believe anyone is that gullible or willfully deluded. David Adesnik, a senior fellow and director of research at the Foundation for Defense of Democracies, said that neither the Health Ministry nor the Gaza Media Office can be trusted to provide accurate information about civilian death—especially if they are identified as women and children. "[O]ne expects Hamas to lie," he said. "What's much harder to explain is how the supposed experts at the U.N. could be so credulous for so long."[197]

Hamas knows that the numbers game is its only winnable strategy. Through libelous statistics, manipulated military rules, and international pressure brought to bear on the Jewish state, Western nations have halted, and in some cases, withheld weapons to Israel. Proportionality is the red herring. Civilian casualties is being used to supplant the importance of military necessity—and everyone knows it. But can any those numbers be trusted?

A passing glance at the Gaza Health Ministry's findings leads one to conclude that, "Hamas-produced statistics are inconsistent, imprecise, and appear to have been systematically manipulated to downplay the number of militants killed and to exaggerate the proportion of noncombatants confirmed as dead."[198]

In April 2024, Hamas conceded that its numbers were "flawed." A report issued by the think tank, The Foundation for the Defense of Democracies, revealed that: "The Hamas-run Gaza Ministry of Health said on April 6 that it had 'incomplete data' for 11,371 of the 33,091 Palestinian fatalities it claims to have documented."[199] Apparently, it was missing such key data points as full name, date of birth, or date of death.

One month later, the United Nations acknowledged that it could not rely on Hamas' casualty figures. It lowered its own estimates of fatalities by as much as ten thousand, and sharply reduced the alleged number of childhood deaths from fourteen thousand to around seven thousand eight hundred. The IDF maintains that at least half of the death toll always consists of terrorists.[200]

These were shocking revelations coming roughly fifteen months into a war that was nearly at its end. All those many months, and now even Hamas acknowledged that it had been lying all along. And, yet, the mainstream media regarded the subterfuge as a nonstory. After a year and a half of conning the public with lies about Palestinian deaths, correcting the error should have been Page One!

The Gaza Health Ministry deliberately overcounted women and children by as much as twice the actual number. Half of their women and children are, in fact, "unidentified, which is why even the United Nations decided that the Health Ministry's numbers are worthless."[201] Because they listed eleven thousand as "unidentified," the Health Ministry thought it was a good idea to classify them all as women and children, padding the civilian side of the ledger.

In June 2024, the Associated Press took the extraordinary step of deviating from Hamas' approved death toll edicts and did their own homework. And this is what they discovered: the proportion of children killed in the war is nowhere near what the Health Ministry said it was, and, in fact, the death toll of children was falling each month.[202]

As the war in Gaza was winding down by the end of 2024, the Henry Jackson Society, a think tank, released a Report, titled

"Questionable Counting: Analyzing the Death Toll from the Hamas-Run Ministry of Health in Gaza," that relied upon the actual data the Health Ministry collected from its own registries, but were deceitfully packaged with deliberate falsities.[203] The think tank didn't even have to do its own research. The discrepancies in the Health Ministry's own data were damning enough. For instance, "In the August 2024 list, 103 names were marked as female who had a male first name (e.g. Mohammed)."[204]

How stupid, gullible, and sloppy does Hamas think the West is?

On December 10, the Gaza Media Office reported that nearly 44 percent of 44,758 reported fatalities were children. But most of those casualties were adults registered *as* children. In some cases, those in their mid-twenties were listed as infants! Someone who was twenty-two years old was listed as a four-year-old; a thirty-one year-old was registered as an infant.

And five thousand natural deaths—including cancer patients—were added to the wartime death toll. Yes, cancer patients who died from the disease! Some were listed as wartime casualties while still receiving cancer treatments. That means Palestinian doctors were prescribing chemotherapy for people who were already dead—and died in their sleep! Jihad Mahmoud Adeeb Al-Taweel, ID number 950130153, who in early April 2024 was a child purportedly killed by the IDF, on April 15 was listed as a patient suffering from laryngeal cancer.[205]

Andrew Fox, the lead author of the Report said, "You can't say it's a genocide when half the people that have died are combatants who are still fighting."[206]

The Report reads, "The data behind their figures contains natural deaths, deaths from before this conflict began and deaths of those killed by Hamas itself; it contains no mention of Hamas combatant fatalities; and it overstates the number of women and children killed."[207]

The Report reveals that the Health Ministry made no distinction between those killed in Israeli airstrikes from those who became casualties not of war but of Hamas' own incompetence from misfired rockets. Even worse, while stealing the humanitarian aid that Israel allowed into the Strip, Hamas gunmen killed their own civilians who complained. They, too, were listed as casualties of war instead of casualties of Hamas.[208]

Reading this Report clearly reinforces what the IDF has been saying all along: that Israel is not targeting civilians, and nearly half of the Gazans who they are killing are adult, fighting-aged males (and underaged enlisted teenagers)—most of whom are actual terrorists who, under every principle of international humanitarian law, can never be referred to as collateral damage.

The global public has no way of knowing any of this because the legacy media has no interest doing the same kind of investigative work as was undertaken by the Henry Jackson Society. Even reporting on its blockbuster findings was not even mentioned on a slow news day.

Over a four-month period in the spring of 2024, 1,378 articles calling attention to the casualties of war in Gaza appeared in such "reputable" media outfits as the *New York Times*, *Washington Post*, the *Guardian*, *CNN*, *BBC*, *Reuters*, the *Associated Press*, and the Australian *ABC*. The Report from the Henry Jackson Society revealed that 84 percent of these stories made no distinction between civilian and combatant deaths. And 98 percent relied entirely upon the numbers supplied by the Gaza Health Ministry.[209]

A similar finding was made by the Committee for Accuracy in Middle East Reporting and Analysis (CAMERA) in its own Report profiling the biases against Israel by the *BBC*. Palestinian terrorists killed in Gaza were routinely referred to as "innocent civilians" even though the *BBC* was well aware that the dead were not collateral to the war. They were all armed militants of Hamas and Islamic Jihad.[210]

The metaphorical "fog of war" in Gaza is used in the reverse context: not as an excuse by an aggressor that it couldn't see through the fog, which accounts for a battlefield awash in blood, but by the alleged victims, who declare that so many of their people have been killed, they couldn't keep count. As we have come to learn in Gaza, if one doesn't know for sure, just overcount the fatalities and call them all women and children. Outside sources won't check, anyway.

After conducting its own more thorough investigation, the IDF released its own numbers. Obviously, the tallies are disparate. The overall casualty figures are lower, and it includes actual terrorists. And there is a significant drop-off in the number of women and children. Yet, no one seems interested in the calculations of a state actor fighting in self-defense against a notoriously terroristic and math-phobic nonstate entity. Hamas admits error and the world ignores it; Israel produces its own more exact findings, and the world ignores that, too.

The avowedly incorrect Health Ministry projections reinforce the false narrative of Israel being in violation of international law. Why bother tampering with that? "We would expect everyone to now take [our] figures as a genuine estimate from a free democratic country that fights in strict accordance with the laws of armed conflict in one of the most challenging urban warfare scenarios in history," Avi Hyman, an IDF spokesman, told Fox News. "Let me make it clear: Every civilian casualty is a tragedy. That would not have happened if Hamas hadn't insisted on using their own people as human shields."[211]

Hamas has been exploiting the media's willingness to tell whatever version of events will be most damaging to Israel—regardless of the truth, even if it means that the media, and not Hamas, must falsify the evidence. Most notably, the image that unleashed so much global fury against the Jewish state back in 2002. It was actually the second day of the Second Intifada when this event occurred. The IDF was engaged in crossfire shooting with Hamas at the Netzarim Junction in the Gaza Strip.

Caught between the combatants was Jamal al-Durrah and his twelve-year-old son, Muhammad. Both were ducking behind a concrete cylinder. The boy was crying; the father was waving his arms, trying to alert the combatants on both sides that they were caught in their bullet barrage. A Palestinian cameraman captured footage of the incident.

French television acquired the footage and on that evening's news, aired less than one minute of it. At some point, viewers saw smoke obscuring the father and son, and when it cleared, the boy is shown slumped over in his father's lap, dead.

The immediate accusation was that Israel targeted the boy for death—that the IDF was actually aiming at him. The global legacy media, and the Arab Street, went into immediate action. This was the latest and most damning of all Jewish blood libels. No longer do Jews kill Christian children to make matzah. Now they target little boys for death to rid the region of Palestinians. The rush to judgment was set in motion. What Israel did was in direct violation of the laws of war—specifically, the failure to distinguish between armed combatants and terrified children.

Many investigations followed, conducted by outside entities and the Israeli military, but this was the kind of sensationalism that was not to be undone or even mitigated. This image would last an eternity in the minds of Muslims who will never run out of reasons to call for the death of Jews. There was even a stamp used throughout the Muslim world with the terrified face of Muhammad al-Durrah. Osama bin-Laden used the French video clip as a recruiting pitch for jihad against the Jews.

But when it comes to mortal combat in public relations and propaganda, there is always a catch. The cameraman, who was Palestinian, handed over the raw footage to an antisemitic French television news channel, France 2. The footage that was shown that evening had been edited in ways that violate the best practices of broadcast journalism. For instance, some of the footage shows the boy miraculously lift his hand from his face *after* he was presumably dead. Viewers never saw that image. Also, the smoke that precedes the image of the dead body seems to have been creatively added. The smoke doesn't appear on the original reel.

The viewer also never sees from where the shot was fired or where the bullet was lodged. No autopsy was performed. One investigative team believes that Muhammad is actually still alive—twenty-two-years later! Was this broadcast news, or performance art? We will never know for sure. Another investigator surmised that the entire episode was staged. If it was, it is reminiscent of footage that appeared on Instagram well into the October 7 War. It depicted three Hamas terrorists dressed in IDF uniforms beating up a young Palestinian. Additional footage was accidentally loaded where you see the four of them sitting in the back of an SUV, liftgate up, and laughing. The IDF soldiers were not Israelis, but Gazans dressed in IDF uniforms. Apparently, there are many roles for a human shield to play so long as it helps manipulate an already predisposed general public.[212]

What we do know is that if Muhammad al-Durrah was killed, without a forensic examination of the crime scene, we can't know with any degree of certainty which side fired the bullet. Israel originally took responsibility, but after conducting its own inquiry, concluded that the shots came from a different direction and were fired by Hamas. But Israel haters don't need any further proof. The reel edited in France show evil Israelis killing a twelve-year-old Muslim boy. That's all the world needed to know.

That might explain why a book, published by Duke University Press in 2017, *The Right to Maim: Debility, Capacity, Disability*, received a book award even though there is barely a coherent English sentence to be found within its pages. It goes well beyond the al-Durrah blood libel. It actually claims that the IDF aims its weapons at Palestinian children in order to maim them. Israel also, allegedly, poisons the Palestinian water supply. And most shocking and scandalous at all, the IDF allegedly harvests the organs of dead Palestinians for profit.

Is there any proof for these charges? Well, not in the book, and the author has claimed that she is not obliged to supply any. The killing of Palestinians, generally, makes her claims essentially true, she says, even if not actually true. Not only is she a recipient of a book award; she is an esteemed guest lecturer at universities where she routinely receives standing ovations.

Whatever happened to academic integrity and the pursuit of truth? It exists nowhere nowadays, but it is especially barren when it comes to truths about Israel.

There is an even more recent example of the same blood libel against Jews. The UN Independent International Commission of Inquiry on the Occupied Palestinian Territory, including East Jerusalem and Israel, issued a report alleging that "Israeli authorities have destroyed in part the reproductive capacity of the Palestinians in Gaza as a group, including by imposing measures intended to prevent births, one of the categories of genocidal acts in the Rome Statute and the Genocide

Convention."[213] How is this being achieved, pray tell? No one knows, or cares. Sterilizing Palestinian mothers from a distance, as another genocidal tactic, is too good a story to let facts and impossibilities to get in the way.

Remember the legacy media's initial coverage of the Mavi Marmara, the Turkish flotilla on its way to Gaza in 2010? It tried to penetrate Israel's naval blockade, which was imposed to prevent Hamas from receiving illicit contraband for the making of bombs. The ship illegally entered Israeli waters and refused warnings to turn back. Israeli Seals boarded the ship and was immediately set upon by fifty Palestinian activists wielding clubs. It was all yet another PR stunt, knowing that the media would cover Israel's response, and not the violence that precipitated it—or, for that matter, that the ship was, indeed, carrying cargo intended for use in making weapons.

And, more recently, the media covered Israel's alleged bombing of the Al-Ahli Hospital in Gaza early on in the October 7 War. The hospital doubled as a terrorist haven, with a formidable underground command center and weapons depot. And, yes, above ground, it was a hospital, too, but Israel would ultimately discover that many of the doctors had Hamas credentials. The Health Ministry informed the press that Israel had bombed the hospital, killing five hundred Palestinian patients and hospital personnel. Israel was dubious that it was responsible for the airstrike at all. Turns out: they were right. The crater left by the blast was not wide enough to have been caused by one of its bombs. The destruction was caused by a misfired rocket, launched by either Hamas or Islamic Jihad. Even more deceitfully, the media got the target wrong: the rocket hit the parking lot beside the hospital, and the fatalities were not five hundred, but seven.

Yet, the legacy media was off to the races with the false reportage. "In all, I contacted a dozen reporters or communications departments at news outlets, including the *Times*, the AP, *The Wall Street Journal*, *ABC News*, *The Guardian*, and *Al Jazeera*," said David Zweig, an independent journalist who tried to do his own investigative reporting on the story, believing the civilian death statistics to be false. "Not one reporter from any of these outlets replied to my queries. This was their reporting, on perhaps the most contentious news story in the world at the moment. And none of them would respond with the source behind what they had written."[214]

There was also the tragic fire that killed civilians in a temporary housing facility in Rafah. It was yet another example of how combustible an urban battlefield Israel faces. The area was designated as a humanitarian corridor for the safety of civilians. The Israeli Air Force fired two small thirty-seven-pound bombs at a building in Rafah, targeting two Hamas senior commanders, both of whom were killed. The bombs were too small to ignite a blast radius that would have extended to the refugee site. The IDF could not have known that the two Hamas commanders had surrounded themselves with ammunition and bombs. A jeep was filled with explosives not far from where the airstrikes took place. It ignited a second blast, sparking a fire that spread all the way to the camp. Once again, however, if terrorists were not operating near civilians, this tragedy never would have occurred.

But none of that matters if Israel is one of the parties because the consolidated weight of storytelling and the most compelling plot lines will shift the blame to the Jewish state. The media reported the story as if the IDF was aiming at civilians who were located at the humanitarian corridor that Israel created itself to serve as a safe haven. Does that make any sense at all? The whole point of such a civilian compound was to transform human shields back into regular civilians. They weren't targeted. It was just another tragic manifestation of collateral damage—caused by Hamas always angling for proximity to civilians.[215]

We have seen the very same lazy, irresponsible reporting when it comes to civilian casualties, generally. *CNN* freely acknowledges that it received its total death toll numbers from the United Nations, the Palestinian Authority, or foreign aid agencies. Each of those entities freely admit that they got their numbers from the Gaza Media Office or Health Ministry. The United Nations conceded that it had no idea whether those numbers were reliable. Yet *CNN*, one of the world's foremost media brands, would cite the United Nations anyway rather than investigate further, confirm with sources, and report the truth.[216]

Even if the Health Ministry's civilian death toll numbers are to be believed, the charade behind the Al-Ahli Hospital bombing demonstrates that Hamas and Islamic Jihad are at least responsible for killing some civilians on their own with misfired rockets. It's an ugly twist on friendly fire because these terror groups are no friends of the Palestinian people. Iran reserves its most advanced precision-guided weaponry for Hezbollah, their fellow Shia Muslims. Hamas and Islamic Jihad were left with the scraps. They launch rockets at Israeli civilians indiscriminately with next to no GPS certainty as to where they might land, or whether they even make into Israeli air spare.[217]

The IDF has estimated that 9,500 Palestinian rockets were launched at Israel during the first month of the war. At least twelve percent, or more than one-thousand one-hundred, landed inside the Gaza Strip, which is consistent with earlier wars with Israel. But Hamas never admits to any of these misfires. It doesn't much matter to them if it's their rockets that take the lives of human shields. A kill is a kill, and Israel is to be blamed. Who knows how many hundreds of Palestinians were ultimately killed by their own countrymen who have consigned them to so many different kinds of miserable fates.

But even if the Health Ministry is accurately reporting the Palestinian death toll, and Israel is found responsible for every single Palestinian death, how would the combatant-to-noncombatant death ratio compare with other wars and battlefields?

Let's take the Health Ministry's numbers, as of December 2024, as a given: forty-four thousand. As noted, they make no distinction between terrorists and civilians. And the skeptical statistical experts I mentioned earlier believe that the seventy percent figure that gets reported for women and children is preposterous. Israel itself believes that it has killed twenty thousand terrorists, conservatively. That's nearly a ratio of one combatant for every one noncombatant, or civilian—1:1.

Let's look at the combatant to civilian ratio for other wars fought in that region, and under similar urban, asymmetric circumstances involving terrorists embedded among their people—whether they be the Taliban, al-Qaeda, or ISIS. How well did American-led Coalition Forces do in minimizing civilian casualties? In Afghanistan, the United States and its Coalition Allies killed roughly forty-two thousand civilians and sixty-four thousand combatants. In Iraq, the number was over 150,000 civilians and sixty-two thousand combatants. Against ISIS, the death toll of Iraqi civilians was 1,400, with a combatant to civilian ratio of 1:2.5.[218]

The death toll in Mosul, Iraq, is also an inapt comparison with Gaza. Hamas devoted ten years to building a military force of forty thousand combatants. The entire enclave has no other purposeful industry other than as a training ground for terrorism. Mosul was a real city that offered its residents more than suicide vests. Moreover, ISIS distinctively wears black—they *are* in uniform and thereby distinguishable from civilians. The Iraqis and Syrians have no love for these terrorists. Israeli troops are surrounded by civilians with great sympathy for Hamas. A terrorist in Gaza never goes anywhere without a civilian shield. And yet, the ratio of civilian deaths in Gaza is much lower than it was in Mosul.[219]

The United Nations and the European Union both estimate that in typical urban wartime settings, 90 percent of the casualties are civilians—which is essentially 9:1.[220] Looking at each of America's wars in Syria, Iraq, and Afghanistan, the *New York Times*, *Boston Globe* and the Watson Institute of Brown University concluded the ratio was four civilians for every combatant.

Israel's death toll ratio in Gaza is roughly 1:1—let's say even 2:1. The IDF deserves a global humanitarian medal, and not its condemnation. Given Hamas' penchant for inflated numbers, the civilian death rate might actually be lower! This is all the more remarkable given the suffocating density of the population in Gaza. Israel must be doing something right if one considers the close-quarters and voluntary presence of human shields.[221]

John Spencer, who teaches at West Point and served for twenty-five years as an infantry soldier with two combat tours in Iraq, finds the whole blame-shifting to Israel exasperating. Rather than being excoriated for its military operations in Gaza, Israel should be applauded for the considerable precautions it has taken to protect civilian life. The Jewish state is providing civilians with evacuation warnings in the very same buildings where it is hunting down terrorists! What other army in military history has telegraphed its whereabouts, revealed plans for its next maneuver and freely provided such information to the actual targets?

Despite the unique challenges Israel faces in its war against Hamas, Spencer wrote, "it has implemented more precautions to prevent civilian harm than any military in history—above and beyond what international law requires and more than the U.S. did in its wars in Iraq and Afghanistan."[222]

But in the end, even if you were to trust the Gaza Health Ministry's casualty figures and conclude that Israel is killing more civilians than it claims, one is still left with that imponderable moral question that does have a military solution: What can, and should, Israel do about it then? Recoil in horror and shrink away or press on with its national duty to protect its own citizens and sovereign right to be rid of Hamas—forever?

After two decades of experience with asymmetric warfare, governments and military experts have not come up with a better way to defeat an adversary as menacing as Hamas. The answer can't possibly be that Israeli civilians must pay the price for saving Palestinian civilians—that Jewish lives are worth less, or that Jews have a greater obligation to spare the lives of the people who wish them dead. Moreover, since no one, including Bob Simon back in 2014, has figured out how to go about sparing lives, should Israel do absolutely nothing to defend itself until the world figures it out?

Writing in *Foreign Policy*, the director at the RAND Corporation, Raphael Cohen, stated, "If the international community wants Israel to change strategies in Gaza, then it should offer a viable alternative strategy to Israel's announced goal of destroying Hamas in the Strip. And right now, that alternate strategy simply does not exist."[223]

CHAPTER 10

The Duty to Provide Humanitarian Aid and What Happens the "Day After"

That Hamas and its civilian henchmen initiated a war of aggression on October 7 is not in dispute. The same could be said of Hezbollah in Lebanon. Starting on October 8, 2023, the Lebanese Shi'ite terrorist group, funded by and doing the bidding of its fellow Shi'ites in Iran, attacked Israel. Those attacks never abated throughout Israel's war in the south. From the first days of the October 7 War, Israel was strained to fight on two fronts. Daily airstrikes forced sixty thousand Israelis to evacuate their homes in northern Israel.

Beginning in the fall of 2024, when the fighting in Gaza receded, Israel decided to strike more aggressively at Hezbollah. That resulted in a bit of clever counterespionage and wartime derring-do in the form of walkie-talkies and beepers rigged with explosives. This simultaneous assassination out of science fiction eliminated nearly all of Hezbollah's senior commanders. In an earlier assassination, Israel killed Hezbollah's longtime titular head, the murderous cleric, Hassan Nasrallah.[224]

On both of those fronts, Article 51 of the United Nations Charter entitled Israel to abolish these threats to its southern and northern borders, pursuant to its inherent right to self-defense. The statements made by Hamas leaders that they were planning future attacks of the same magnitude, provided even greater latitude to do what was necessary to bring this war, and Hamas itself, to an end. It cannot be forgotten that Hamas crossed Israel's border, invaded its nation, and violated its sovereignty. It then proceeded to commit heinous, unimaginable, and unforgivable acts against Israeli infants, teenage girls, and the elderly. The military campaigns in both Gaza and Lebanon constituted just wars.

Where Israel has come under criticism, and not for the first time, is the manner in which it has been fighting. Its success rate is too good. The collateral damage it leaves behind is too high. In a world that demands equity for people of dark skin, there, apparently, must be dead Jews to even the score.

The world has curiously shown little interest in the fate of Lebanese civilians, however. One can surmise two reasons for that: the Lebanese are not Palestinians, and only Palestinian death evokes global outrage; and unlike Gazans, when you warn a Lebanese civilian that his building will soon be destroyed, he grabs his family and finds shelter elsewhere.

What a novel concept.

One person who did express concern about civilians, specifically in Hezbollah's orbit, was Michael Walzer himself. Curiously, Walzer, who agreed that Israel's military response to Hamas and Hezbollah's aggression in Gaza and Lebanon, respectively, constituted a just war, was of a different opinion when it came to Israel's covert espionage operation with those exploding cell phones and walkie-talkies. In Walzer's view, Israel failed to minimize the risk to civilians who may have been standing nearby an unlucky Hezbollah terrorist. In an article he published in the *Times* shortly after, he deemed the entire operation to be reckless and a breach of the wartime obligation to mitigate civilian harm. The killing or maiming of a civilian in such a situation crossed the line into the gray area of *jus in bello*—constituting an unjust manner of conducting war.

"[T]he attacks..." Walzer wrote, "came when the operatives were not operating; they had not been mobilized and they were *not militarily engaged.* Rather, they were at home with their families, sitting in cafes, shopping in food markets—among civilians who were randomly killed and injured."[225]

Walzer seemingly wants it both ways. He recognizes that Just War Theory, which he is often associated with, depends on making distinctions between combatants and civilians, which is nearly impossible to do when Islamic terrorists conflate those categories into a single fighting force. If he is right, and he is right, then it is the rare moment when Hezbollah commanders are *not* "militarily engaged." Their entire lives, every waking breath, is dedicated to killing Jews and infidels.

Surely Walzer realizes that Islamic terrorism is a twenty-four-hour job. Unlike office workers, terrorists are always on the clock. If Israel believed that terrorists were faithful family men who never miss dinner with their children, they would have made sure not to detonate those five thousand devices between the hours 6 to 8 PM. Actually, Israel's intelligence service, Mossad, sent encrypted messages that set off those explosions at 3:30 PM.

The whole point was to schedule the blasts when it was most likely that those in possession of boobytrapped phones and pagers would answer them. But given the dirty but faithful business of terrorism, there probably would never be a time when they wouldn't.

The insurmountable problem with going to war against fanatical Islamists is that Israel has no way of knowing when a terrorist is not standing next to family members or civilians. Given the ubiquity of human shields, the IDF must conclude that there is no time of day or night when terrorists distance themselves from their favorite form of protection. Remember, they kept Israeli hostages chained to beds in adjoining rooms. As long as Islamist terror groups devote their days to killing Jews, Israel can't be held responsible for the precise whereabouts of the people who want them dead and with whom they keep the most company.

Walzer is essentially saying: it's better to be safe than sorry. Don't even consider an Operation Radio Shack because a civilian might be present. But in a warzone teeming with civilians, generally, Walzer's logic would require exactly what Israel's enemies are saying: no targeting of terrorists because they are always surrounded by civilians, and casualties of war are not permissible in Gaza.

Under the principles of proportionality, the military advantage of taking five thousand terrorists out of commission clearly overrides the accidental killing of some civilians.

It is Israel's moral duty to place a priority on the safety of its own people. Walzer knows that Israel is not required to forfeit opportunities to win a just war simply because its adversary makes it impossible to distinguish combatants from noncombatants. The military necessity remains vital and can't be ignored. The risk to civilians is always present, largely because Hamas and Hezbollah have made it so, no matter what Israel does to try to minimize that risk.

When the Western world acknowledges Israel's right to self-defense, is it just lip service? It should mean that Israel has the sovereign right to ensure that its people will never experience an October 7 attack again. Israel's allies surely can't reserve the right to dictate how Israel is to achieve victory. Acknowledging that Hamas must be eradicated is meaningless if the world allows Hamas to fight dirty and tie Israel's hands in meeting the threat.

As of late March, 2025, of the two-hundred and fifty hostages taken, under sixty remain captive—either in tunnels, or the homes of civilians, and most of them are already dead. The entire nation of Israel has been left traumatized. The savagery of October 7 speaks directly to the justness of this war. The shock it registered must be equal to the retribution Israel seeks.

Given the enormity of October 7, and the celebration from Gaza's civilian population—in spitting upon half-naked hostages, dragging corpses through cheering streets, treating the return of some of the emaciated hostages like a high school pep rally—and evidence that thousands of them took part in some facets of this war, what obligation is Israel under to provide humanitarian aid to their mortal enemies who, frankly, don't deserve it? Morality aside, what demands does international humanitarian law make of the Israelis?

The landscape of Gaza is now a place of utter devastation. Yes, Israeli firepower made it so, but a democratically elected and wildly popular Hamas brought this upon the Palestinian people. The nation fighting in self-defense surely can't be thinking simultaneously about rebuilding what it had just destroyed.

But soon after the October 7 massacre, nations and NGOs demanded that Israel make sure that Gazans have enough food, water, and electricity. As a reward for butchering Israeli babies, is Israel expected to ensure that Palestinian babies are well fed? Never before in the annals of siege warfare has a nation been held to clean up whatever it just broke and give aid and comfort to those with so much blood on their hands.

Is this what the British did for the Germans during World War II, or the United States with Japan, Vietnam, Afghanistan, and Iraq?

Much of the criticism against Israel has to do with the allegation that it has been deliberately withholding aid. This accusation is also being applied to the genocide charge.

A report from the World Health Organization decried that there was a severe shortage of food in Gaza with "a strong likelihood that famine is imminent in areas within the northern Gaza Strip," where Israel was concentrating its operations at the end of 2024.[226] The report cited data showing that by October 2024, the average number of trucks entering Gaza Strip was only fifty-eight per day, while before the war began, monitors with the World Food Programme estimated that five hundred commercial and aid trucks entered Gaza each day.

If true, that's a severe deficit, but is Israel to blame?

The Biden administration gave Israel a thirty-day ultimatum to increase humanitarian assistance allowed into Gaza. Failing to do so, Biden warned, would result in restrictions on military assistance and weapons deliveries. Israel apparently also missed deadlines on similar obligations requested in a letter from Secretary of State Antony Blinken and Defense Secretary Lloyd Austin, demanding that Israel ramp up its aid assistance to three hundred and fifty trucks per day. Its data, supplied by the United Nations, showed that only seventy-one trucks were entering Gaza each day.[227]

But even the Biden administration has acknowledged false claims of famine in Gaza. When the Famine Early Warning Systems Network (FEWS Net) released a report in late December 2024 alleging famine in northern Gaza, falsely stating that sixty-five thousand to seventy-five thousand individuals were starving, United States Ambassador Jack Lew angrily denied the report, accusing FEWS of "causing confusion,...rel[ying] on data that is outdated and inaccurate. We have worked closely with the Government of Israel and the UN... and it is now apparent that the civilian population in that part of Gaza is in the range of 7,000-15,000, not 65,000-75,000."[228]

No one seems to mind that FEWS acknowledges that it issued these findings without hard data, relying instead "on extrapolation, inference, empirical evidence, logic, and expert judgment."[229]

If a human rights agency is going to accuse a nation of committing a crime as horrific as mass starvation, shouldn't they have been obligated to look at verifiable numbers instead of self-serving, bias-ridden guess work? Apparently not when that nation is the Jewish state. This isn't even the first time FEWS acted so recklessly and irresponsibly. In June 2024, the United Nations Famine Review Committee, comprised of food security and nutritional experts, rejected a false report from FEWS.

Israel alleges that Hamas has, throughout this war, confiscated aid intended for the Gazan people and used it for their own fighters. The *New York Times* reported as recently as November 2024 that convoys of trucks carrying aid have been "violently looted." The trucks came to a halt when their tires became target practice for AK-47-toting terrorists. Pointing assault rifles at the drivers, terrorists demanded that they unload what they were carrying. Some were shot. UNRWA reported that one hundred and nine trucks were confiscated upon reaching the Kerem Shalom border crossing in southern Gaza. As few as eleven trucks arrived at their intended destinations.[230]

One of UNWRA's own tweets, since deleted, complained that Hamas seized fuel and medical equipment from UNWRA's storage facilities that were intended for hospitals and civilians.[231] A Palestinian social media influencer, Hamza Howidy, living in the Gaza Strip throughout the war, desperately wondered, "Why is the media ignoring what is going on in central and southern Gaza? Hamas is assassinating Gazans, particularly tribe leaders, in order to deter anyone other than Hamas from delivering humanitarian relief and participating in Gaza."[232]

American college students and Marxist antisemites are marching on streets carrying posters that read: "We are Hamas!" and "We love your rockets!" What manner of psychotic love are we talking about here? Is terrorism truly becoming a career ambition among those who attend Ivy League universities?

Here's something else the legacy media didn't feel was "fit to print" because it reflected so poorly on a terrorist organization bent on wiping out the Jewish people. Hamas actually fired a projectile at a UNICEF humanitarian aid convoy. Yes, when Hamas wasn't stealing aid, it was destroying humanitarian aid while in transit. In coordination with Israel, the trucks were seeking to reunite children from northern Gaza Strip with their families in the south. Howidy observed, "[The attack on the] UN aid workers…demonstrate[s] that Hamas is determined to destroy the humanitarian situation in Gaza and is willing to sacrifice thousands of lives in order to pressure Israel to end the war so they can survive."[233]

Let us all hope that Hamza Howidy is still alive.

Terrorist organizations in Gaza have complete run of the place. Nothing happens without them knowing about it, or actually doing it. The humanitarian aid supplied by the international community is not fulfilling the purpose for which it was intended. That's because the aid is being co-opted by terrorist groups, themselves.[234]

One of the few hostages who survived his captivity and returned to Israel near the end of the second negotiated ceasefire, Eli Sharabi, testified before United Nations Security Council on

March 20, 2025—specifically about how the international aid was ultimately used.

"I saw Hamas terrorists carrying boxes with the UN and UNRWA emblems on them into the tunnel," Sharabi said. "Dozens and dozens of boxes, paid by your government, feeding terrorists who tortured me and murdered my family. They would eat many meals a day…and we never received any of it… Hamas eats like kings while hostages starve."

Sharabi weighed just ninety-seven pounds when he was finally released.

His indictment continued: "Since Oct. 7, you have passed seventy-seven resolutions…[but]…not passed a single resolution condemning Hamas.… You have debated humanitarian assistance without acknowledging the humanitarian catastrophe Hamas is deliberately inflicting on the hostages."[235]

Even though Hamas and the other gangs of Gaza may be stealing most of the humanitarian aid set aside for civilians, it is not necessarily true that the aid situation in Gaza is as dire as the mainstream media, and the United Nations, is portraying it to be. Humanitarian aid, and its alleged shortfall, is yet another thing that can be pinned on Israel—even if the deprivations don't actually exist.

A leading expert in behavioral economics, Ron Kivetz, ran the numbers and relied on data supplied by Israel's Coordinator of Government Activities in the Territories (COGAT). He concluded that between November 1, 2023 and May 20, 2024, Gazans actually received over two-thousand tons of food each day. This amounted to more than three-thousand calories per person each day, which, according to the UN's World Food Programme (WFP), surpassed one-hundred and thirty percent of the population's daily dietary needs.

Yet, the endlessly propagated lie of mass starvation, which has been taken before the ICC, is perceived as true simply because it gets repeated so often. Negative news delivered in a visual manner tends to grab headlines and become widely shared.[236]

It clearly suckered the Biden administration and other manipulated Western nations. They all cling to a lie. The data was there all along for anyone who bothered to look. After all, the only evidence of emaciated human beings belonged to freed hostages, and not Gazans. (Photos that purport to show malnourished Gazan children appear to be recycled from other parts of the world.)

Right from the very beginning, the United Nations watchdog, UN Watch, observed that "as of April 4, 2024, approximately six months into the war, some 13,000 trucks of food have entered Gaza, which amounts to 272,000 tons of food, more than double the required amount according to the WFP. Moreover, while the total number of trucks entering Gaza since before October 7th has decreased overall, the number of food trucks entering Gaza since October 7th has doubled."[237]

The UN's Integrated Food Security Phase Classification (IPC) issued a report on June 4, 2024, well into the war, concluding that famine in Gaza was not "plausible" because there was no "supporting evidence" indicating mass starvation of any kind. Moreover, only thirty-two deaths had been attributable to malnutrition, twenty-eight of whom were children under five-years-old.[238]

Not a single international human rights or humanitarian aid agency, nor the mainstream media that magnified the lies, have acknowledged that they either got the story wrong, or more simply, falsely manufactured a crisis. With full knowledge of the truth, the *New York Times*, on June 18, 2024, reported that Gaza "is facing extreme levels of hunger." Yet another IPC report, issued just a week after the *Times*' story, on June 25, concluded that the food supply in Gaza had actually increased.[239]

And, yet, the International Criminal Court has issued arrest warrants for Israeli Prime Minister Benjamin Netanyahu and former Defense Minister Yoav Gallant, specifically charging them with, among other things, the deliberate starvation of the Gazan people as a method of warfare. (Syrian President Bashar al-Assad, having fled his country with the blood of five hundred thousand of his former citizens still on his hands, many of whom were gassed with chemical weapons, isn't especially worried that the ICC will issue an arrest warrant for him).

These frantic charges against Israeli leaders require a proving of intent that Netanyahu is fighting a war specifically to starve Gazans, and that he is "willfully impeding relief." The ICC knows there is no actual evidence that a single Gazan has died of starvation as a result of Israel's border policies. And there is even less evidence that Israel is fighting this war to intentionally inflict starvation on the Palestinian people.[240]

The entire case against Netanyahu and Gallant is legally baseless and factually groundless. It also charges them with crimes against humanity and deliberately targeting civilians. No leader of a democratic country has ever been so charged, and it sets a dangerous precedent whenever a law-abiding nation goes to war against a nonstate actor in an urban environment swarming with civilians. Any resulting collateral damage, even if minimal, will give the ICC a legal pretext to prosecute Western nations.

As law professor Eugene Kontorovich eloquently put it, "The ICC was already a failing institution when it seized onto the oldest hatred to revive its relevance. Now it has issued arrest warrants against leaders of a democratic non-member state for crimes that did not happen, in a state that does not exist, against leaders who have overseen the most humane urban war in modern history."[241]

The United Nations persists in blaming Israel for famine in Gaza while completely ignoring countries like Sudan, where more than eighteen million people face starvation, two hundred twenty thousand are severely malnourished, and seven thousand new mothers are likely to die in the coming months.[242] For instance, in 2022, as an example, the United Nations General Assembly passed fifteen anti-Israel resolutions, while passing only thirteen for the rest of the world.

As for Israel's obligation to supply Gaza with humanitarian aid, on an ordinary week in December 2024, COGAT, the agency within the Israeli Defense Ministry that oversees civilian policies in the West Bank and resolves logistical tensions in Gaza, reported that 242 trucks carrying 7,260 tons worth of flour entered Gaza, along with 600 tons of winter clothing, 120 tons of tents, 170 tons of medical equipment (including 75,800 doses of flu vaccines), and 125 tons of hygiene products.

Similarly, in yet another representative week, sixty-four patients were permitted to leave Gaza for medical treatment in Jordan, the United States, Romania, Spain, and Belgium, and sixty-six patients were transferred from Kamal Adwan and Shifa hospitals to other operational hospitals in Gaza. Five ambulances from the United Arab Emirates entered Gaza on December 2 through the Kerem Shalom border, and the COGAT facilitated the delivery of hundreds of crutches and wheelchairs into Gaza.

If one were to examine the humanitarian situation in Gaza honestly, the problem is not the availability of humanitarian aid or the amount of food and medical supplies that the enclave needs, or the number of trucks that Israel permits entry through border crossings infested with terrorists. Put simply, the issue comes down to distribution—why is the aid not getting to the people who need it?

Both Hamas and Israel accuse each other of creating the impasse. COGAT stated that more than one thousand five hundred aid trucks are anchored at Kerem Shalom, the main border crossing between Israel and the Gaza Strip. Israel is happy to allow them access into Gaza, but the drivers are too frightened to navigate through this nightmare of an urban warzone. And who can blame them? All sorts of criminal enterprises lurk within the shattered concrete, pockmarked streets and hollowed out buildings. Hamas will pirate the trucks. The IDF will fire upon terrorists scavenging around those supply chains. The United Nations has declared Gaza the deadliest place in the world for humanitarian aid workers. Since the war began on October 7, least 250 have been killed.[243]

Whose burden then is it to undertake the risk of delivering the aid? International law seems to suggest that it depends on who is determined to be the occupying power on the ground—"Territory is considered occupied when it is actually placed under the authority of the hostile army… [It must] take measures to restore and ensure, as far as possible, public order and safety" and "the provision of food and medical care to the population."[244]

Good luck answering that.

Israel officially withdrew from Gaza in 2005. Jews haven't lived in the enclave ever since. It has no "effective control over the territory." The scope and success of Hamas' surprise attack on October 7 is pretty clear evidence that Israel is neither in control nor in charge of the region. It is too busy trying to distinguish snipers from civilians.[245]

Israel's position is simple: Does it look like we have control over Gaza? Everywhere we turn a mortal danger is present. We aren't policing streets or feeding the people. That job belongs to the popularly elected government in Gaza, Hamas, the same entity that is stealing the food designated for people who will soon assume their positions as human shields.

British columnist Melanie Phillips rationally stated, "[W]hy should Israel be held responsible for providing Gaza with humanitarian assistance? Israel has been under bombardment from the coastal enclave for two decades. Gaza's population elected Hamas to rule them. Opinion polling consistently reveals that even among those who now hate Hamas, the vast majority support the killing of Israelis."[246] Raphael Cohen, the RAND Corporation director put it more bluntly: "If the Israeli military takes over distributing humanitarian aid to Gaza, they will likely lose soldiers in the process. And so Israelis are asking why should their boys die providing aid to someone who wants to kill them."[247]

Why, indeed? What does international humanitarian law require under the fraught and extreme circumstances of Gaza? Israel already warns the enemy where it will be conducting its combat and bombing operations. Now it must also expose its soldiers to certain death by requiring them to drive trucks inside Gaza and distribute humanitarian aid, knowing that, in all likelihood, it will be stolen by Hamas, anyway? Under international law, the Fourth Geneva Convention, and the ground rules of siege warfare, given that this aid is ultimately being diverted to feed terrorists, Israel isn't obligated to allow *any* humanitarian assistance at all—and yet it has been doing so since the war began.[248]

Now we come to another gray area that has been arrayed against Israel all throughout this war: Can a country order its military to pursue a scorch-the-earth strategy, as the Israelis have done in Gaza, without first contemplating what the "Day

After" would look like? Did President Abraham Lincoln and his most ruthless generals, Ulysses S. Grant and William Tecumseh Sherman, plan Reconstruction while they were burning down Atlanta? Did Reconstruction mean acquiring actual hammers and nails to reconstruct the South before General Lee surrendered at Appomattox? Was the Marshall Plan already in place before the bombings over Dresden and Hiroshima?

Of course not. But once more, Israel is being held to a higher standard, and very few are intellectually honest enough to at least acknowledge that the world has never placed such laughably absurd demands on any other nation.

Rules for Israel, alone: "Don't break anything unless you have plans to rebuild it. Don't focus so much on winning the war and eliminating Gaza. Spend more time with city planners and construction crews on how best to restore the Strip and give the Palestinians a chance to regroup and hate you even more."

To rebuild and regroup it into what, exactly, on the Day After? Israel would love to have a thriving and majestic Macao or Singapore to its south. What it doesn't want is yet another reconstituted training ground for terrorists, financed by Iran and Qatar, dedicated to eliminating the Jewish state. Why should it be contemplating any Day After plan until there is some reassurance that the Palestinians are hoping to build hotels along the Mediterranean rather than subterranean tunnels?

Most military experts would probably say that this is precisely what international humanitarian law requires. "You break it; you fix it." But then again, none of these "experts" in military doctrine have ever faced terrorists on their home urban, trip-wired turf.

It's one thing to say you have a plan for the Day After. It is something else entirely for it to have any hope of succeeding. For instance, President Joe Biden repeatedly expressed his desire to see the Palestinian Authority take control of Gaza. Perhaps a neighboring Arab nation, along with UN Peacekeepers can help establish a buffer-zone to satisfy Israel's national security concerns. All that matters is that Hamas does not emerge from the wreckage.

But that's no easy task or deliverable wish. The Palestinian Authority (PA) is corrupt and has little support from the people of the West Bank. Those Palestinians now worship Hamas after October 7. They, too, have only held one democratic election for president since 2005. Fatah controls the PA, and it probably would not be able to win another election. Gazans already chose Hamas over Fatah in the 2007 election. There has not been a second election in Gaza, either. It is doubtful that Gazans would suddenly favor Fatah. So, who or what, exactly, was President Biden envisioning? Because neither of those options would be acceptable to Israel.

Israeli Prime Minister Benjamin Netanyahu has stated, emphatically, "I will not allow Israel to repeat the mistake of Oslo." The Oslo Accords created the Palestinian Authority, which is responsible for putting bounties on the heads of Israelis by rewarding convicted or martyred terrorists with lifetime salaries, lump-sum cash payments, stipends, civil service jobs, and benefits for family members. "After the great sacrifice of our civilians and our soldiers, I will not allow the entry into Gaza of those who educate for terrorism, support terrorism and finance terrorism," he said.[249]

What Netanyahu has in mind is for Israel to maintain control over Gaza, militarily, but not necessarily politically. He doesn't care who runs the place so long as it's not another iteration of Palestinian terrorism. But he wants Israel to maintain its own security presence. What that will look like, and whether it will require displacing Palestinians in order to create a sufficient buffer along the border, is anyone's guess. That will not go over well. Many will instantly decry yet another variation of an Israeli occupation.

What also hasn't been well received is the idea circulated by newly elected American president, Donald Trump. He wishes to transfer the entire two million plus Gazan population to neighboring Arab nations. Taking Palestinians in and integrating them among existing Arab and Muslim citizens has never been the will of any of these nations—Egypt and Jordan, especially.

These countries, all theocracies or autocracies, have enough problems controlling their own populations. Adding Islamists with a demonstrated penchant for terrorism is not a very appealing immigration story.

And Trump has been silent on whether he envisions the new Gaza as a Palestinian homeland. He sees the Strip like a developer looking to convert a dilapidated slum into a true Shangri-la—a paradise on Earth rather than the one Islamists aspire to, which can only be visited upon death. What we know about Trump from his first term in office is that unlike his many predecessors, Palestinian petulance does not move him. He does not believe that the economic and diplomatic success of the region depends on a political resolution to the Conflict. Placating Palestinian demands is not a priority.

Remember that it was Trump's first administration that was responsible for the Abraham Accords. He already once tried convincing Palestinians to accept a Peace Through Prosperity plan. It would have made them among the wealthiest Arabs in the world. The plan was less grandiose on political solutions, however. As they had done four prior times in the past, Palestinians rejected the plan on arrival. Trump might be of the view that they lost their opportunity, especially after PA President

Mahmoud Abbas lied to him in the Oval Office in denying that he used American funds to compensate martyrs.[250]

Before Trump was elected, David Makovsky, a fellow with the Washington Institute for Near East Policy, believed that the United States would demand more from Israel when it comes to the cleanup and rebuilding of Gaza. "The Americans want to know, like, OK, you have a military strategy. I get that. And maybe a very reasonable one, but tell me how it leads to political outcomes? The outcome is no Hamas. Okay. That's good. That's necessary. But is it sufficient?"[251]

The *Wall Street Journal* reported that the United Arab Emirates, one of the signatories to the Abraham Accords, might agree to help fund the rebuilding of Gaza, but only if they see a meaningful pathway to a two-state solution.

And therein lies the problem. Who is Israel to negotiate with? What partner in peace actually exists? Two generations of Gazans have been indoctrinated with anti-Israel dogma. Children see maps that erase the Jewish state. They sing songs about killing Jews. They do math exercises that incorporate subtracting Jewish life from the Middle East. They learn how to carry assault rifles and slit throats. The PA pays salaries to those who commit murder and violence against Jews. Once such a terrorist is freed from an Israeli prison, he or she is guaranteed a high-level civil service appointment.

Not exactly a recipe for peaceful coexistence. There is no leadership class among Palestinians that has accepted the reality that Israel isn't going anywhere. And there is no training ground for civil servants to learn how cities and states are governed and operate. A background in munitions is not helpful for the person suddenly placed in charge of clean water and sewage. Knowing the fine points of designing a suicide vest is not a transferable skill in operating an energy grid or building schools not focused on antisemitic indoctrination.

There cannot be a Two-State Solution when one side demands that there be just one, and that state can't have any Jews in it. Given the long history of Palestinian rejectionism, dating back to 1947, it is folly to believe that the Palestinians possess any of the tools and tact necessary for true statehood. They can't make peace with the idea of living beside Jews. Claims of a "right of return," or the recovery of homes in greater Israel—in cities like Haifa and Jaffa—that now belong to Jews, are nonstarters. There cannot and never will be an Arab state on the same land that incorporates what is now a Jewish state.

It is important to remember that at the conclusion of World War II, Germany and Japan did not magically transform themselves overnight into liberal democracies. You don't go from bombings over Dresden and Hiroshima to instantly pacified, democratized countries. It took the Nuremberg Trials, the Tokyo War Crimes Tribunal, the Marshall Plan, and years of re-education to purge Germans and Japanese of their idolatry of Chancellor Hitler and Emperor Hirohito, and to fully reject the authoritarian and empire-seeking ideologies that led them to national ruin.

The Day After, realistically, won't be accomplished in a day.

Given the success of the Palestinian PR strategy in turning half the world against Israel, as well as transforming the Democratic Party into a hotbed of anti-Zionism, they might be excused for holding out hope for the end of Israel. Palestinians have shown an enormous capacity to simply wait. They don't grow weary from refugee camps; they don't seem to mind consigning their grandchildren to the same fate.[252] They can grit their teeth and clutch keys to homes that once existed until they are toothless and their hands bleed. It won't change the existence of a Jewish state exactly where they don't want it to be. What they lack in statesmanship they more than make up in patience and stamina—never accepting defeat, even after they are thoroughly, repeatedly, and resoundingly defeated. The realities of the situation never seem to sink in.

General David Petraeus served as a four-star general in several high-ranking positions for both NATO and United States forces in Afghanistan and Iraq, along with a stint as director of the CIA. When the war in Iraq started to shift in America's favor, Petraeus was at the center of that successful war strategy. It was called, "The Surge," and it included an entirely new feature, counterinsurgency, which he developed into a Field Manual.[253] It was designed to be highly effective when the battlefield was irregular, and the warfare asymmetric, involving nonstate actors.

What counterinsurgency seeks to accomplish is to win the "hearts and minds" of the civilian population, a strategy that is as much political, economic, and psychological as it is focused on military gains. It is the art of public diplomacy, adapted to wartime conditions where diplomats are scarce. For instance, soldiers handing out candy to children, restoring movie theaters, and reopening universities—even doling out money—is a way to win a war by disconnecting the enemy insurgents from the people without having to endure a conventional battle. Bribery works in warfare, it seems. The people who are suffering the most from the ravages of war need to be incentivized to reject the terrorists they have long come to know. Any separation in national bonds is good. Assassinations are part of counterinsurgency, too. It is not solely a pacified way to win a war.

Would something like that work in Gaza? Are hearts and minds winnable? Gaza has become synonymous with dead civilians who have presumptively sworn their allegiance to terror outfits such as Hamas and Islamic Jihad. Polling shows the strong religious and political belief system Gazans have adopted in their embrace of terror. There are abiding loyalties to Hamas. Could they be persuaded to look elsewhere, to see that terrorism is their enemy, not the Israelis?

Perhaps it's worth a try, but I would not hold out much hope. The very same people who are comfortable martyring their children and refusing to flee when warned of an oncoming airstrike are not likely to be motivated by candy, an IMAX theater, cash payments and reopened universities. The Palestinians rejected Trump's Peace for Prosperity Plan. Their dreams, apparently, can't be bought off. Gazans have continued to show that they are a breed apart. They have certain olive trees in mind that they insist beautified their forsaken homes, and won't accept anything less than their complete return.

Are there Gazans, and Palestinians more broadly, who are ready to imagine co-existence with Israel? A complete overhaul of values and expectations? The transformation of Gazan society into a reimagined future? If there are such people, counterinsurgency techniques might be helpful in opening hearts and minds and gestures of good will might be become well received, as they were during the Surge.

An entirely new generation of Gazans would have to somehow emerge out of the anti-Zionist ruins of Gaza. Some other nation is going to need to do in Gaza what was successfully done in Germany and Japan after World War II—namely, assist in deprogramming a fully indoctrinated population. All that pernicious hatred for the existence of a Jewish state must somehow be expelled from the region.

Palestinians will have to undergo a radical transformation in their worldviews. And they must begin to see possibilities for their future in a more conciliatory, life-affirming light.

CONCLUSION

Beyond Proportionality: Why Israel Must Set Aside the Laws of War to Establish Deterrence

If you are a parent with an infant at home, what took place in southern Israel on October 7, 2023, must have affected you deeply. Imagine if your neighbor, who had already made it known that he or she denied your existence and wished for your house to be burned down with you and your family in it, broke into your home and slit your baby's throat.

I will allow that to sink in for a moment. It deserves contemplation. I fear most people have not given the reality of such barbarism very much thought. But that is precisely the barbarism that those who attended the Nova Music Festival, or who happened to live in small, ransacked *kibbutzim* on that fateful October 7 morning, experienced.

If you are a father with teenage daughters, there was barbarism for you, as well. Imagine if your similarly monstrous next-door-neighbor invaded your home with a rapacious group of his male relatives and friends, and brutally gang raped your daughter—and made you watch. When finished, they mutilated her breasts and genitalia with knives and machine guns. Can you imagine surviving something like that—as in, psychologically survive such an assault on your flesh and blood? One would have to acclimate to an eternity of agonizing, nightmarish sleep.

I have daughters. To the Israeli fathers of October 7 who live with the knowledge that this was the last miserable, unimaginable moments of their daughters' lives, I am in awe of your resilience and courage. I am quite sure I could not endure it.

The next time some pink-haired progressive or anti-American Muslim is shouting "I am Hamas!" or "Globalize the Intifada!" or "Death to America!" please, at the very least, assume a facial expression that signals an appropriate level of disgust.

It is with these vulgarities in mind that the obvious must be stated: The laws of war were fashioned by military strategists who lived in civilized nations, men who believed that even in war there must be rules. There was honor in going to battle to defend a nation, but wars must be fought honorably—especially when facing adversaries committed to following the same set of rules. The laws of war provide a framework for how civilized nations can resolve their disputes, even if it requires going to war.

Nonstate actors, however, terrorists—who abide by no rules at all, who have no pretenses about civility, and who believe themselves to be exempt from the laws of war—should expect that the civilized nations they face in battle will set at least some of those rules aside, too. It's only fair, it is often necessary, and to do anything less is a betrayal of one's own people.

I conclude this book with those indelible images of what occurred on October 7, 2023, and how impossible it is to imagine yourself confronted with and forever changed by such agonies. I would like these dark thoughts to stay with you. But I am also reminded of what happened when the leader of the progressive movement in the United States, back in 2008, first visited Israel, and what he had to say about fathers.

I am not referring to Bernie Sanders, but Barack Obama, the true holder of the progressive mantle in America. When Obama was running for president, he made his first visit to Israel, the summer before the election—a sideways campaign stop. He had already sewed up the Democratic nomination. The Democratic Party, at least back then, was solidly supportive of the Jewish state—as it had been since President Harry Truman became the first foreign leader to congratulate Israel on its independence and welcomed it to the family of nations.

Obama wanted to burnish his foreign policy credentials, but mostly he needed to reassure American Jews, many of whom are Democrats, that a biracial man from Hawaii and Indonesia understood the moral purpose and strategic necessity of Israel, a nation created a mere three years after the liberation of Auschwitz. A majority of Americans have always supported Israel on a bipartisan basis. He certainly was not going to deviate from the party line, or drastically alter American foreign policy when it came to the only democracy in the Middle East.

At least not then.

But something happened to Obama when he visited the Holy Land. Israel has been known to have such effects on the least likely of people. There are many wonders, and eyesores, of the Jewish state. At the time, Obama was a very young father of two small daughters. Unexpectedly, probably improvising from the scripted campaign materials, he responded to something he saw in Israel as a protective father would and should, and not as a cynical, gladhanding candidate.

Israeli officials escorted him around the country but made sure to schedule a visit to the southern city of Sderot. Ironically, it happens to be located not far from where the Nova Music

Festival took place fifteen years later. These are the southern most cities, villages, and *kibbutzim* along Israel's border with Gaza.

Sderot has been target practice for Hamas and Islamic Jihad since 2007. The people who live there have grown accustomed to hearing sirens that cause them to enter outside bomb shelters and indoor safe rooms, or duck behind concrete barriers dredged along roads built for this very purpose. Obama spoke with Israeli families who told him that Sderot has faced tens of thousands of rockets in the time they have lived there. One such family had a small boy who lost a leg to one of those Qassam rockets.

When the visit was over, Obama held an impromptu press conference. He had prepared some remarks, and planned to take questions. His trip was already a success. The Israelis enjoyed meeting the charismatic young American. But it came as a surprise to many who were skeptical of his support for Israel when Obama read these words out loud:

"The first job of any nation state is to protect its citizens. And so, I can assure you that if—I don't even care if I was a politician. If somebody was sending rockets into my house where my two daughters sleep at night, I'm going to do everything in my power to stop that. And I would expect Israelis to do the same thing."[254]

We know the story from there. The candidate won the presidency, and almost instantly upon entering the Oval Office, forgot all about his visit to Israel. The memory of Sderot, a small city teeming with vulnerability, obviously did not stay with him. During his second term in office, when Israel was at war with Hamas in 2014, Obama repeatedly warned Israel to "show restraint," "de-escalate the fighting," and seek avenues for a "ceasefire."

How soon he forgot.

Under international law and Article 51 of the United Nations Charter, Israel's right to self-defense against Hamas is virtually limitless. October 7 was a genocidal assault for the ages. Given Israel's small population, it is the equivalent death toll of fifty thousand Americans—which translates to roughly seventeen 9/11's. Factor in the decapitations and gang raping and the promise to renew this savage attack "again and again," Israel should never have to stop the fighting in Gaza if that is what it takes to put an end of Hamas and Islamic Jihad, and to choke the appetite for terrorism out of the people.

All they must do is ensure that in its wartime conduct, what it chooses to target achieves appropriate military objectives, steps are taken to minimize civilian death, intelligence exists to justify the attack, and humanitarian aid is permitted.

Israel has the law on its side even if most of the world is always against them and is willing to misapply the law.

The Jewish state has been in compliance with each of the relevant doctrinal principles. It should be granted the same right of every other sovereign nation to eliminate the threat that Hamas and Islamic Jihad have posed for nearly twenty years. Israel should have been able to engage in a just war without interference and browbeating, without sanctimonious moralizing and hypocritical double standards.

These have been strange times for Jews all around the world. Truly shocking episodes of antisemitic fervor have dominated the headlines and sullied the streets throughout Western Europe, the United States, Canada, and Australia—with almost daily occurrences of menacing violence masquerading as free speech. Large demonstrations throughout the West have occurred—marching through cities and creating encampments on college campuses—roving gangs wearing masks or shielding their identities with keffiyeh scarves. The World Zionist

Organization cited data showing an 800 percent increase in antisemitic incidents in Sweden, a 680 percent increase in Spain, a 450 percent increase in the Netherlands, a 442 percent increase in the UK, and a 433 percent increase in France.[255] It has been reported that half the world's population now has a negative view of Israel. What can Israel possibly do to improve its global standing and public approval ratings by means other than ceasing to exist?

It appears that many of the protestors are Muslims, but given the cowardice of their anonymity, it's difficult to know for sure. What we do know is that large numbers of Muslim immigrants were foolishly allowed into Western nations where they formed alliances with leftist radicals, sharing in a mutual contempt for Western civilization. Israel is now beside the point.

Yet, they call for the death of Jews and the rape of Jewish daughters in London. Ransacking of Jewish businesses and homes in America. Desecration of synagogues globally. Upheavals on college campuses and the praising of Hamas—red hands becoming a metaphorical symbol of the desire for dead Jews.[256]

It simply won't stop. Before the year 2024 came to a close, a twenty-eight-year-old rabbi was kidnapped and murdered in Abu Dhabi by Iranian terrorists. An Israeli locksmith was murdered in Memphis. In Canada, eighty-five thousand students across thirteen universities went on strike calling for divestment from Israel. Pro-Hamas extremists in Montreal shouting "Globalize the Intifada!" vandalized Jewish stores and set cars on fire.

Anti-Israel rallying in Toronto featured mobs inciting violence against Jews while Jewish figures were torched in effigy. In New York and New Jersey, keffiyeh-masked hoodlums targeted Jewish homes, businesses, and schools. Hamas supporters in Greece hurled firebombs after burning Israeli and American flags. The Israeli Foreign Affairs Ministry in Greece warned

Israelis and Greek Jews to avoid wearing identifying symbols of Judaism.

Days after Jews were chased through the streets of Amsterdam, five Muslims were arrested in Belgium on November 10 for using social media to call for a "Jew Hunt" in the Jewish Quarter of Antwerp.[257] A terror threat was issued for Jewish travelers in Thailand. Dutch, French, and Irish Jews are shedding yarmulkes and Stars of David. Europeans are afraid to carry Israeli passports. Nine students from the University of Athens Law School are facing deportation for "disruptive anti-Israel demonstrations."[258]

In France, antisemitic incidents have risen by over 1,000 percent. Jews are removing mezuzahs from their doorways. They avoid taking Uber because it employs so many Muslim drivers. Some, acting out of complete desperation, have changed their surnames to avoid being targeted while receiving deliveries.[259] In 2024, 1,570 antisemitic incidents were recorded; in 2023, 1,676 incidents compared with 436 the prior year.[260] About 1,200 French Jews submitted applications to emigrate to Israel in 2023, an increase of 430 percent from 2022.

A man riding the Paris metro was photographed wearing a sports jersey with the words "Anti-Jew." Three men assaulted a Jewish woman in front of her home, reminding her that it was the one-year anniversary of October 7. An elderly Jewish woman was punched in the face, pushed to the ground, and kicked while the assailant said, "Dirty Jew, this is what you deserve." A kosher restaurant in Lyon was defaced with "Free Gaza" in red paint. An Algerian was arrested for trying to set fire to a synagogue in La Grande-Motte.

Perhaps most horrifying of all, a twelve-year-old Jewish girl was gang raped by three Muslim boys in a Paris suburb.

Similarly, a Jewish woman was beaten and raped, as "vengeance for Palestine."

The Anti-Defamation League reported that antisemitism in Germany has grown by 95 percent, although it believes that the number is much larger because Jews are afraid to report it. This following incident did get reported, however: on November 7, an under-seventeen Jewish soccer team was "chased and assaulted" by a gang of Muslim teenagers brandishing knives and sticks and screaming, "Free Palestine!"[261]

Meanwhile, over the past ten years, almost on a daily basis, the Chinese government has committed unspeakable crimes against a Muslim minority of one million people, the Uyghurs. During this time period, sixteen thousand mosques have been razed. The Uyghurs have been interned in concentration camps. They have been subjected to forced sterilizations and murder. But this is no civil war. The Uyghurs have never engaged in acts of aggression or terrorism. Their crime is entirely one of existence.

China's clear intent is to destroy a racial and ethnic group, which constitutes an actual genocide under the Genocide Convention. Yet, has anyone walked into a Chinese restaurant in San Francisco, Los Angeles, Chicago, or New York and screamed, "Shame!" and "Stop the Genocide!", or splattered walls and windows with red paint, or caused any form of public disturbance on behalf of the beleaguered Uyghurs?

What we do see, instead, is a worldwide crusade to end the one Jewish state. And for what: defending itself against terrorists who want them all dead.

Jews are being persecuted without anyone bothering to ask whether any of them are actually Zionists. Israel is a convenient excuse to revive old-world antisemitism with new twists. Gaza has become a license to hate Jews—wherever they may be found. The treatment of Jews throughout Europe today is painfully reminiscent of the Dreyfus Affair in France at the end of the nineteenth century.

Where's the equivalent outrage against China for committing an actual genocide? Where's the anti-Asian backlash by Muslims for crimes against humanity committed by China against their co-religionists? And that's not the world's lone genocide taking place at this very moment. It is happening to the Tigrayans of Ethiopia, for instance. Are the media reporting those stories? I don't see college encampments with human barricades preventing Chinese students from walking safely to class. No one is seizing campus buildings and destroying school property for the sole purpose of calling attention to the poor Tigrayans.

Closer to home, would university officials stand by and protect the free speech rights of pro-KKK activists? I seriously doubt it. For racism, the Code of Student Conduct, and Supreme Court precedent on the First Amendment, would properly render these protests unlawful. But neither Codes of Student Conduct nor legally recognized restrictions on free speech were applied to protect Jews on campus for what has now been the second academic year in a row.

Israel's retaliation against Hamas for the October 7 massacre has unearthed antisemitic sentiments that many had believed to be dormant, if not altogether eradicated. Something is responsible for this global fixation on Gaza when other warzones have resulted in more civilian deaths but far less, if not nonexistent, calls to action.

A lot of loose talk has resulted in lost lives, not to mention fraught atmospheres of harassment and intimidation. Choosing one's words carefully is crucial under such strained and intemperate circumstances. But such economies with language—prudence and mutual respect—are not to be found. We see the frightening consequences of inflammatory speech used to promote propaganda, instill indoctrination, and cause incitement. "Genocide," "ethnic cleansing," "apartheid," "white supremacy," and "settler colonialism" are invoked casually. They have become rallying cries screamed by brainwashed students who have no understanding of Middle East history and no idea what any of those terms mean.

There are also mischievous Muslims who are very well aware that Israel is home to two million of their people who would choose to live nowhere else. But these anti-Israel, anti-American Muslims don't want anyone to know what life is really like in Arab and Muslim societies.

These chants—"From the River to the Sea, Palestine will be free!," "Death to Israel!," "Death to America!"—the burning of Israeli and American flags, and the defacing of monuments with hateful graffiti are all reminiscent of decades of rage-filled demonstrations in the Middle East and Persian Gulf. Americans, finally, have become introduced to the Arab Street,[262] which still takes center stage in town squares in places like Tehran, but over the past few decades, has gravitated to European and Canadian cities like London, Berlin, Stockholm, Madrid, Barcelona, Amsterdam, Toronto, Montreal, Brussels, Antwerp, and Paris, and more recently has made its way to New York, Los Angeles, and Patterson, New Jersey and Dearborn, Michigan.

Masks can't fully disguise radical Islamists who glorify death, are prepared to martyr children, and threaten to erase Israel from the map. And PhD's can't mask academic frauds who are using tenured platforms to spread lies, close minds, and foment hate among impressionable teenagers who thought college was supposed to be about mind expansion and open inquiry.

Columnist Jonathan Tobin has written, "[T]he safety of American Jews and their ability to study safely on college campuses and walk on the streets of major cities is called into question by the way mainstream culture, the media and politicians continue to refuse to draw a line in the sand and unreservedly condemn the lies that fuel the surge in antisemitism."[263]

And what are some of those lies?

Israel and Jews are colonialists and white oppressors around the world.

Israel is an apartheid society, exactly like South Africa.

Israelis, like all Jews, have white privilege, even though more than 50 percent of Israelis are persons of color from the Middle East, Persian Gulf, and North Africa.

Jews control the media and banking.

Jews are capitalists and major donors.

Jews are greedy and care only about themselves.

Try challenging any of these presumptions in intellectual circles, polite society, and elite company. You would instantly be labeled a racist, Islamophobe, and an enabler of genocide. Among Muslims, you would be beaten senseless.

Many are true believers, natural antisemites, and Jew-haters of the first order who are now having their day. Others have been turned. Both private and public schools indoctrinate hateful attitudes toward Jews. Even many Jews are reciting the same anti-Israel refrains, having joined the other side as the new Hellenized Jews.

Why would they do this? Many were targets of a well-coordinated campaign to pollute the West with anti-Israel, anti-American, anti-white claptrap. And some made personal and professional calculations that developing antisemitic predilections were terrific career moves. All they had to do is disavow and denigrate their own people. Publicly proclaim that Jews are the worst of the worst—when it comes to almost any sin. And Israel stands alone as the world's most vile human rights violator.[264] Neither the Nazis, nor the Huns, have anything on the Jewish state. There are no other people as despicable and debased.

The most ignorant among them don't realize that if they were sincere in their beliefs, they would be directing their recriminations against extremist Muslims around the world, and not ordinary Israelis. Many either don't know, or don't care to know, that Arabs enjoy civil rights equal to that of Jews in Israel. There is no apartheid in Israel—not even close. No racial separation at all.

The apartheid states are actually the Muslim ones where Jews are not permitted to live. Palestinians have long made it known that should they ever have a state of their own, Jews would not be welcome there. So much for diversity and inclusion—so very popular and obligatory on college campuses—being applied to Islam.

Israel is the only nation in the Middle East where women stand equal to men, do not walk behind them, do not allow themselves to be covered up for ostensible Islamic reasons of modesty. In Israel, Sharia law does not allow Arabs to beat, stone, and lash their wives. Israel is also the only nation in the region where homosexuals are not tossed from rooftops and hanged from cranes.

And yet, there is actually a group called "Queers for Palestine." Really? Is it stupidity or something more sinister? The group UN Women, "feminists," and women's advocacy entities in the West disgracefully remained silent in failing to denounce and demand justice for the mass raping of Israeli teenagers and the mutilation of their organs. What does #MeToo mean if it can't, at the very least, stand against the violence committed against Israeli women by Muslim men who learned how to treat the subservient sex in the Koran?

When an American student pledges sympathy for Hamas, are they even remotely aware how offensive this is not only to Jews, but to their own parents? If you have the misfortune of being the parent of such a morally disabled college student, wrapped in a keffiyeh scarf, choking on bile against Israel, screaming chants they don't understand, and carrying a sign that reads: "Hamas we love you! We support your rockets, too!"—God help you. This is the return on your investment for the colorless privilege of attending an Ivy League university.

Message to the brainwashed, at best, and brain dead, at worst, students who protested so fiercely and self-righteously on college campuses against Israel's retaliation in Gaza, along with the cadre of antisemitic progressives who hijacked bridges, libraries, campus walkways, and railroad stations: Hamas is a terrorist organization that won a democratic election and then summarily murdered its rivals. They would castrate a homosexual in a Greenwich Village minute. Their Muslim Brotherhood despises women, who are condemned to miserable and abusive lives under Sharia law.

That's the team whose jerseys you are shamelessly wearing.

In the end, it doesn't matter what hardcore antisemites or deluded students think or believe. All that matters is what Israel must do to survive. And what all Israelis and the generals that command their armed forces know—learned from hard-won lessons adhering strictly to the laws of war and yet never fully vanquishing their enemies—is that to defeat Hamas and Islamic Jihad, given the suicidal and genocidal aspirations of terrorist organizations, Israel must go *beyond* proportionality.

That's right: wars that are won, especially those that involve relentless foes, feature armies that realize they must surpass the *lex talionis* of merely getting even.[265] Observe the laws of war, if possible, but forsake them entirely when the actions of terrorists make it abundantly clear that adherence to rules is tantamount to surrender.

In asymmetric urban warzones, where terrorists mock the laws of war, the gloves have to come off. Israel has repeatedly fought just wars against terrorists, but they have been criticized for the manner in which they fight—the *jus in bello*—even though they make every effort to comply with the rules of engagement. But if the same enemy keeps coming back—renewed and emboldened with better weapons and deeper tunnels—Israel must be allowed, and should be expected, to cross the Rubicon of disproportion.

For the most part, Israel has always toed the correct legal line. But there are times that call for the dropping of two-thousand-pound bombs with a larger kill radius. Why? Because Hamas commanders are hiding in tunnels far below the Gazan ground, and they are responsible for the ungodly crimes of October 7. The IDF should not be hesitating for an instant. Those who cheered on and still have no remorse for October 7 do not deserve Israel's sympathy. Mitigating damage cannot, and should not, be Israel's highest priority. The cold reality of wars that are fought against monsters is the inevitability that civilians will die. But so, too, must terrorists and their cache of weapons be completely destroyed.

Without some degree of disproportion, nations cannot declare victory against nonstate actors who famously ignore the laws of war and refuse to surrender. Terrorists have nothing to lose. They are playing with Qatari and Iranian money. And they are not afraid to die. Moreover, the civilians they should be protecting are satisfied with apocalyptic endings.

Even when facing conventional armies on battlefields where the rules of engagement are mutually reinforced, the dark truth of warfare is that it often takes proportion-plus to get the other side to surrender. America took a crash course in these realties when bombing Hiroshima and Nagasaki. These cities had mostly industrial significance, although slightly less true of Hiroshima, which housed an army headquarters. Neither qualified as true military necessities. And America failed the distinction test since the point was to get the attention of Japanese civilians and shatter their morale.

Churchill chose German cities to firebomb that had little military significance, as well, although there were some weapons manufacturers—including poisonous gas. The objective was to get the German people to despise the Nazis and pressure them to put down their weapons and turn off the gas. The United States failed to recall these truths in Vietnam, but relearned them all over again during the first Gulf War with the implementation of the Powell Doctrine and its focus on overwhelming military force.

"Shock and Awe" was the American battle cry against the Taliban and al-Qaeda immediately after 9/11. The detention centers in Abu Ghraib and Guantánamo Bay were unsightly but necessary. These were all representations of disproportionate American might.

You want to win a war? You want the other side to surrender? Hit them not with mathematical precision but wrath of God vengeance. By the time Joe Biden had dropped out of the presidential race, Kamala Harris feared alienating Jewish Democratic voters, and the American people were on summer holidays. Israel, for the first time in nearly a year, was given a free hand to operate. The return of President Trump created even more opportunities to unleash the full weight of their military might. And they took marvelous advantage of it.

Sinwar and many of his chief commanders had been killed in Rafah, the last stronghold with fractured battalions still carrying on the fighting. The titular head of Hamas, Ismail Haniyeh, who had been holed up throughout the war in a lavish five-star hotel in Qatar, was assassinated while visiting Iran. Israel soon turned its attention to Hezbollah, eliminating its longtime cleric, Hassan Nasrallah, who headed Iran's primary-proxy, along with the entirety of his senior command.

The war turned rapidly when Israel was not hounded about what size bomb it was dropping or whether it should matter that Hamas concealed its main communications centers under hospitals and mosques, or whether the IDF was not doing enough to deliver humanitarian aid. Finally, Israel was given the green light to get the job done.

Student protests on Ivy League campuses meant little to the Israeli War Cabinet. But pressure from the White House was not welcome, being all too reminiscent of the Obama years. Given all the horror on October 7, President Biden's initial reaction to it, and his immediate visit to Israel, the mixed messaging came as a surprise. It took nearly a year, but when the Biden administration began to focus on other distractions as the summer months brought the Olympics, Taylor Swift's Eras Tour, and the presidential election, Israel's military ingenuity and technological edge finally was unleashed, and the heavy price Israel promised was finally delivered to Hamas, Islamic Jihad, Hezbollah, the Houthis, and Iran.

I realize that to the legions of antisemitic international law "experts"—and there are many; Amal Clooney has many like-minded friends, including some of the self-hating Jewish variety—the very title of this book will generate a negative reaction, at best, and total denunciation at worst. But everything about Israel, manifested in calling for its removal from the community of nations, ignites antisemitic passions and deep-seated prejudices. There will be those who say that there is no doctrinal authority for going beyond proportionality. But the history of warfare itself, and realities of the Middle East, would suggest otherwise.

Most wars come to an end in ugly ways that have proven General Sherman right when he said: "War is hell." Atlanta was in the path of Sherman's March, and that's why nearly half of it was burned beyond recognition. Given the challenges of urban combat and its own unique elements in the Middle East, Israel has adapted the rules when applied to the unconventional warzones that have been its misfortune to endeavor. The special asymmetries and go-for-broke fighting spirit of terrorists who mock the laws of war and revere Charters that call for annihilating all Jews, perhaps requires proportionality to undergo a bit of tweaking.

The Dahiya Doctrine, first applied in the 2006 Lebanon War against Hezbollah, is a military strategy that addressed those situations when Israel must target buildings knowingly occupied by civilians. Never widely discussed but given serious thought within the Israeli defense establishment, the Dahiya Doctrine empowers the IDF, under certain circumstances, to go beyond proportionality. Whether it was implemented, even implicitly, in the October 7 War is not yet known. But I suspect that on some levels, it was.

It contemplates a revamping of the rules of engagement and provides a strategic calculus on whether to bomb urban terror complexes with airstrikes, instead of invading with ground troops. It doesn't concern itself with disproportionate civilian loss. The fact that the IDF believed it was necessary to have boots on the ground in Gaza suggests that a maximalist implementation of the Dahiya Doctrine was not completely applied.

The Dahiya Doctrine cuts to the very essence of Fourth Generation, asymmetric urban warfare. It speaks directly to the challenges placed on conventional armies in urban settings. The Doctrine does not address whether Palestinian "civilians" are actually noncombatants, rather than an auxiliary militia or fully committed aiders and abettors. It doesn't have to. It takes as a given that civilians are present in the targeted building. And it freely accepts that they will be harmed—whether they provide material assistance to Hamas or not.

This military doctrine operates independently of whether the civilians harmed in war are wholly innocent. And that's why it is not openly discussed in public forums. Collateral damage is treated as an unavoidable cost of such wars. Israel's right to take out a military target and accomplish a military objective does not wait for the ideal circumstances when no one is home.

Dahiya is an actual place, a suburb of Beirut, which to this day serves as Ground Zero for Hezbollah's military command and the repository for its weapons and communications systems. That's why Dahiya received a good deal of attention during the Fall of 2024 when Israel took a multifront military turn and decided to stop toying with Hezbollah. It was time to simply eliminate them altogether. Most of the airstrikes were directed at Dahiya.

Back in 2006, top commanders of the IDF came to the conclusion that these urban compounds with embedded terrorists and rocket launchers are tantamount to military bases—except that they happen to be located in civilian neighborhoods. If Israel is at war, then those strategic military installations—civilians aside—must be abolished. No other army has ever had to contend with an adversary that positions its headquarters, intelligence and communications centers, and its arsenal of weapons inside homes and apartment buildings. The conventional laws of armed combat, and its focus on distinction and proportionality, simply cannot be made to fit this nightmarish situation—unless an army is amenable to defeat.

General Gadi Eisenkot, who led the IDF's northern division and is one of the IDF brass that many believe developed the Dahiya Doctrine, wrote that Israel "should target economic interests and the centers of civilian power that support the organization" with an outcome similar to what Winston Churchill sought to achieve with his firebombing of German cities: suffering, overwhelmed, and demoralized civilians will turn against and blame the terrorists who terrorize them, too.[266] After leveling Dahiya, he said, "What happened in the Dahiya quarter of Beirut in 2006 will happen in every village from which Israel is fired on,...[w]e will apply *disproportionate force* on it and cause a great deal of damage and destruction there. From our standpoint, these are not civilian villages, they are military bases... This is not a recommendation. This is a plan. And it has been approved."[267]

The Doctrine clearly was not fully applied in Gaza because of the large troop movements that constituted a siege of the enclave. But to some degree, when it comes to collateral damage, the Dahiya Doctrine seems to have influenced the mindset of Israel's military echelon.

It may make the world recoil, but a counteroffensive that goes beyond proportionality is something Israel has long considered and even experimented with—at least as far back as 2006. The decision to implement these ideas into actual military practice was not lightly undertaken or made without rational and moral thought. It's just that Israel's own self-defense generates all too much internal psychological conflict and outside moral confusion.

Jews have had a long history of abysmally appeasing their enemies; the warrior culture is still a novel, not easily embraced, concept for liberal Jews. And as for moral confusion, the world can't think straight when it comes to Jews fighting back. Both calcified and inchoate antisemitism always interferes. Introducing new moral criteria is instantly rebuffed. Most armies have never fought under such distress. Pundits watching the aftermath of a terrorist strike from the comfort of their homes on high-definition television sets are truly unfit to judge.

Unless you have tens of thousands of rockets and missiles launched toward your civilian population centers or have geographic neighbors capable of the barbarism Hamas was not ashamed for all the world to see, you should be disqualified from rendering an opinion. Israel rediscovered on October 7, as if it needed any reminders, that Gaza is a moral black hole. Palestinians commit unspeakable crimes. Israel responds with overwhelming force. Women and children are killed, and Israel is ostracized as a rogue state that should be expelled from the community of nations. But much to my old and departed friend Bob Simon's chagrin, there's simply no way to defeat Hamas without dead children. The only alternative is for Israel to do nothing and attend the funerals of their own.

The Dahiya Doctrine may be the military tactic that knows no name. But unfortunately, its necessity is not in dispute. The IDF's main priority must be the protection of Israelis, the maintenance of its national security, and establishing deterrence against Iran and its proxies. If civilian facilities are secreting Hamas or Hezbollah's madmen and war machines, they must be destroyed.

It may be true that the Doctrine is easier to apply in Lebanon than in Gaza. The Lebanese people are not Palestinians. Hezbollah is a guest of the country—and an unwelcome one. Most Lebanese regard Hezbollah as a menace and would be happy to see it find another base of operations. And there is no love lost for their patron saint, Iran, either. And unlike Gazans, the Lebanese will not grant Hezbollah any public support once it is reminded of the consequences of giving up their homes to hide the weapons and hatch the strategies of terrorists.

General Eisenkot concluded, "Hezbollah understands well that its fire from within villages will lead to their destruction. Before Nasrallah [who Israel assassinated in the October 7 War] gives the order to fire at Israel, he will need to think 30 times if he wants to destroy his support base in the villages. This is not a theoretical matter for him. The possibility of harm to the population is the main factor restraining Nasrallah."[268]

It is ironic that when the war shifted to Lebanon, the IDF finally put some elements of the Dahiya Doctrine to the test. Beirut may not have received the same pummeling as Gaza, but Dahiya, as a suburb of Beirut, is no longer the same. That's where Israel's heaviest bombing was centered in 2024—back where it all started, in 2006. Asymmetric warfare requires a redefinition of the laws of armed conflict. Collateral damage is having less relevance in the Middle East than usual, and perhaps that's how it should be—not that it gave me much pleasure writing that last sentence.

Going beyond proportionality should be permitted, and expected, only when military necessity is especially severe. That does not mean that the moral calculations of making such military decisions are suspended. It just means that this is how Fourth Generation Warfare must be waged. There is little doubt that cadets enrolled at West Point at this very moment are familiar with the Dahiya Doctrine and are struggling with its moral and military dimensions. But that doesn't make the outside urgency more impetrative and the internal conflict any less real.

The Dahiya Doctrine is disturbing, but it is not without a rationale. Israel values the lives of its own people over the lives of Palestinians and owes special duties to them. In this respect, the Jewish state is no different from any other sovereign nation. Israel naturally also has a visceral attachment to its own children. Unfortunately, the same cannot be said of Hamas.

Throughout history, wars are won when the losing nation has lost its will to fight, when its casualty counts become unbearably too high, when suing for peace is the only logical option for saving what's left of the country. This was true in Germany and Japan, which required two years of additional warfare for the Allied Powers to defeat these armies and destroy the people's will to see the fighting continue. Going beyond proportionality, in many of these cases, resulted in enormous carnage at war's end—of homes, schools, factories, and hospitals—and, of course, people.

With the rebuilding of Europe and Japan, and a rejection of prior ideologies that drove their nations to crave empire, World War III was averted.

Israel's critics have been implicitly saying all along that its right to self-defense comes with caveats and is limited in scope. It can only respond to the October 7 massacre defensively and in a measured fashion—proportionality par excellence. Fighting to win and defeat the enemy, to ensure its total eradication is simply not allowed. Those who wish to kill Jews must be permitted to stay alive and try again.

What other country has ever received such wartime directives from other sovereign states? As Israel has discovered with the terrorists to its north and south, such a passive approach to existential dangers only guarantees another round of violence sometime in the near future.

The moral challenge Israel faces is unique. When one side is torching infants and gang raping teenagers, what is to be done with such an enemy who exists right next door—especially when the martyrdom of its own people will redound against you? The surreal nature of such a lawless war inevitably leads into a maze of muddled moral thinking. The irrationality of it all creates the temptation to ignore the barbarism of Hamas and, instead, chastise the fighting methods of Israel in self-defense. After all, Israel is a democratic country founded on Western, liberal values. It must not resort to the same methods of their evil adversary. And besides, as a civilized nation, it can be reasoned with.

But doesn't such logic depend on a racist vision of the Palestinian people, the soft bigotry of diminished expectations? Failing to apply widely accepted moral standards to a particular group. Refusing to hold them accountable, concluding instead that they are a people incapable of functioning in a civilized world, and cannot be expected to adjust. The inherent racism in such depraved excuse-making seems to be lost on the West: "We can't understand the inhumanity of Hamas. They are wholly alien to us. They won't listen to us."

What's the takeaway? A civilized nation is being asked to endure whatever barbarians can imagine. This is one of the reasons why Israel's war strategy in Gaza has come under such heavy criticism: It cringingly offends our basic notions of civilized society. Israel must be better than Hamas. How does one define "better" in such situations? Like, dead?

Israel is not at war with a civilized society, and that's why the legal indictment and moral criteria against Israel is so cavalier, misapplied, and plainly wrong. And that's also why a strict application of the laws of armed conflict, under these maddening circumstances, only prolongs the lives of terrorists and plays right into their hands.

There is a perilous Western tendency, born of a toxic brew of moral relativism, to refuse to confront and acknowledge the truth of what entities such as Hamas, ISIS, the Iranian regime, the Houthis, Boko Haram, the Taliban, and al-Qaeda represent: a direct challenge to liberal moral ideals and to Western civilization, itself. The impulse is to ignore all the evidence and not take their actions and motives seriously.

This book has sought to bring much-needed clarity to the nature of this new urban warfare that weaponizes every building and purposely puts civilians in harm's way. This new theater of war must continue to inform the evolution of international law and find its way into Western military doctrine.

Liberal platitudes make for good sound bites, but they are wholly inadequate when the war sirens sound. Given the aftermath of October 7, with its social upheavals, political gamesmanship, and eruption of antisemitic violence, Americans must decide whether it is prepared to stand beside its lone democratic ally in the Middle East, or lecture them about the enemies they face—and that America will someday surely face, as well.

It's time to choose sides—without ambivalence and fear of social ostracism. The consequences of not doing so are great, much greater than the risk of momentary discomfort at fashionable cocktail parties. The questions presented in this book are important for American foreign policy, and especially for Europe and its own problems with *jihadist* sentiments that could literally explode at any moment. But first we need to be more honest about the world in which we live.

This kind of warfare is not going away—indeed, given the incitement and recruitment chatter on the internet, it may be getting worse. One way to lose the fight is to be deluded about the true nature of the enemy. We cannot afford such delusions. The moral morass cannot be used to subvert an honest assessment about the dangers we face. The blurring of moral categories is making us all blind—too harshly judging Israel's responses to terrorism while refusing to judge terrorists at all.

Now, on a lighter note.

You may recall that earlier in this book, I referenced two iconic motion pictures from the early 1960s: *Lawrence of Arabia* and *Exodus*. Indeed, there were several occasions in which I noted works of dramatic art that depict how the broader culture learns about the ethics of war. Art can capture the moral and emotional complexity of war and vengeance, and, in doing so, shape cultural attitudes in unique and profound ways.

Lawrence of Arabia, set during World War I, shows how the Arab Revolt helped Britain defeat and oust the Ottoman Empire from the Middle East. *Exodus* is set soon after World War II, when the remnants of European Jewry were readying themselves to return to their ancestral homeland to build a new state. After defeating Turkey in World War I, the British had promised to return the lands it had occupied to both Arabs and Jews. But neither the British nor Palestinian Arabs were too keen on Israel realizing its dream.

Both films left viewers with two distinct impressions: Arabs do not shy away from bloody wars—in fact, they rather enjoy violence; and killing Jews—including children—is a tribal obsession among far too many Arabs and Muslims.

But there is a third film, *Ben-Hur* (1959), another movie blockbuster released during the same time period as the other two films, that tells a much different story. This one is about biblical Arabs and Jews. And I think it leaves the perfect coda with which to end this book.

Based on a bestselling 1880 novel by Lew Wallace, a former Civil War general and devout Christian, the film broadly depicts the Roman conquest of Jerusalem and the crucifixion of Jesus Christ. Between those epochal moments, a prince of one of the most prominent Jewish families in Jerusalem is shipped off into slavery and returns to exact vengeance on the childhood friend who betrayed him and rose to become a Roman tribune.

But it is the action-packed chariot race that most people remember about the movie. What is often overlooked, however, is the solidarity between Arabs and Jews against the invading Romans. That's a shame. *Ben-Hur* offers a redemptive message that would serve the offspring of these biblical brothers quite well.

The highly bred white horses that Judah Ben-Hur races to victory are Arabian—they bear the names of Arabic constellations—and the proud possession of an Arab Sheik. Given that the story takes place simultaneous with the New Testament, there is no Arab religion at this moment in history. Islam is more than half a millennium away from its founding. The movie relies upon Judaism, and the earliest days of Christianity, for its religious underpinnings. Although rabbis didn't love this plot twist, the film ambiguously intimates that Judah Ben-Hur may ultimately become a follower of this new religion.

But here's the beauty of the plot: Arabs and Jews are allies and friends. The Sheik asks Ben-Hur to take the helm of the Arabian horse-drawn chariot. He inspires him by declaring that a victory will signal to these Roman *occupiers* that the "people of this land" cannot be easily defeated—that means, Arabs *and* Jews. The Sheik recognizes the obvious—this region of the world is populated by Jews and Arabs. The Romans are the unwelcome conquerors—non-indigenous colonizers, if you will. He even hands Ben-Hur a Star of David amulet as a good luck charm and as a reminder of the true stakes of this race.

When the teams are presented to the crowded stadium, Ben-Hur is announced as hailing from "Judea." Yes, the kingdom that Jews once controlled several hundred years before the Ancient Greeks. That was the first Jewish homeland. And, perhaps most tellingly, as the chariots dangerously circle the course nine times, the loudest cheering for Judah Ben-Hur comes from the Arabs that have jammed the stadium to see him represent the semitic peoples.

Why aren't there mandatory screenings of this movie on college campuses across the country? It might not do much to alter the thinking of hardcore antisemitic professors and students. But for those who are simply misinformed about the Middle East, and foolishly utter words and phrases like "settler colonialism" and "land-grabbing," this acclaimed film can provide a more accurate and instructive tutorial on the region.

Yes, the Jews of the Middle East are not solely from Brooklyn and Brentwood. They are indigenous to the land—especially in Jerusalem. And Jews and Arabs don't have to be enemies.

Perhaps the Abraham Accords provided an inkling that such solidarity is still possible. Imagine if Palestinians and Israelis could trade in all those weapons for just one chariot and, for old times' sake, take it out for a joy ride?

But that would be a Hollywood movie, the kind of happy ending that is unimaginable for anyone who knows the bitter realities and sharp tensions of life in the Middle East for Arabs and Jews. *Ben-Hur* provides a cinematic curtain call that may never have been true. After all, the nations that normalized relations with Israel in the Abraham Accords did not share a border with the Jewish state. At the same time, Egypt and Jordan, which are actual neighbors of Israel, have signed enduring peace treaties that have remained in effect for decades.

Israel has been willing to share a border with a Palestinian state. There are five rejected offers of statehood to show for it. Such a more sanguine future for Arabs and Jews will only be possible when the images of October 7 are as repulsive to Arabs as they are to Jews.

ENDNOTES

Introduction

1 Niha Masih, "What is Hamas, and Why Did It Attack Israel Now?" *Washington Post*, October 31, 2023.

2 Yasmine Salam, "Gaza Strip explained: Who Controls It and What to Know," *NBC News*, October 8, 2023.

3 Yousef Munayyer, "How the Al-Aqsa Mosque Became a Flashpoint in the Israeli-Palestinian Conflict," October 8, 2023, in *Weekend Edition Sunday*, produced by NPR, podcast.

4 Raz Segal, quoted in Solcyré Burga, "Is What's Happening in Gaza a Genocide? Experts Weigh In," *Time* Magazine, November 14, 2023.

5 David Suissa, "Israel Just Took Down a Terrorist who Loves Room Service," *Jewish Journa*l, July 30, 2024.

Chapter 1

6 David M. Litman, "Hamas Counted on Biased Western Journalism—and They Got It," *Algemeiner*, June 21, 2024.

7 Ayaan Hirsi Ali, *Heretic: Why Islam Needs a Reformation Now* 117 (New York, NY: Harper, 2015).

8 Thane Rosenbaum, "Hamas's Civilian Death Strategy: Gazans Shelter Terrorists and Their Weapons in Their Homes, Right Beside Sofas and Dirty Diapers," *Wall Street Journal*, July 21, 2024.

9 Matthew Rosenberg and Maria Abi-Habib, "As Gazans Scrounge for Food and Water, Hamas Sits on a Rich Trove of Supplies," *New York Times*, October 27, 2023.

Chapter 2

10 Adam Rasgon, "U.S. Strikes Militant Group in Yemen That Has Kept Up Attacks on Ships," *New York Times*, December 31, 2024.

11 Muhammad Ali Khalidi, "'The Most Moral Army in the World'": The New 'Ethical Code' of the Israeli Military and the War on Gaza," *Journal of Palestine Studies* 39, no. 3, (2010).

12 Eyal Ben-Ari, Zeev Lerer, Uzi Ben-Shalom, and Ariel Vainer, *Rethinking Contemporary Warfare: A Sociological View of the Al-Aqsa Intifada* (Albany, NY: SUNY Press, 2011), 152.

13 Summer Said and Rory Jones, "Gaza Chief's Brutal Calculation: Civilian Bloodshed Will Help Hamas," *Wall Street Journal*, June 10, 2024.

14 Christopher F. Schuetze, "German Prosecutor Says Islamic State Terrorist Link Is Suspected in Festival Stabbings," *New York Times*, August 26, 2024.

15 Rick Noack, "Leaked document says 2,000 men allegedly assaulted 1,200 German women on New Year's Eve," *Washington Post*, July 11, 2016.

16 Peter Savodnik, "Islamists Keep Stabbing People. Why Aren't We Talking About It?" *The Free Press,* June 6, 2024.

17 Thane Rosenbaum, "Rushdie and the Satanic Clerics of Iran," *Jewish Journal*, August 14, 2022.

18 Stefanie Dazio, "The Plot to Attack Taylor Swift's Vienna Shows Was Intended to Kill Thousands, a CIA Official Says," *Associated Press*, August 29, 2024.

19 Thane Rosenbaum, "Of Dutch Pogroms and American Politics," *Jewish Journal*, November 10, 2024.

Chapter 3

20 "IDF probing alleged violations of regulations and international law during war on Hamas," *The Times of Israel*, February 6, 2024.

21 Thane Rosenbaum, "The Year of Living Insanely Dangerously," *Jewish Journal*, October 20, 2024.

22 "Most Palestinians Support October 7 Attack, Dissatisfied With Abbas and Fatah," *Foundation for Defense of Democracies*, June 14, 2024.

23 Adam Taylor, "Poll: Hamas Popularity Surges After War with Israel," *Washington Post*, September 2, 2014.

24 Jay Loschky, "Palestinians Lack Faith in Biden, Two-State Solution," *Gallup*, October 18, 2023.

25 "Most Palestinians Support October 7 Attack, Dissatisfied With Abbas and Fatah," *Foundation for Defense of Democracies*, June 14, 2024; Deborah Danan, "'They Are All Hamas,'" *Tablet*, January 24, 2024.

26 Thane Rosenbaum, "Tenuous Tears at Israel's Birthday Bust," *Jewish Journal*, May 3, 2023; Thane Rosenbaum, "Palestinians' Revisionist History Chains Them to a Lie," *Jewish Journal*, May 19, 2020.

27 Nan Jacques Zilberdik, "Terrorist Bragged He 'Killed 10 Jews with My Own Hands' in Call to Parents During Hamas Onslaught," *Algemeiner*, October 31, 2023; "IDF Publishes Audio of Hamas Terrorist Calling Family to Brag About Killing Jews," *The Times of Israel*, October 25, 2023.

28 Jeremy Sharon, "Several UNRWA Staffers Praised Hamas's October 7 Massacres, Report Finds, *The Times of Israel*, November 6, 2023.

29 Troy O. Fritzhand, "UN Agency Staff Praised Hamas' Oct. 7 Massacre in Telegram Channel, Watchdog Reveals," *Algemeiner*, January 11, 2024.

30 Bassam Tawil, "UNRWA Hires Palestinian Terrorists, Glorifies Violence and Terrorism," *Gatestone Institute*, November 18, 2024.

31 Ben Hubbard, "How a U.N. Agency Became a Flashpoint in the Gaza War," *New York Times*, September 12, 2024.

32 Ohad Merlin, "UNRWA Schools in Gaza: Principals, Staff Identified as Members in Terror Units," *Jerusalem Post*, November 14, 2024.

33 Adam Kredo, "Biden State Dept Privately Downplayed Use of 'Jihad' and 'Occupation' in UNRWA-Made Study Materials, Saying Only 'Some Other Audiences' View the Terms as 'Inappropriate,'" *Washington Free Beacon*, February 6, 2025.

34 Yardena Schwartz, "October 7 Happened Before, in Hebron," *Tablet*, November 7, 2023.

35 Joel Fishman, "The 'Two-State Solution' and the Arab Palestinians: Partition or Politicide?" *Jerusalem Center for Security and Foreign Affairs*, February 16, 2023.

36 Elliot Kaufman, "History Goes to War in the Holy Land," *Wall Street Journal*, March 29, 2024.

37 Jacob Frankel, "Hamas Official Says Terror Group 'Would Do Oct. 7 Attack Again' if Possible to Go Back in Time," *Algemeiner*, June 19, 2024 (emphasis added).

38 Jacob Frankel, "Hamas Official Says Terror Group 'Would Do Oct. 7 Attack Again' if Possible to Go Back in Time," *Algemeiner*, June 19, 2024.

39 "Hamas Official Ghazi Hamad: We Will Repeat The October 7 Attack, Time And Again, Until Israel Is Annihilated; We Are Victims—Everything We Do Is Justified," *MEMRI*, November 1, 2023.

40 Bassam Tawil, "Palestinian Leaders Prefer Murderers and Rapists Over Reforms," *Gatestone Institute*, July 19, 2024.

41 Summer Said and Rory Jones, "Gaza Chief's Brutal Calculation: Civilian Bloodshed Will Help Hamas," *Wall Street Journal*, June 10, 2024.

42 Thane Rosenbaum, "In Israel's Time of Need, Jewish Hollywood Has Failed the Audition," *Jewish Journal*, December 17, 2023.

43 Haley Ott, "Israel Shows Photos of Weapons and a Tunnel Shaft at Gaza's Al-Shifa Hospital as Search for Hamas Command Center Continues," *CBS News*, November 16, 2023.

44 Kassy Akiva, "These Gaza Hospital Leaders Are Also High-Ranking Hamas Members," *Daily Wire*, January 24, 2025.

45 Yaakov Lappin, "How Hamas Turned Gazan Homes Into Weapons Depots," *Jewish News Syndicate*, June 3, 2024; Yoav Zitun, "IDF Soldiers Find Pictures of Women, Children Holding Rifles in Gaza Home," *Ynet News*, December 26, 2023; "More Weapons Hidden Under Children's Beds in Gaza Discovered by IDF," *National Post*, November 24, 2023.

46 "Report: New IDF Assessment Shows Some 6,000 Gazans Invaded Israel on Oct. 7," *The Times of Israel*, August 31, 2024.

47 Deborah Danan, "'They Are All Hamas.': Let me know of one Palestinian in Gaza who tried to save a Jew and maybe I'll change my mind," *Tablet*, January 24, 2024.

48 Danan, "'They Are All Hamas.'"

49 Steve Hendrix, Shira Rubin, Loveday Morris, Heba Farouk Mahfouz and, Hajar Harb, "Inside Israel's Hostage Rescue: Secret Plans and a Deadly 'Wall of Fire,'" *Washington Post*, June 9, 2024.

50 Danan, "'They Are All Hamas.'"

51 Bart Schut, "UK Journalist who Blew Whistle on BBC Gaza Documentary: 'I caught them in bed with Hamas,'" *The Times of Israel*, March 7, 2025.

52 Danan, "'They Are All Hamas.'"

53 Thane Rosenbaum, "Anne Frank's Baby Brothers," *Jewish Journal*, February 21, 2025.

54 Deborah Danan, "Oct. 7 Was Worse Than a Terror Attack. It Was a Pogrom," *Tablet*, January 24, 2024.

55 Danan, "'They Are All Hamas.'"

56 Danan, "'They Are All Hamas.'"

57 Andrew Bernard, "Reform Rabbi: 'Hamas is the Palestinians,' Two-State Solution a Delusion," *Jewish News Syndicate*, February 28, 2025.

58 Deborah Danan, "Oct. 7 Was Worse Than a Terror Attack. It Was a Pogrom," *Tablet*, January 24, 2024.

59 Gianluca Pacchiani, "Street Rallies Celebrate Hamas Onslaught in West Bank and Throughout the Middle East," *The Times of Israel*, October 8, 2023.

60 Liel Leibovitz, "Israel's Two Big Lies," *Tablet*, July 1, 2024.

Chapter 4

61 Michael Walzer, *Just and Unjust Wars: A Moral Argument with Historical Illustrations*, fifth edition 19 (New York City, NY: Basic Books, 2015).

62 Walzer, *Just and Unjust Wars*, 254.

63 Walzer, *Just and Unjust Wars,* 263 (quoting Truman's address to the American People on August 12, 1945).

64 Walzer, *Just and Unjust Wars,* 263 (emphasis added).

65 Walzer, *Just and Unjust Wars*, 258.

66 Anthony King, *Urban Warfare in the Twenty-First Century* (Oxford, UK: Polity, 2021).

67 King, *Urban Warfare*, 22.

68 King, *Urban Warfare*, 1.

69 King, *Urban Warfare*, 9-12.

70 King, *Urban Warfare*, 28.

71 Ben-Ari, Lerer, Ben-Shalom, and Vainer, *Rethinking Contemporary Warfare*, 50.

72 Ben-Ari, Lerer, Ben-Shalom, and Vainer, *Rethinking Contemporary Warfare*, 50.

73 Ben-Ari, Lerer, Ben-Shalom, and Vainer, *Rethinking Contemporary Warfare*, 43.

74 Ben-Ari, Lerer, Ben-Shalom, and Vainer, *Rethinking Contemporary Warfare*, 97.

75 Ben-Ari, Lerer, Ben-Shalom, and Vainer, *Rethinking Contemporary Warfare*,106.

76 Loveday Morris, Sarah Cahlan, Jonathan Baran, and Louisa Loveluck, "Revenge, Fire and Destruction: A Year of Israeli Soldiers' Videos from Gaza," *Washington Post*, December 3, 2024.

77 Loveday Morris, Sarah Cahlan, Jonathan Baran, and Louisa Loveluck, "Revenge, Fire and Destruction."

78 Saranac Hale Spencer and D'Angelo Gore, "What We Know About Three Widespread Israel-Hamas War Claims," *FactCheck.org*, March 5, 2024.

79 Edward N. Luttwak, "Why Israel is Winning in Gaza," *Tablet*, February 8, 2024.

80 David Adesnik and Kevin Chen, "The Gaza Health Ministry Flimflam," *Commentary*, June 2024.

81 Amos Harel, "The Philosopher Who Gave the IDF Moral Justification in Gaza," *Haaretz*, February 6, 2009.

82 Ben-Ari, Lerer, Ben-Shalom, and Vainer, *Rethinking Contemporary Warfare*, 105.

83 Patrick Kingsley, Natan Odenheimer, Bilal Shbair, Ronen Bergman, John Ismay, Sheera Frenkel, and Adam Sella, "Israel Loosened Its Rules to Bomb Hamas Fighters, Killing Many More Civilians," *New York Times*, December 26, 2024.

84 Bassam Tawil, "Why Are Hamas's Crimes Ignored by Western Media?" *Gatestone Institute*, July 2, 2024.

85 "'Greedy Monsters' Ruled Church," *Washington Times*, May 15, 2002.

86 "PA Official Admits 'Nativity Siege' Staged," *Ynet News*, October 1, 2007.

87 "PA Official Admits 'Nativity Siege' Staged."

88 Robert Williams, "Big Lies About Israel," *Gatestone Institute*, July 4, 2024.

89 Williams, "Big Lies About Israel."

90 Adam Goldman, Ronen Bergman, and Natan Odenheimer, "'Moving in the Dark': Hamas Documents Show Tunnel Battle Strategy," *New York Times*, September 2, 2024.

91 Goldman, Bergman, and Odenheimer, "'Moving in the Dark.'"

92 Dylan Martinez, "Hamas Had Command Tunnel Under UN Gaza HQ, Israel Says," *Reuters*, February 11, 2024; Pamela Falk, "Israel Says These Photos Show How Hamas

Places Weapons In and Near U.N. Facilities in Gaza, Including Schools," *CBS News*, November 8, 2023.

93 Goldman, Bergman, and Odenheimer, "'Moving in the Dark.'"

94 Daphné Richemond-Barak, "Is Israel Winning the War on the Tunnels in Gaza?" *Foreign Policy,* January 6, 2024.

Chapter 5

95 Jack Cunningham, "Just War Theory: Fighting with One Hand Bound, Not Both," *Open Canada*, May 6, 2024.

96 *Bosnia and Herzegovina* v. *Serbia and Montenegro*, 91, (ICJ, 2007).

97 Eric Posner, "Terrorism and the Laws of War," *Chicago Journal of International Law* 5, no. 2, (2005): 432.

98 Posner, "Terrorism and the Laws of War," 431.

99 (emphasis added).

100 Marc Champion, "Meet the US Military Expert Defending Israel," *Bloomberg*, August 19, 2024; Clifford D. May and Col. Richard Kemp, "Colonel Richard Kemp on Israel's Long War," *Foreign Podicy*, Foundation for Defense of Democracies, January 27, 2024; Gabriel Emanuel, "Douglas Murray, Col. Richard Kemp Explain Uphill Battle for Israel," *Jerusalem Post*, December 29, 2023.

101 Walzer, *Just and Unjust Wars,* 325.

102 Walzer, *Just and Unjust Wars*, 258.

103 Michael Walzer, "Gaza and the Asymmetry Trap," *Quillette*, December 1, 2023.

104 David Brooks, "What Would You Have Israel Do to Defend Itself?" *New York Times*, March 24, 2024.

105 Jeremy Diamond, Kareem Khadder, Zeena Saifi and Benjamin Brown "Israeli Airstrike Kills Three Sons of Hamas Political Leader in Gaza as Ceasefire Talks Stutter," *CNN*, April 11, 2024.

106 Amichai Cohen and David Zlotogorski, *Proportionality in International Humanitarian Law* (Oxford University Press, 2021), 149.

107 Linda Kinstler, "The Bitter Fight Over the Meaning of 'Genocide,'" *New York Times*, August 20, 2024 (emphasis added).

108 Tova Zimuki, "'International Defenders': How Israeli Jurists Back IDF in War," *Ynet News*, October 22, 2023; Yonah Jeremy Bob, "IDF Lawyer to 'Post': Why the Israel-Hamas War is Like No Other," *Jerusalem Post*, December 25, 2023; Marc Garlasco, "Legal Questions Answered and Unanswered in Israel's Air War in Gaza," *Lawfare*, January 2, 2024.

109 Garlasco, "Legal Questions Answered and Unanswered."
110 Thane Rosenbaum, "Worse Than War," *Huffington Post*, November 17, 2009.
111 "Palestine Population 2024," World Population Review, accessed February 25, 2025; Wael R. Ennab, "Population and Demographic Developments in the West Bank and Gaza Strip Until 1990," United Nations Conference on Trade and Development, 1994.
112 Harel, "The Philosopher Who Gave the IDF Moral Justification in Gaza."
113 Avishai Margalit and Michael Walzer, "Israel: Civilians & Combatants," *New York Review of Books*, May 14, 2009.
114 Asa Kasher and Amos Yadlin, "Military Ethics of Fighting Terror: An Israeli Perspective," *Journal of Military Ethics* 4, no. 1 (2005).
115 Harel, "The Philosopher Who Gave the IDF Moral Justification in Gaza."
116 Kingsley, Odenheimer, Shbair, Bergman, Ismay, Frenkel, and Sella, "Israel Loosened Its Rules."
117 Kingsley, Odenheimer, Shbair, Bergman, Ismay, Frenkel, and Sella, "Israel Loosened Its Rules."
118 Jonathan S. Tobin, "Debunking the Gaza 'Genocide' Blood Libel Won't Dissuade Israel-Haters," *Jewish News Syndicate*, December 27, 2024.
119 Rashid Khalidi, "The Dahiya Doctrine, Proportionality and War Crimes," *Journal of Palestine Studies* 44, no. 1 (2014): 8.
120 Thane Rosenbaum, "If You Repeat 'Occupation' Often Enough," *The Times of Israel*, February 25, 2017.

Chapter 6

121 Eugene Scott, "Sanders Accuses Israel of 'Disproportionate' Response in Gaza," *CNN*, April 10, 2016.
122 Thane Rosenbaum, *Payback: The Case for Revenge* (Chicago: University of Chicago Press, 2013).
123 Thane Rosenbaum, "Numbers Don't Tell the Mideast Story," *Daily Beast*, July 10, 2014.
124 David B. Rivkin Jr. and Lee A. Casey, "Israel, Hamas and the Law of War," *Wall Street Journal*, May 29, 2024.
125 United Nations, Office of Human Rights, *Report of the Independent International Commission of Inquiry on the Occupied Palestinian Territory, including East Jerusalem, and Israel*, September 11, 2024.
126 Walzer, "Gaza and the Asymmetry Trap."

127 Walzer, *Just and Unjust Wars*, 258.
128 Walzer, *Just and Unjust Wars*, 299.
129 Litman, "Hamas Counted on Biased Western Journalism—and They Got It."
130 Shlomo M. Brody, "How Israel Missed Its Chance to Elimination the Leadership of Hamas," *Tablet*, December 4, 2023.
131 Harel, "The Philosopher Who Gave the IDF Moral Justification in Gaza."
132 Steven Erlanger, "Under the Rules of War, 'Proportionality' in Gaza is Not About Evening the Score," *New York Times*, December 3, 2023 (emphasis added).
133 Cohen and Zlotogorski, *Proportionality in International Humanitarian Law*, 169.
134 Thane Rosenbaum, "Bibi's Bind," *Jewish Journal*, January 19, 2025.
135 Rosenbaum, "Hamas's Civilian Death Strategy."
136 Cunningham, "Just War Theory."
137 Cohen and Zlotogorski, *Proportionality in International Humanitarian Law*, 149.
138 Thane Rosenbaum, "ICC Kangaroo Court in Session," *Jewish Journal*, November 25, 2024.
139 Rivkin Jr. and Casey, "Israel, Hamas and the Law of War."
140 United States Department of Defense, *Law of War Manual* (2016), para. 5.12.3.4.
141 Tim Lister, Ibrahim Dahman and Tamar Michaelis, "Around 70% of Deaths in Gaza are Women and Children, Says UN," *CNN*, November 9, 2024.

Chapter 7

142 *Protocol Additional to the Geneva Conventions* (Article 51(5)(b)): Protection of the Civilian Population (1977) (emphasis added).
143 *Protocol Additional to the Geneva Conventions* (Article 51(7) (emphasis added).
144 *Protocol Additional to the Geneva Conventions* (Article 58).
145 *Draft Rules for the Limitation of the Dangers Incurred by the Civilian Population in Time of War*, International Committee of the Red Cross (1956) Article 8.
146 *Draft Rules for the Limitation of the Dangers Incurred by the Civilian Population in Time of War*, Article 9. (emphasis added).
147 John Spencer, "I'm An Expert in Urban Warfare. Israel is Upholding the Laws of War," *CNN*, November 7, 2023.

148 "The U.N.'s Anti-Israel 'Genocide' Purge," *Wall Street Journal*, November 26, 2024.

149 Marni Rose McFall, "Netanyahu Arrest Warrant: Full List of Countries That Will Comply With ICC," *Newsweek*, November 22, 2024.

150 "Amnesty International Investigation Concludes Israel is Committing Genocide Against Palestinians in Gaza," *Amnesty International*, December 5, 2024.

151 "Amnesty International's Israel Branch Distances Itself From 'Genocide' Claim," *Guardian*, December 5, 2024.

152 The Convention On The Prevention And Punishment Of The Crime of Genocide (1948).

153 Seth Mandel, "Amnesty International and Balaam's Talking Ass," *Commentary*, December 5, 2024.

154 Rosenbaum, "ICC Kangaroo Court in Session."

155 Nigel Biggar, "Why the ICC Is Mistaken About Israel," *Spectator World*, November 25, 2024.

156 Allister Heath, "Israel's Bravery Has Exposed the Lie at the Heart of Starmer's Foreign Policy," *The Telegraph*, September 18, 2024.

157 Jack Cunningham, "Here's What Canada Should (and Should Not) Do in Shaping Its Middle East Policy," *Hub*, December 7, 2024.

158 Thane Rosenbaum, "'Ocean's Eleven' May Yet Become 'From the River to the Sea,'" *Jewish Journal*, May 26, 2024.

159 Rosenbaum, "ICC Kangaroo Court in Session"; Eugene Kontorovich, "The ICC's Brazen Anti-Israel Bias," *Wall Street Journal*, June 9, 2024.

160 Erlanger, "Under the Rules of War."

161 Cohen and Zlotogorski, *Proportionality in International Humanitarian Law*, 39.

162 Yoram Dinstein, *The Conduct of Hostilities under the Law of International Armed Conflict*, 3rd ed. (Cambridge, UK: Cambridge University Press, 2004), 127.

163 United Nations Office of Human Rights, *Report of the Independent International Commission of Inquiry.*

164 Report of the United Nations Fact Finding Mission on the Gaza Conflict, September 24, 2009.

165 Gal Beckerman, "Goldstone: 'If This Was a Court Of Law, There Would Have Been Nothing Proven,'" *Forward*, October 7, 2009.

166 Thane Rosenbaum, "The Ghost of the Goldstone Report," *Jewish Journal*, April 8, 2024; Thane Rosenbaum, "Find Israel Guilty," *Forbes*, June 19, 2013.

167 Martin Peretz, "Tel Aviv Journal: Richard Goldstone Recants a Blood Libel," *New Republic*, April 5, 2011.

168 "Former Head of ICJ Explains Ruling on Genocide Case Against Israel Brought by S Africa," *BBC*, April 26, 2024 (emphasis added).

Chapter 8

169 Jeff McMahan, "Gaza: Is Israel Fighting a Just War?" *Prospect*, August 5, 2024.

170 Rushdi Abualouf, "Gaza's Top Islamic Scholar Issues Fatwa Criticising 7 October Attack," *BBC*, November 8, 2024.

171 (emphasis added).

172 Abualouf, "Gaza's Top Islamic Scholar Issues Fatwa Criticizing 7 October Attack."

173 Michael N. Schmitt, "The IDF, Hamas, and the Duty to Warn," *Articles of War*, Lieber Institute of Law and Land Warfare at West Point, October 27, 2023.

174 Thane Rosenbaum, "The Agony of IDF-Envy," *Jewish Journal*, January 31, 2024.

175 Thane Rosenbaum, "Palestinians are Rewarding Terrorists. The U.S. Should Stop Enabling Them," *Washington Post*, April 28, 2017.

176 Walzer, *Just and Unjust Wars,* 159.

177 Walzer, *Just and Unjust Wars*, 185.

178 Cohen and Zlotogorski, *Proportionality in International Humanitarian Law*, 137.

179 Walzer, *Just and Unjust Wars*, 200.

180 Walzer, *Just and Unjust Wars*, 200 (emphasis added).

181 Shlomo M. Brody, "How Israel Missed Its Chance to Eliminate the Leadership of Hamas," *Tablet*, December 4, 2023.

182 Brody, "How Israel Missed Its Chance to Eliminate the Leadership of Hamas."

183 Revisions to the United States Department of Defense, *Law of War Manual*, revised ed. (2023), para. 5.4.3.2; *see* Geoff Corn, "2023 DoD Manual Revision—What's in a Presumption?" *Articles of War*, Lieber Institute of Law and Land Warfare at West Point, August 3, 2023.

184 Thane Rosenbaum, "No More Walkie-Talkie for Terrorists," *Jewish Journal*, September 22, 2024.

185 Arsen Ostrovsky and John Spencer, "It's Time to Start Using the Term 'Palestinian Civilian' Correctly," *Newsweek*, June 17, 2024.

186 Ostrovsky and Spencer, "It's Time to Start."

Chapter 9

187 Kassy Akiva, "How Hezbollah Scared Journalists Out Of Embedding With The IDF In Lebanon," *Daily Wire*, November 26, 2024.

188 Lister, Dahman and Michaelis, "Around 70% of Deaths in."

189 Gabriel Epstein, "How Hamas Manipulates Gaza Fatality Numbers: Examining the Male Undercount and Other Problems," *Washington Institute for Near East Policy*, no. 144, January 2024.

190 Mike Wagenheim, "After Faulting 'Fog of War' for Cloudy Hamas Casualty Numbers, UN's New Stats Still Don't Appear to Add Up," *Jewish News Syndicate*, May 14, 2024.

191 Benjamin Weinthal, "Biden Use of Hamas Death Count Challenged by Prominent Statistician, Says Numbers 'Aren't Accurate,'" *Fox News*, March 23, 2024.

192 Weinthal, "Biden Use of Hamas Death Count Challenged."

193 Weinthal, "Biden Use of Hamas Death Count Challenged."

194 David Adesnik and Kevin Chen, "The Gaza Health Ministry Flimflam," *Commentary*, June 2024.

195 Adesnik and Chen, "The Gaza Health Ministry Flimflam."

196 Weinthal, "Biden Use of Hamas Death Count Challenged."

197 Wagenheim, "After Faulting 'Fog of War.'"

198 Epstein, "How Hamas Manipulates Gaza Fatality Numbers."

199 "Hamas-Run Gaza Health Ministry Admits to Flaws in Casualty Data," *Foundation for Defense Democracies*, April 9, 2024.

200 Wagenheim, "After Faulting 'Fog of War.'"

201 "Hamas-Run Gaza Health Ministry Admits to Flaws in Casualty Data," *Foundation for Defense Democracies*; *see also* Andrew Fox, "Questionable Counting: Analyzing the Death Toll from the Hamas-Run Ministry of Health in Gaza," *Henry Jackson Society*, December 2024.

202 Litman, "Hamas Counted on Biased Western Journalism—and They Got It."

203 Zoe Strimpel, "Those Who Put Trust in the Hamas Casualty Figures Should Hang Their Heads in Shame," *Telegraph*, December 16, 2024.

204 Andrew Fox, "Questionable Counting: Analysing the Death Toll from the Hamas-Run Ministry of Health in Gaza."

205 Canaan Lidor, "Hamas Vastly Inflated Gaza Death Statistics, Study Shows," *Jewish News Syndicate*, December 15, 2024.

206 Debbie Weiss, "Gaza Death Toll Figures Inflated to Bolster Genocide Claims, Study Finds," *Algemeiner*, December 15, 2024.

207 Andrew Fox, "Questionable Counting: Analysing the Death Toll from the Hamas-Run Ministry of Health in Gaza."

208 Weiss, "Gaza Death Toll Figures Inflated."

209 Strimpel, "Those Who Put Trust in the Hamas Casualty Figures."

210 Weiss, "Gaza Death Toll Figures."

211 Greg Norman, "Israel Releases New Gaza Civilian Death Toll, says Hamas' Numbers Are 'Fake and Fabricated,'" *Fox News*, May 14, 2024.

212 Richard Landes, "A Look Back at the Muhammad al-Dura Affair, 20 Years Later," *Jerusalem Post*, September 30, 2020.

213 "UN accuses Israel of destroying 'reproductive capacity of Palestinians' in the Gaza Strip," *Reuters*, March 13, 2025.

214 Clayton Fox, "Anatomy of a Blood Libel," *Tablet*, October 30, 2023; *see also* Aaron Poris, "In the Battle for Israel-Hamas War Narrative, Truth Falls Away," *Jerusalem Post*, November 25, 2023.

215 Wafaa Shurafa and Samy Magdy, "Israeli Army Says It Used Small Munitions in Rafah Airstrike, and Fire Was Caused by Secondary Blast," *Los Angeles Times*, May 28, 2024; *see* Emanuel Fabian, "IDF Says Hidden Store of Terror Munitions May Have Caused Deadly Rafah Blaze," *The Times of Israel*, May 28, 2024.

216 Litman, "Hamas Counted on Biased Western Journalism—and They Got It."

217 Fox, "Anatomy of a Blood Libel."

218 Harry Stevens, Missy Ryan, and Mustafa Salim, "Behind the tally, names and lives," *Washington Post*, November 18, 2020.

219 Bob, "IDF Lawyer to 'Post.'"

220 United Nations Security Council Meeting, "Ninety Per Cent of War-Time Casualties Are Civilians, Speakers Stress, Pressing Security Council to Fulfil Responsibility, Protect Innocent People in Conflicts," SC/14904, May 25, 2022.

221 Shlomo Cohen, "Israel, Gaza, and Proportionality," *Quillette*, November 20, 2023.

222 John Spencer, "Israel Has Created a New Standard for Urban Warfare. Why Will No One Admit It?" *Newsweek*, March 25, 2024.

223 Brooks, "What Would You Have Israel Do to Defend Itself?"

Chapter 10

224 Rosenbaum, "No More Walkie-Talkie for Terrorists."
225 Michael Walzer, "Israel's Pager Bombs Have No Place in a Just War," *New York Times*, September 21, 2024 (emphasis added).
226 Lister, Dahman and Michaelis, "Around 70% of Deaths in Gaza."
227 "Israel is falling far short of a US ultimatum to surge aid to Gaza," *Associated Press*, November 1, 2024.
228 Corey Walker, "Biden Admin Slams US Agency's Claim of 'Famine' In Northern Gaza," *Algemeine*r, December 25, 2024.
229 Walker, "Biden Admin Slams US Agency's Claim of 'Famine' In Northern Gaza."
230 Hiba Yazbek and Erika Solomon, "Looters Strip Aid From About 100 Trucks in Gaza, U.N. Agency Says," *New York Times*, November 18, 2024.
231 Pnina Sharvit Baruch and Tammy Caner, "Israel's Humanitarian Obligations Toward the Civilian Population in Gaza," *INSS*, October 26, 2023.
232 Tawil, "Why Are Hamas's Crimes Ignored by Western Media?"
233 Tawil, "Why Are Hamas's Crimes Ignored by Western Media?"
234 Merlin, "UNRWA schools in Gaza."
235 Vita Fellig, "'Hamas Eats Like Kings While Hostages Starve,' Eli Sharabi Tells UN," *Jewish News Syndicate*, March 20, 2025.
236 Ran Kivetz, "Time For Justice At The International Criminal Court Over Israel," *Chicago Tribune*, February 10, 2025.
237 Williams, "Big Lies About Israel."
238 Williams, "Big Lies About Israel."
239 Williams, "Big Lies About Israel."
240 Rosenbaum, "ICC Kangaroo Court in Session."
241 Stephen Pollard, "ICC's Arrest Warrants Expose the West's Inability to Defend the Values on Which Freedom and Democracy Are Built," *The Jewish Chronicle*, November 24, 2024; *see also* Eugene Kontorovich, "The ICC's Brazen Anti-Israel Bias," *Wall Street Journal*, June 9, 2024.
242 Pallabi Munsi, Nima Elbagir, Barbara Arvanitidis and Mark Baron, "'Enlist or Die': Fear, Looming Famine and a Deadly Ultimatum Swell the Ranks of Sudan's Paramilitary Forces," *CNN*, March 21, 2024.

243 Max Boot, "Israel Won't Take Responsibility for Gaza Governance or Humanitarian Aid," *Washington Post*, July 1, 2024.

244 Boot, "Israel Won't Take Responsibility for Gaza Governance or Humanitarian Aid."

245 Baruch and Caner, "Israel's Humanitarian."

246 Melanie Phillips, "The UNRWA Meltdown," *Jewish News Syndicate*, October 31, 2024.

247 Brooks, "What Would You Have Israel Do to Defend Itself?"

248 Cunningham, "Here's What Canada Should (and Should Not) Do"; Rosenbaum, "ICC Kangaroo Court in Session."

249 Ron Kampeas, "The Debate Over What Should Happen in Gaza After the war, Explained," *The Times of Israel*, December 14, 2023.

250 Rosenbaum, "Palestinians are Rewarding Terrorists."

251 Kampeas, "The Debate Over What Should Happen in Gaza."

252 Rosenbaum, "Palestinians' Revisionist History Chains Them to a Lie."

253 "Understanding General David Petraeus's Counterinsurgency Strategy," *Total Military Insight*, July 22, 2024.

Conclusion

254 Barack Obama, "Speech in Sderot, Israel," *New York Times*, July 23, 2008.

255 Itamar Eichner, "New Hate Records: Amsterdam Pogrom Reflects Alarming Trend Across Europe," *Ynet News*, November 11, 2024.

256 Thane Rosenbaum, "Jewish Hollywood's Jewish Problem," *Jewish Journal*, March 2, 2025.

257 Yuval Barnea, "Antwerp Police Arrest Five, as Fears of a 'Jew Hunt' Rise Following Calls to Action on Social Media," *Jerusalem Post*, November 11, 2024.

258 Beth Bailey, "Calls for US to Do More as Antisemitic Acts Skyrocket in Europe: 'Enormously Painful,'" *Fox News*, November 24, 2024.

259 Colette Davidson, "Amid Fresh Wave of Antisemitism, Some French Jews Resort to Fake Names," *Christian Science Monitor*, October 17, 2024.

260 Ailin Vilches Arguello, "Antisemitism Continues to Skyrocket in France, With Over 1,500 Incidents Recorded in 2024, New Report Finds," *Algemeiner*, January 22, 2025.

261 "Berlin Police Chief Warns Jews, Gay People to 'Be Careful' in Arab Neighborhoods," *The Times of Israel*, November 19, 2024.

262 Thane Rosenbaum, "Gaza Masquerade Parties Can't Mask Ugliness," *Jewish Journal*, May 6, 2024; Thane Rosenbaum, "Where Sesame and Arab Streets Meet," *Jewish Journal*, April 28, 2024; Thane Rosenbaum, "Progressive Terrorism," *White Rose*, June 23, 2024; Thane Rosenbaum, "When that Other Ball Drops," *Jewish Journal*, January 2, 2024; Thane Rosenbaum, "Blasphemy, Fatwas + Jihad," *White Rose*, November 15, 2023.

263 Jonathan S. Tobin, "Affirming the 'Genocide' Smear Against Israel Fuels Antisemitism," *Jewish News Syndicate*, October 21, 2024.

264 Thane Rosenbaum, "We Shouldn't Overdo It With the Apologies," *Jewish Journal*, October 3, 2023; Thane Rosenbaum, "Israel, It's Not You—It's Them," *The Times of Israel*, August 4, 2016.

265 Rosenbaum, *Payback*.

266 Paul Rogers, "Israel's Use of Disproportionate Force is a Long-Established Tactic—With a Clear Aim," *Guardian*, Dec. 5, 2023; Ishaan Tharoor, "The Punishing Military Doctrine that Israel May Be Following in Gaza," *Washington Post*, November 10, 2023; Yaron London, "The Dahiya Strategy: Israel Finally Realizes That Arabs Should Be Accountable For Their Leaders' Acts," *YNET News*, Oct. 6, 2008 (emphasis added); Gabi Siboni, "Disproportionate Force: Israel's Concept of Response in Light of the Second Lebanon War," *INSS*, October 2, 2008.

267 "Israel warns Hezbollah war would invite destruction," *Reuters*, October 3, 2008 (emphasis added).

268 Ian Curr, "Opening the Gates of Hell…Armageddon," *Workers BushTelegraph*, July 31, 2024.

ACKNOWLEDGMENTS

Each of my books have received assistance from family, friends, and colleagues who made the writing of it possible. This book, especially, for various reasons owing to its subject matter, presented a number of challenges, some obvious, others less so, that requires special acknowledgment.

First, my editor, publisher, and friend, Adam Bellow, who reached out to me soon after Israel's war in Gaza commenced, proposing that we undertake such a project. He correctly surmised that no other publisher and writer would, arguably, dare do so.

My agent, Murray Weiss, provided a steady presence and encouraging voice.

My colleagues at Touro University—the leadership team of Alan Kadish, Moshe Krupka and Patricia Salkin—have given me a true home to speak and write freely. Most universities have much to learn from Touro's example as a true citadel of academic freedom. I received invaluable assistance and friendship from Touro Law Center's head librarian, Irene McDermott. And special gratitude to Ronnie Myers, David Katz, Alan Jurim, and Jay Rubin.

A number of friends made the path in writing this book easier to traverse: Marty Bodzin, David Boies, Linda Carlsen, Carolyn Gilbert, Danny and Sarah Goldhagen, Angela Himsel,

Tracey Hughes, Annette Insdorf, Carolyn Jackson, Thomas Kaplan, Alex Mauskop, George Klein, Paula Rackoff, Andrew Steinmetz, David Stern, and Robert Wertheimer.

My faithful friends and fellow directors of the FOLCS Board: Hugo Barreca, Warren Bloom, Joe Feshbach, Amanda Halter, the Hollweg Family, Jim Leitner, Jeffrey Lenobel, Shareef Malnik, Jay Newman, Brett Paul, Veronica Relea, Rich Rofe, Diane Sapir, Joel Simon, Olivia Simon, and John Thomas.

And my children: Basia Tess, Solenne Rose and Eric.

ABOUT THE AUTHOR

Photo credit: Bruce Gilbert

Thane Rosenbaum is an essayist, novelist, and law professor. He is a Distinguished University Professor at Touro University, where he directs the Forum on Life, Culture & Society (FOLCS.org). His writings have appeared in the *New York Times*, *Wall Street Journal*, *Washington Post*, *Los Angeles Times*, *CNN*, and the *Daily Beast*, among other publications. He is a columnist for the *Jewish Journal* of Los Angeles, for which he has received the Louis Rapoport Award for Excellence in Commentary, and the Rockower Award for Excellence in Cultural Criticism. He serves as the Legal Analyst for CBS News Radio, and as a Contributor to *White Rose* magazine and Newsmax. Rosenbaum is the author of *Saving Free Speech...from Itself*; *Payback: The Case for Revenge*, and *The Myth of Moral Justice: Why Our Legal System Fails to Do What's Right*. He has also published five novels including *The Golems of Gotham*, *Second Hand Smoke*, and *Elijah Visible*.

www.ingramcontent.com/pod-product-compliance
Ingram Content Group UK Ltd.
Pitfield, Milton Keynes, MK11 3LW, UK
UKHW021706190726
13853UKWH00001B/447

9 798888 457894